THE RENAISSANCE OF THE
TWELFTH CENTURY

THE RENAISSANCE

OF THE

TWELFTH CENTURY

BY

CHARLES HOMER HASKINS

HARVARD UNIVERSITY PRESS

CAMBRIDGE, MASSACHUSETTS, AND LONDON, ENGLAND

TO

MY CHILDREN

SIXTH PRINTING, 1976
ISBN 0-674-76075-1

PRINTED IN THE UNITED STATES OF AMERICA

PREFACE

THE title of this book will appear to many to contain a flagrant contradiction. A renaissance in the twelfth century! Do not the Middle Ages, that epoch of ignorance, stagnation, and gloom, stand in the sharpest contrast to the light and progress and freedom of the Italian Renaissance which followed? How could there be a renaissance in the Middle Ages, when men had no eye for the joy and beauty and knowledge of this passing world, their gaze ever fixed on the terrors of the world to come? Is not this whole period summed up in Symonds' picture of St. Bernard, blind to the beauties of Lake Leman as he bends "a thought-burdened forehead over the neck of his mule," typical of an age when "humanity had passed, a careful pilgrim, intent on the terrors of sin, death, and judgment, along the highways of the world, and had scarcely known that they were sightworthy, or that life is a blessing"?

The answer is that the continuity of history rejects such sharp and violent contrasts between successive periods, and that modern research shows us the Middle Ages less dark and less static, the Renaissance less bright and less sudden, than was once supposed. The Middle Ages exhibit life and color and change, much eager search after knowledge and beauty, much creative accomplishment in art, in literature, in institutions. The Italian Renaissance was preceded by similar, if less wide-reaching movements; indeed it came out of the Middle Ages so gradually that historians are not agreed when it began, and some would go so far as to abolish the name, and perhaps even the fact, of a renaissance in the Quattrocento.

To the most important of these earlier revivals the present volume is devoted, the Renaissance of the Twelfth Century which is often called the Mediaeval Renaissance. This century, the very century of St. Bernard and his mule, was in many respects an age of fresh and vigorous life. The epoch of the Crusades, of the rise of towns, and of the earliest bureaucratic states of the West, it saw the culmination of Romanesque art and the beginnings of Gothic; the emergence of the vernacular literatures; the revival of the Latin classics and of Latin poetry and Roman law; the recovery of Greek science, with its Arabic additions, and of much of Greek philosophy; and the origin of the first European universities. The twelfth century left its signature on higher education, on the scholastic philosophy, on European systems of law, on architecture and sculpture, on the liturgical drama, on Latin and vernacular poetry. The theme is too broad for a single volume, or a single author. Accordingly, since the art and the vernacular literature of the epoch are better known, we shall confine ourselves to the Latin side of this renaissance, the revival of learning in the broadest sense — the Latin classics and their influence, the new jurisprudence and the more varied historiography, the new knowledge of the Greeks and Arabs and its effects upon Western science and philosophy, and the new institutions of learning, all seen against the background of the century's centres and materials of culture. The absence of any other work on this general theme must be the author's excuse for attempting a sketch where much must necessarily rest upon second-hand information.

Some portions of the book are the result of the author's independent investigations, as set forth more fully in his *Studies in the History of Mediaeval Science* (second edition, Cambridge, 1927) and in a parallel volume of *Studies in Mediaeval Culture* now in course of preparation. For the rest the reader is referred to the bibliographical notes at the close of the several chapters, with the reminder that on most subjects there is still room for further research. The topical order has seemed preferable to the biographical or geographical; and while the index partially corrects the resultant inconvenience of breaking up the accounts of particular individuals or countries, it is hoped at the same time that the share of the principal countries in the movement has been made reasonably clear, and that some individuality still remains to such figures as Abaelard, John of Salisbury, and the Latin poets.

For the critical reading of portions of the manuscript my grateful thanks are due to my colleagues Messrs. E. K. Rand, C. H. McIlwain, and George Sarton, and to M. Étienne Gilson of the Sorbonne. In all its later stages this book owes much to the accurate scholarship and sound judgment of Mr. George W. Robinson, Secretary of the Graduate School of Arts and Sciences of Harvard University. I am glad also to acknowledge the assistance of Miss Irma H. Reed, Dr. Josiah C. Russell, and, especially, Mrs. Margaret G. Comiskey. Such aid has advanced my labors in many ways and has saved me from many errors and oversights.

CHARLES H. HASKINS.

CAMBRIDGE, MASSACHUSETTS,
    January, 1927.

CONTENTS

THE RENAISSANCE OF THE
TWELFTH CENTURY

THE RENAISSANCE OF THE TWELFTH CENTURY

CHAPTER I

THE HISTORICAL BACKGROUND

THE European Middle Ages form a complex and varied as well as a very considerable period of human history. Within their thousand years of time they include a large variety of peoples, institutions, and types of culture, illustrating many processes of historical development and containing the origins of many phases of modern civilization. Contrasts of East and West, of the North and the Mediterranean, of old and new, sacred and profane, ideal and actual, give life and color and movement to this period, while its close relations alike to antiquity and to the modern world assure it a place in the continuous history of human development. Both continuity and change are characteristic of the Middle Ages, as indeed of all great epochs of history.

This conception runs counter to ideas widely prevalent not only among the unlearned but among many who ought to know better. To these the Middle Ages are synonymous with all that is uniform, static, and unprogressive; 'mediaeval' is applied to anything outgrown, until, as Bernard Shaw reminds us, even the fashion plates of the preceding generation are pronounced 'mediaeval.' The barbarism of Goths and Vandals is thus spread out over the following centuries, even to that 'Gothic' architecture which is one of the crowning achievements of the constructive genius of the race; the ignorance and superstition of this age are contrasted with the enlightenment of the Renaissance, in strange disregard of the alchemy and demonology which flourished throughout this succeeding period; and the phrase 'Dark Ages' is extended to cover all that came between, let us say, 476 and 1453. Even those who realize that the Middle Ages are not 'dark' often think of them as uniform, at least during the central period from *ca.* 800 to *ca.* 1300, distinguished by the great mediaeval institutions of feudalism, ecclesiasticism, and scholasticism, and preceded and followed by epochs of more rapid transformation. Such a view ignores the unequal development of different parts of Europe, the great economic changes within this epoch, the influx of the new learning of the East, the shifting currents in the stream of mediaeval life and thought. On the intellectual side, in particular, it neglects the mediaeval revival of the Latin classics and of jurisprudence, the extension of knowledge by the absorption of ancient learning and by observation, and the creative work of these centuries in poetry and in art. In many ways the differences between the Europe of 800 and that of 1300 are greater than the resemblances. Similar contrasts, though on a smaller scale, can be made between the culture of the eighth and the ninth centuries, between conditions *ca.* 1100 and those *ca.* 1200, between the preceding age and the new intellectual currents of the thirteenth and fourteenth centuries.

For convenience' sake it has become common to designate certain of these movements as the Carolingian Renaissance, the Ottonian Renaissance, the Renaissance of the Twelfth Century, after the fashion of the phrase once reserved exclusively for the Italian Renaissance of the fifteenth century. Some, it is true, would give up the word renaissance altogether, as conveying false impressions of a sudden change and an original and distinct culture in the fifteenth century, and, in general, as implying that there ever can be a real revival of something past; Mr. Henry Osborn Taylor prides himself on writing two volumes on *Thought and Expression in the Sixteenth Century* [1] without once using this forbidden term. Nevertheless, it may be doubted whether such a term is more open to misinterpretation than others, like the Quattrocento or the sixteenth century, and it is so convenient and so well established that, like Austria, if it had not existed we should have to invent it. There was an Italian Renaissance, whatever we choose to call it, and nothing is gained by the process which ascribes the Homeric poems to another poet of the same name. But — thus much we must grant — the great Renaissance was not so unique or so decisive as has been supposed. The contrast

---

[1] New York, 1920.

of culture was not nearly so sharp as it seemed to the
humanists and their modern followers, while within the
Middle Ages there were intellectual revivals whose influence was not lost to succeeding times, and which par-
took of the same character as the better known movement
of the fifteenth century. To one of these this volume is
devoted, the Renaissance of the Twelfth Century, which
is also known as the Mediaeval Renaissance.

The renaissance of the twelfth century might conceiv-
ably be taken so broadly as to cover all the changes
through which Europe passed in the hundred years or
more from the late eleventh century to the taking of
Constantinople by the Latins in 1204 and the contemporary events which usher in the thirteenth century, just as
we speak of the Age of the Renaissance in later Italy; but
such a view becomes too wide and vague for any purpose
save the general history of the period. More profitably
we may limit the phrase to the history of culture in this
age — the complete development of Romanesque art and
the rise of Gothic; the full bloom of vernacular poetry,
both lyric and epic; and the new learning and new literature in Latin. The century begins with the flourishing
age of the cathedral schools and closes with the earliest
universities already well established at Salerno, Bologna,
Paris, Montpellier, and Oxford. It starts with only the
bare outlines of the seven liberal arts and ends in possession of the Roman and canon law, the new Aristotle, the
new Euclid and Ptolemy, and the Greek and Arabic

physicians, thus making possible a new philosophy and a new science. It sees a revival of the Latin classics, of Latin prose, and of Latin verse, both in the ancient style of Hildebert and the new rhymes of the Goliardi, and the formation of the liturgical drama. New activity in historical writing reflects the variety and amplitude of a richer age — biography, memoir, court annals, the vernacular history, and the city chronicle. A library of *ca.* 1100 would have little beyond the Bible and the Latin Fathers, with their Carolingian commentators, the service books of the church and various lives of saints, the textbooks of Boethius and some others, bits of local history, and perhaps certain of the Latin classics, too often covered with dust. About 1200, or a few years later, we should expect to find, not only more and better copies of these older works, but also the *Corpus Juris Civilis* and the classics partially rescued from neglect; the canonical collections of Gratian and the recent Popes; the theology of Anselm and Peter Lombard and the other early scholastics; the writings of St. Bernard and other monastic leaders (a good quarter of the two hundred and seventeen volumes of the Latin *Patrologia* belong to this period); a mass of new history, poetry, and correspondence; the philosophy, mathematics, and astronomy unknown to the earlier mediaeval tradition and recovered from the Greeks and Arabs in the course of the twelfth century. We should now have the great feudal epics of France and the best of the Provençal lyrics, as well as the earliest works in Middle High German. Romanesque art would have reached and passed its prime, and the new Gothic style would be firmly established at Paris, Chartres, and lesser centres in the Île de France.

A survey of the whole Western culture of the twelfth century would take us far afield, and in many directions the preliminary studies are still lacking. The limits of the present volume, and of its author's knowledge, compel us to leave aside the architecture and sculpture of the age, as well as its vernacular literature, and concentrate our attention upon the Latin writings of the period and what of its life and thought they reveal. Art and literature are never wholly distinct, and Latin and vernacular cannot, of course, be sharply separated, for they run on lines which are often parallel and often cross or converge, and we are learning that it is quite impossible to maintain the watertight compartments which were once thought to separate the writings of the learned and the unlearned. The interpenetration of these two literatures must constantly be kept in mind. Nevertheless, the two are capable of separate discussion, and, since far more attention has been given to the vernacular, justification is not hard to find for a treatment of the more specifically Latin Renaissance.

Chronological limits are not easy to set. Centuries are at best but arbitrary conveniences which must not be permitted to clog or distort our historical thinking: history cannot remain history if sawed off into even lengths of hundreds of years. The most that can be said is that the later eleventh century shows many signs of new life, political, economic, religious, intellectual, for which, like the revival of Roman law and the new interest in the classics, specific dates can rarely be assigned, and that, if we were to choose the First Crusade in 1096 as a convenient turning-point, it must be with a full realization that this particular event has in itself no decisive importance in intellectual history, and that the real change began some fifty years earlier. At the latter end the period is even less sharply defined. Once requickened, intellectual life did not slacken or abruptly change its character. The fourteenth century grows out of the thirteenth as the thirteenth grows out of the twelfth, so that there is no real break between the mediaeval renaissance and the Quattrocento. Dante, an undergraduate once declared, "stands with one foot in the Middle Ages while with the other he salutes the rising star of the Renaissance"! If the signature of the thirteenth century is easy to recognize in the literature, art, and thought of *ca.* 1250, as contrasted with the more fluid and formative epoch which precedes, no sharp line of demarcation separates the two. We can only say that, about the turn of the century, the fall of the Greek empire, the reception of the new Aristotle, the triumph of logic over letters, and the decline of the creative period in Latin and French poetry, mark a transition which we cannot overlook, while two generations later the new science and philosophy have been reduced to order by Albertus Magnus and Thomas Aquinas. By 1200 the mediaeval renaissance is well advanced, by 1250 its work is largely done. In a phrase like 'the renaissance of the twelfth century,' the word 'century' must be used very loosely so as to cover not only the twelfth century proper but the years which immediately precede and follow, yet with sufficient emphasis on the central period to indicate the outstanding characteristics of its civilization. For the movement as a whole we must really go back fifty years or more and forward almost as far.

Furthermore, the various phases of the movement do not exactly synchronize, just as in the later Renaissance there is not complete parallelism between the revival of classical learning, the outburst of Italian art, and the discoveries of Columbus and Copernicus. Certainly the revival of the Latin classics begins in the eleventh century, if indeed it may not be regarded as a continuous advance since Carolingian times, while the force of the new humanism is largely spent before the twelfth century is over. The new science, on the other hand, does not start before the second quarter of the twelfth century, and once begun it goes on into the thirteenth century in unbroken continuity, at least until the absorption of Greek and Arabic learning is completed. The philosophical revival which starts in the twelfth century has its culmination in the thirteenth. Here, as throughout all history, no single date possesses equal importance in all lines of development.

Unlike the Carolingian Renaissance, the revival of the twelfth century was not the product of a court or a dynasty; and, unlike the Italian Renaissance, it owed its beginning to no single country. If Italy had its part, as regards Roman and canon law and the translations from the Greek, it was not the decisive part, save in the field of law. France, on the whole, was more important, with its monks and philosophers, its cathedral schools culminating in the new University of Paris, its Goliardi and vernacular poets, its central place in the new Gothic art. England and Germany are noteworthy, though in the spread of culture from France and Italy rather than in its origination; indeed, the period in Germany is in some respects one of decline as we approach the thirteenth century, while England moves forward in the closest relation with France, as regards both Latin and vernacular culture. Spain's part was to serve as the chief link with the learning of the Mohammedan world; the very names of the translators who worked there illustrate the European character of the new search for learning: John of Seville, Hugh of Santalla, Plato of Tivoli, Gerard of Cremona, Hermann of Carinthia, Rudolf of Bruges, Robert of Chester, and the rest. Christian Spain was merely a transmitter to the North.

Such names, for the most part only names to us, suggest that the twelfth century lacks the wealth and variety of striking personalities in which the Italian Renaissance abounds. It has no such mass of memoirs and correspondence, its outstanding individuals are relatively few. Nor can it claim the artistic interest of portraiture. Its art is rich and distinctive both in sculpture and architecture, but it is an art of types, not of individuals. It has left us no portraits of scholars or men of letters, very few even of rulers or prelates. It has not even given us likenesses of its horses, such as adorn the palace of the Gonzaga dukes at Mantua.

Of the antecedent conditions which produced this intellectual revival, it is not easy to speak with much definiteness. The eleventh century is in many ways obscure, while the tenth is obscurer still, and the origins of intellectual movements are not easy to trace under the most favorable circumstances. One very obvious fact in the later eleventh century is the rapid development of trade and commerce, particularly in Italy, and the consequent quickening of urban life in the same region. One is tempted to draw a parallel with the economic and urban antecedents which recent writers have emphasized as explaining the Italian Renaissance of the Quattrocento; but the renaissance of the twelfth century was not specifically Italian, indeed it was in some respects most marked beyond the Alps, where economic revival had scarcely begun, so that the movement cannot be explained solely in the terms so dear to economic determinism. There was also a certain amount of political advance, as seen in the Norman lands of England and Sicily, in

Catalonia, and in the process of feudal consolidation in France, an advance which promoted a certain degree of peace and the travel and communication which go on best in a peaceful society. All these influences counted in the Mediterranean and also in the intercourse between the Mediterranean and the Northern lands, while the more prosperous feudal and royal courts were, as we shall see in the next chapter, centres which favored literature both Latin and vernacular. The church, of course, shared in the growing prosperity, so that among both regular and secular clergy there was more to spend for travel and for the buying and copying of manuscripts, and thus greater physical opportunity for learning and study. The growth of the papal monarchy drew clerks and laymen in ever increasing numbers along the road to Rome, also frequented, like the other great routes of pilgrimage, by a crowd of religious wayfarers for whom many of the *chansons de gestes* were produced. Moreover, the closer definition of the ecclesiastical system was reflected in the pamphlet literature of the investiture controversy, in the canonistic writings which followed, and in general in a larger and better organized body of written records of every sort.

While a general quickening of the spirit naturally accompanied the more active life of this age, a more direct connection with the intellectual movement can, in some instances, be shown. Thus the revival of the Roman law in Italy toward 1100 was closely associated with the growth of economic and social conditions to which this superior jurisprudence was applicable. The formation of the pilgrimage romances went with the growing number of pilgrims who took the road to Rome and Compostela. The translations of scientific and philosophical works from the Arabic depended upon the Christian reconquest of Northern Spain, which reached Toledo in 1085 and Saragossa in 1118, thus opening the learning of the Saracens to the Christian scholars from the North who turned eagerly to the Peninsula. The translations from the Greek were facilitated by the Norman conquest of Sicily and Southern Italy, and by the commercial and diplomatic relations maintained with Constantinople by the city republics of the North. The geographical position of Salerno undoubtedly assisted its rise to dominance in mediaeval medicine. History grew more voluminous and varied as action increased in variety and interest; histories of the Crusades required Crusaders even before historians!

Time was when the Crusades themselves would have served as an ample explanation of this, as of every other change of the twelfth and thirteenth centuries. Did not 'these costly and perilous expeditions' strengthen (or weaken!) monarchy, exalt the Papacy, undermine feudalism, create the towns, set free the human spirit, and in general usher in a new age? Does not Gibbon, for example, declare that the poverty of the crusading barons "extorted from their pride those charters of freedom which unlocked the fetters of the slave, secured the farm of the peasant and the shop of the artificer, and gradually restored a substance and a soul to the most numerous and useful part of the community"? Unfortunately for all such easy guesses and facile rhetoric, historians now distinguish between the Crusades and the age of the Crusades, and point out that they were only one phase, and that not the most important, of the life of a vigorous epoch. They brought East and West into closer contact, stimulated trade, transportation, and the use of money, and helped to accelerate many tendencies already at work; but their specifically intellectual consequences are less tangible and probably less significant. Gibbon rightly saw that "the ardor of studious curiosity was awakened in Europe by different causes," if not entirely by "more recent events"; and a recent writer has pointed out that "a man may travel much and yet see little," so that "St. Louis, as Joinville shows him to us, or Joinville himself, was not intellectually changed by his crusading."[1] In any case the Crusades fail us as a cause of the Latin Renaissance, for it began well before the First Crusade, and the two movements scarcely touch.

When we have exhausted all such explanations, good or bad, there remains a final residuum which does not yield to these methods of proximate analysis. Anselm, Abaelard, Irnerius, Turold (or whoever be the author of the *Song of Roland*), Adelard of Bath at one end of the

---

[1] E. J. Passant, in *Cambridge Medieval History*, v. 331.

century, Frederick II, Francis of Assisi, and the great schoolmen at the other, cannot be accounted for by reckonings of time and milieu, still less by an inheritance which (save perhaps for Frederick II) we can no longer trace. Between such manifestations of individual genius and the vague generalization that so active an age in men's affairs was likely to be active also in the things of the mind, there is still room for further inquiry as our knowledge grows. Such inquiry needs particularly to be pushed back into the eleventh century, that obscure period of origins which holds the secret of the new movement, well before those events of crusade and conquest which fail as explanations chiefly because they come too late. Meanwhile we may simplify the problem in some degree by remembering that we have to deal with an intensification of intellectual life rather than with a new creation, and that the continuity between the ninth and the twelfth centuries was never wholly broken. While it is true in general that "each succeeding mediaeval century, besides inheriting what had become known in the time immediately preceding it, endeavored to reach back to the remote past for further treasure,"[1] the twelfth century reached out more widely and recovered more.

The resurgence of learning and literature in the ninth century which is generally known as the Carolingian Renaissance had its source and centre at the court of

---

[1] H. O. Taylor, *Thought and Expression in the Sixteenth Century*, i, p. viii.

Charles the Great and his immediate successors. Originally confined to the establishment of a decent standard of education among the Frankish clergy, this movement had developed an interest in learning for its own sake, bringing into Gaul scholars from England, Italy, and Spain, and training the new generation which was to carry on their work. It was a revival rather than a new birth, a revival of the Latin Fathers, the Latin classics, and the Latin tongue which had suffered so severely in the 'Dark Ages' just preceding. Its theological treatises were compilations of material from the Fathers; its Latin prose and verse dealt largely with old subjects, though they set new standards of composition for the period which followed. The movement conserved rather than originated; yet it reformed the handwriting of Europe by creating that Caroline minuscule which we still use as our alphabet, and its scribes saved to the modern world the Latin classics, nearly all of which have come down to us, directly or indirectly, through Carolingian copies. Libraries had been collected; humanists had appeared in men like Lupus of Ferrières and John the Scot. The Latin language never fell back into the depths of the Merovingian age, and the European intelligence never lost the great gains of the ninth century.

So far as the Carolingian renaissance centred in the court and the palace school, it came to an end with the dissolution of the Frankish empire in the later years of the ninth century and left no immediate representatives at the courts of the lesser kingdoms which succeeded. The official annals come to an end in 882; "the stream of capitularies ceased to flow"; the imperial officers no longer go about on their vigilant rounds. Fortunately, however, Charlemagne had insisted upon the establishment of schools in every monastery and cathedral, and it was in these local centres that the intellectual movement had chiefly flourished. They include great monastic establishments like Tours and Fulda, Reichenau, St. Gall, and Lorsch, Fleury and Saint-Riquier and Corbie; cathedral centres like Metz and Cambrai, Rheims, Auxerre, and Chartres. With the wealth and exemptions which these establishments had acquired under Carolingian protection, there was no inherent reason why teaching and writing should not go on there, irrespective of the fate of the Carolingian dynasty; but they owed their origin to the peace and good order which Charlemagne had established, and they might easily disappear when these were destroyed. The tenth century, that 'century of iron,' furnished the acid test. This was an age of anarchy and 'fist law,' when "no one thought of common defence or wide organization: the strong built castles, the weak became their bondsmen, or took shelter under the cowl: the governor — count, bishop, or abbot — tightened his grasp, turned a delegated into an independent, a personal into a territorial authority, and hardly owned a distant and feeble suzerain." [1] And what the king or the local

[1] James Bryce, *The Holy Roman Empire*, edition of 1909, p. 80.

lord left to the monastery in theory, he might take over in practice as lay abbot. If these local princes, who were at least nominally Christian, might still treat the church with a certain respect, this could not be expected from the Christless invaders, Saracens, Hungarians, and Northmen, who now poured into the Frankish empire and found monasteries and cathedrals rich subjects for plunder and destruction. Each year "the steel of the heathen glistened." In 846 the Saracens looted St. Peter's at Rome; in 843 the Northmen killed the bishop of Nantes before his high altar; in 854 they burnt St. Martin's church at Tours; in 886 they were with difficulty bought off from Paris. Whole regions were devastated, like Flanders, the valleys of the Meuse, Seine, and Loire, and the territory which was to become Normandy. So the cloisters of Bavaria fell before the Hungarians, and those of Central Italy before the Saracens. Many great monasteries were entirely destroyed, and the monks who fled for their lives took with them few books and fewer pupils. Even the walled cathedral cities were not wholly spared.

Throughout the tenth century it is Germany that best maintains the Carolingian traditions, so that under the Saxon Ottos German historians love to speak of an 'Ottonian Renaissance.' Whereas invasion and localism caused decline in France and Italy, the region of Saxony showed the results of its conquest and Christianization by Charlemagne and of the establishment of the monasteries and bishoprics of the new faith. And just as Otto the Great followed Charlemagne in his revival of the Empire, so he brought Italian grammarians and theologians to strengthen the intellectual movement to which he and his brother Bruno, archbishop of Cologne, gave strong support. Connecting links of this sort may be seen in the grammarian Stephen of Pavia, the theologian Ratherius, bishop of Liége and Verona, the poet Leo of Vercelli, and the famous Liutprand of Cremona, whom Otto used as his ambassador to Constantinople.

As we come into the eleventh century, German culture shows little vitality from within. True, certain of the Emperors, Henry II, Henry III, and Henry IV, had a respectable education and possessed intellectual interests, while the Latin literature of the early eleventh century could boast the canonistic treatise of Burchard of Worms (d. 1025), the visions and temptations of the monk Otloh of Regensburg, the schools of Notker of Liége (d. 1008), the translations of Notker of St. Gall (d. 1022), and a very considerable body of annals and biography. There was, however, no real court-centre of learning, and the monastic centres of earlier times were on the decline. Intellectual advance in the late eleventh and twelfth centuries came less from within than through contact with Italy and France. With Italy relations were perforce kept open, after the revival of the Empire by Otto the Great, by the *Römerzug* for the imperial crown and by the scholars and books which came north in the Emperor's train, as in the case of the manuscripts for Henry II's cathedral at Bamberg. However unfortunate were the political consequences of the Holy Roman Empire for the German lands, the results of the connection with Italy were of the first importance for German culture. With France the ties were quite different, created chiefly by the studies of German ecclesiastics in the schools of Northern France, and later by the colonizing activities of Cluni and Cîteaux in reforming and extending monasticism in Germany. Such relations are well known in the twelfth century, but we read much earlier that Bishop Heribert of Eichstädt (1021–42) despised one "who had been educated at home rather than in the valley of the Rhine or in Gaul." We must beware, however, of stressing the political frontier in an age when such frontiers meant very little. Cologne and Liége seem to have been in closer intellectual relations with Rheims, Chartres, and Fleury than with the North and East of the German kingdom.

In Italy the revival of culture was first manifest in the South, where the contact was direct with the Greek and Mohammedan worlds. Southern Italy had remained a part of the Byzantine empire until well into the eleventh century, and after the Norman conquest it preserved its Greek monasteries and a considerable Greek-speaking population, especially in Calabria. Sicily was under Arab domination from 902 to 1091, and here too Greek and Arab elements survived under the Norman rulers.

Both of these regions maintained trade with Northern Africa and the East, as we see in the commerce of a city like Amalfi, which traded with Syria and possessed its own quarter at Constantinople. Already we can discern the background for the brilliant court of Frederick II two hundred years later. While, however, it is natural to assume an important part for Greek and Arab civilization in the Latin revival, such influences are not easy to trace specifically in this early period. The clearest case is that of Constantine the African, *ca.* 1015–87, who made translations and adaptations of important medical works; but Constantine himself is a hazy figure, and scholars are generally of the opinion that the development of medical studies at Salerno antedates his translations and is connected rather with an older local tradition. Certainly versions of Dioscorides and the Greek physicians meet us in manuscripts of the Beneventan hand between the ninth and eleventh centuries, so that some knowledge of these writers preceded Constantine. The important fact for our purpose is that by the eleventh century Salerno has become the chief medical centre in Europe. While the fame of Salerno as a school lay entirely in the field of medicine, there is some evidence of early activity in other directions. Archbishop Alfano (1058–85) showed uncommon skill in the metre of his Latin verse, which covered a variety of subjects, occasional as well as ecclesiastical, and indicates a respectable acquaintance with the Roman poets, while his name is attached to a version from the Greek of the *De natura hominis* of Nemesius. At Monte Cassino we read of the historian Amatus and the computist Pandulf of Capua, while Constantine the African ended his days here and the monk Alberic wrote the first manual of the new art of epistolary composition (*dictamen*). We shall later have occasion to speak more fully of Monte Cassino as an intellectual centre; here it is only necessary to emphasize its connection with the revival of learning in the eleventh century.

In Northern Italy this is the age of the reëmergence of the Roman law, in the sense of a full course of study based on the text of the *Corpus Juris*. Whatever the earlier influence of the Lombard lawyers and whatever the facts about the earliest Roman schools, it is in 1076 that we meet the first citation of the *Digest*, after nearly five centuries, and the first notable Bolognese master in the person of Pepo, "the bright and shining light of Bologna." By the end of the century Bologna is the acknowledged leader and Irnerius the acknowledged master. In two other fields this period in Italy is marked by new works of wide influence, the *Glossary* of the Lombard lexicographer Papias (*ca.* 1050), and the musical writings of Guido of Arezzo, which remain significant even if their author is no longer credited with the introduction of the modern system of notation. In all, a respectable showing for Italy, well before we are in sight of the Crusades!

A further fact to be noted in the Italy of the eleventh century is the survival of education among the laity.

Without taking too literally the lines of the German historian Wipo which make all Italian youth sweat in the schools, we can see clear evidences of the persistence of the older traditions of lay culture here long after they had disappeared beyond the Alps. The Italian layman, says Wattenbach, "read his Virgil and Horace though he wrote no books." If this class did not express itself in literature, it at least furnished the soil for the lay professions of law and medicine, which early rose to prominence in Italian society; it also comprised the important group of the notaries, transmitting from father to son an office which had preserved through the Dark Ages the institution of the Roman *tabelliones*. The notaries constituted an element of much importance in the Italian cities, where they distinguished themselves as local historians, and the notariate passed to other countries with the spread of the Roman law.

If Italy was the cradle of law and medicine, France was in this age superior in the liberal arts, and preëminent in philosophy, theology, and Latin poetry, not to mention the vernacular verse. To what extent France was influenced by Italy at this time is an obscure question, in learning as well as in architecture and sculpture. Certainly Gerbert had visited Italy, while Lanfranc of Pavia brought the light of learning to the Norman school of Bec, where he was succeeded by another Italian, Anselm of Aosta; yet we should be careful in using such facts to support wide conclusions. Gerbert had been in

Spain before he went to Italy, nor is it clear that his mathematics had its origin outside of the limits of Gaul; Lanfranc was by temper a lawyer rather than a theologian; Anselm, a real theologian, shows no discoverable indebtedness to Italian masters. In all essential respects the French learning of the eleventh century seems to root directly in the soil of the Carolingian tradition.

The continuity is perhaps most evident at Rheims, where Flodoard carries his valuable annals to 966 and Gerbert begins to teach in the cathedral school before 980. Gerbert's teaching covered the whole range of the seven liberal arts, logic and rhetoric (with abundant classical illustrations) no less than mathematics and astronomy, but he dazzled contemporaries by his treatises on arithmetic and geometry, and by his use of astronomical instruments which, simple though they were, appeared to them 'almost divine.' Also he eagerly collected manuscripts. He was, says Taylor,[1] "the first mind of his time, its greatest teacher, its most eager learner, and most universal scholar." His pupil Abbo, who became abbot of Fleury-sur-Loire in 988, did much for logic and astronomy at this ancient centre of Carolingian culture, whence Orleans was later to derive its literary traditions. Another pupil probably was Fulbert, chancellor and from 1007 to 1029 bishop of Chartres, which from now on takes first rank as a cathedral school. Indeed, as early as 991 the monk Richer of Rheims has

[1] *The Mediaeval Mind* (1925), i. 286.

left us a curious description of a journey to Chartres for
the study of Hippocrates. Fulbert's many-sided education is seen especially in his poems, in both classic metre
and the later rhyme, and in his voluminous correspondence, written in an excellent style, the letters touching
on medicine, canon law, and all sorts of questions of contemporary politics. The influence of this 'Socrates' of
the schools is illustrated by a poem of one of his pupils,
Adelman of Liége, an alphabetical *planctus* of the Carolingian type, lamenting the death of his former fellow students of Chartres: Hildeger, chancellor of Chartres, and
the masters Ralph and Sigo; the rhetoricians Lambert
of Paris and Engelbert of Orleans; Reginbald, teacher
of grammar at Tours; Gerard of Verdun, pilgrim to the
Holy Sepulchre, and Walter of Burgundy; Reginbald of
Cologne, the mathematician; and three others of the
school of Liége. This is far from a complete list of Fulbert's pupils who reached distinction, but it gives us a
glimpse of the large and active group of teachers and
writers in the field of the liberal arts in the first half of
the eleventh century, as well as of the more specifically
mathematical tradition which passed from Gerbert to
the schools of Lorraine and Chartres and is reflected
ca. 1025 in a curious correspondence between Reginbald
of Cologne and Ralph of Liége. So toward the middle of
the century Franco of Liége is struggling with the problem of squaring the circle, while Hermann, the lame
monk of Reichenau, has learned of the astrolabe from

some source which goes back to the Arabic. A generation later Lotharingian abacists have passed into England, where they may have introduced the abacus into the reckoning of the Exchequer.

Another of the liberal arts, dialectic, now pushes into the foreground in a way that foreshadows its later preponderance and the later disputes of scholasticism. Berengar of Tours, one of Fulbert's most brilliant pupils, carries on a running controversy, from 1049 until his death in 1088, with Lanfranc of Bec and a whole school of conservative theologians. The question is the ever recurring one of the real presence in the elements of the Lord's Supper; Berengar's method is to turn from authority to reason or, as he calls it, dialectic: "it is the part of courage to have recourse to dialectic in all things, for recourse to dialectic is recourse to reason, and he who does not avail himself of reason abandons his chief honor, since by virtue of reason he was made in the image of God." A little later Roscellinus of Compiègne raises that issue of universals which was to form the central problem of scholastic debate, and in 1092 his nominalist doctrine is condemned by the council of Soissons on the ground that it made three Gods of the indivisible Trinity.

In Latin poetry the eleventh century begins with Fulbert of Chartres and closes with Hildebert of Le Mans, whose writings were confused with ancient classics by certain modern editors. Here Carolingian influences are evident, but the new verse is more abundant and more varied, so that it became perhaps the most characteristic expression of this age. Many of these poems are still unpublished. The subjects are of every sort: theology, lives of saints, the virtues of plants and precious stones, monastic biography, events like the burning of Saint-Amand in 1060, satires on contemporaries, many *tituli* or epitaphs on friends or patrons. The valley of the Loire is the most important centre, but the movement extends throughout the whole of Northern France and adjacent Lorraine. Before the close of the century, poets of this type appear in England in the person of Reginald of Canterbury and Geoffrey of Winchester.

Finally, besides the activity shown in these new works, there is a development of libraries and collections of ancient authors. In this respect the tenth century had been more active than we should expect, as illustrated in scattered catalogues of manuscripts and especially in important codices of the principal Latin classics. The eleventh century continued this work and extended it. *Ca.* 1000 Otto III has in Italy copies of Orosius, Persius, Livy, Fulgentius, Isidore, and Boethius. His successor Henry II carries many other manuscripts northward to his cathedral of Bamberg. Bishops Bernward (993–1022) and Godehard (1022–38) collect classics for Hildesheim, as does Abbot Fromund for Tegernsee. We have long lists of the manuscripts now copied at Monte Cassino. The extensive library of Fleury was completed in the eleventh century. The dating of such manuscripts is at best only approximate, for the differences in handwriting are very slight between the tenth century and the eleventh century, between the eleventh century and the twelfth. In palaeography as in learning one age merges in the other.

So much for the period of origins. Vague, obscure, tantalizing, as all such periods are, it at least shows us clearly that the new movement is nothing sudden or catastrophic, but reaches far back into the eleventh century and even earlier. One other fact is equally clear, namely, that so far we have to deal with a Roman renaissance, for it antedates the Crusades, the new learning of Spain, the Greek translators of Sicily. Save for the medical adaptations of Constantine the African and a certain tradition of the astrolabe, it has no contacts with Arabic science; save for some hagiography and the single treatise of Nemesius, it as yet derives nothing immediately from the Greek. All this will come in good time in the twelfth century. Until then the renaissance is a Latin movement, a revival of Roman law, of the Latin classics, of Latin poetry, of a philosophy and theology which root in Boethius and the Latin Fathers. Each of these topics we shall go on to trace by itself through the twelfth century. Meanwhile, however, we shall need to gain some idea of the chief intellectual centres and their intercommunication and of the libraries and manuscripts in which the learning and literature of this age were contained.

BIBLIOGRAPHICAL NOTE

There is no general work on the intellectual life of the twelfth century. Various brief characterizations of the period are listed by L. J. Paetow, *Guide to the Study of Medieval History* (Berkeley, 1917), pp. 384-385, a work of much value for all students of the Middle Ages, and particularly full on the intellectual conditions of the twelfth and thirteenth centuries. H. O. Taylor, *The Mediaeval Mind* (fourth edition, New York and London, 1925), is a useful general account which gives a good sketch of the eleventh century but does not discuss the twelfth as such. R. L. Poole, *Illustrations of the History of Mediaeval Thought and Learning* (second edition, London, 1920), has some excellent chapters on our period; while for general reference the fifth volume of the *Cambridge Medieval History* (Cambridge, 1926), with its full bibliographies, can be recommended. Ordinarily the general histories are of little help for intellectual matters; the church histories and cyclopaedias and the biographical dictionaries are more useful.

Much for our purpose is contained in the histories of Latin literature. Unfortunately, the best of these, the *Geschichte der lateinischen Litteratur des Mittelalters* of M. Manitius (Munich, 1911-23), with full bibliographies, though useful for the field of the present chapter, has not yet advanced further than *ca.* 1050; while the valuable survey of the late F. Novati, *Le origini* (Milan, n. d.), in the coöperative *Storia letteraria d'Italia*, likewise abandons us in the eleventh century. See also Novati, *L'influsso del pensiero latino sopra la civiltà italiana del medio evo* (Milan, 1897); and his paper on Franco-Italian intellectual relations in the eleventh century in *Comptes-rendus de l'Académie des Inscriptions*, 1910, pp. 169-184. The outline of G. Gröber, "Uebersicht über die lateinische Litteratur von der Mitte des 6. Jahrhunderts bis 1350," in his *Grundriss der romanischen Philologie*, ii, 1 (Strasbourg, 1902), covers the whole period and all countries. The *Histoire littéraire de la France* is quite full on Latin writers, but most of the articles for our period are now rather old. The admirable volumes of Ch. V. Langlois, *La vie en France au moyen âge* (new edition, Paris, 1924-   ), touch intellectual as well as social history, but they deal with the vernacular literature. On the relation of the Middle Ages to later times, *The Legacy of the Middle Ages*, edited by C. G. Crump and E. F. Jacob (Oxford, 1926), is suggestive.

It must not be forgotten that, while the writers of the twelfth century are largely represented in the great publications of historical, literary, and theological texts, many of their works are still unpublished and a host of problems still await closer study and monographic investigation. There is no single guide to this new material as it appears; perhaps the most useful is the current bibliography of the *Revue d'histoire ecclésiastique*, published at Louvain.

CHAPTER II

INTELLECTUAL CENTRES

THE intellectual life of Western Christendom in the Middle Ages was not widely diffused throughout the population. It conspicuously lacked both the pervasiveness and the rapidity of intercourse to which the modern world is accustomed. Relatively few could read and write, these chiefly ecclesiastics, and, save for the very moderate attainments of the individual parish priest, men of education were concentrated in certain definite groups separated one from another by wide stretches of rural ignorance. Communication was rendered difficult by the primitive modes of travel, yet a certain amount of communication was required, especially by the ecclesiastical system, so that extreme localism in some respects coexisted with a common European civilization in others. At the same time this intercourse was largely between intellectual centres of the same sort, however distant, rather than between disparate centres in the same region; and while the more composite local relations must ultimately not be overlooked, we must fix our attention in the first instance upon the primary types. These intellectual centres, representing different social strata, consisted chiefly of monasteries, cathedrals, courts, towns, and universities. These several types were not of equal importance throughout the mediaeval period; indeed some of them are unknown to the early Middle Ages, and the development of the new types is a characteristic phase of the twelfth-century renaissance.

Throughout the earlier Middle Ages the chief centres of culture had been the monasteries. Set like islands in a sea of ignorance and barbarism, they had saved learning from extinction in Western Europe at a time when no other forces worked strongly toward that end. True, they too were affected by the localism of the epoch, as well as by the human difficulties of maintaining the ascetic life, but they were kept in some sort of relation with one another by the influence of Rome, by the travels of the Irish monks, by the centralizing efforts of Charles the Great, and by the Cluniac reforms of the tenth and eleventh centuries, so that books and ideas often passed over long distances with a rapidity which surprises the modern student. We should not, however, assume that monasteries were everywhere and always centres of light and learning, and we must try to form a more concrete idea of the nature of their intellectual life.

First of all, we should note the reminder of a modern Benedictine abbot that "all the services of Benedictines to civilization and education and letters have been but by-products." [1] A monastery might be a refuge for travellers, an economic centre, a lamp of architecture, an exchange of ideas and information, a source of new types

[1] Dom Butler, in *Cambridge Medieval History*, i. 538.

in music and literature; but it was all or any of these things only incidentally and by no means necessarily. In the rule of St. Benedict, which came to prevail generally throughout the West, the central point was the *opus Dei*, the daily chanting of the office in the choir, which consumed originally four to four and one-half hours and tended with its later developments to occupy six or seven. From three to five hours daily, depending on the season, were left free for reading, by which was meant study and meditation on the Bible or the Fathers, such as Basil and Cassian, not discursive reading in other works. At the beginning of Lent the monks were to receive a book apiece from the library, "which they shall all read entirely through in order"; but no limit of time is set, and it is plain from Lanfranc's revised decrees that the book was normally kept a year, being solemnly returned on the first Monday of the succeeding Lent, when the monks who had not finished their respective volumes were required to make public confession of the fact. Contrary to a common modern impression, the Benedictine rule likewise says nothing about copying books, but room is left for that under the prescribed manual labor, and some copying there would naturally be in order to produce the necessary volumes for choir and library, not to mention the importance of "fighting the Devil by pen and ink," to use the phrase of Cassiodorus. So the Benedictine rule says nothing about another famous monastic institution, the schools, though we hear of them in the later customs.

"Schools in the modern sense," says Pijper,[1] "namely, institutions in which instruction is given at fixed times by a specifically designated teacher in specifically designated branches to specifically designated pupils, formed in the cloisters of the Middle Ages not the rule but the exception." It is hard to find traces of any special schoolrooms. Instruction is primarily religious teaching: prayers, the rule of the order, sermons, collations, and especially the Bible. The seven liberal arts do not occupy the first place, nor are the whole seven found everywhere.

Let us try to be more precise. By the terms of its origin, every monastery had a library of service books, with usually some copies of Bibles and theological works. It had a school for novices, at least, and therewith often certain elementary textbooks, though these cannot always be assumed. As a landowner, it had its charters and title deeds, sometimes copied into cartularies and perhaps constituting archives of some importance which might require a special custodian. It also kept a register of its members, living and dead, and often lists of the deceased members of other monasteries with which it had formed a confraternity to pray for their souls. Its services required a calendar, to which the names of new saints were from time to time added, and in which were noted the obits of monks and benefactors; also tables of the date of Easter which might serve as the basis of annals as news filtered in from the outer world. No his-

[1] *De Kloosters* (The Hague, 1916), pp. 294–295.

torical record was obligatory, but the elements were there, and many monasteries took advantage of them to become centres of local historical writing, for a time, indeed, almost the only centres. A library, a school, an archive, the rudiments of a record of its own, these were incidental to the existence of a monastery and formed the nucleus of a certain amount of intellectual life. Often they remained only a nucleus, for, while monasteries were many, real centres of learning were relatively few, and the best of these had their ups and downs, their periods of activity and of deep decline. Indeed, this is true of monasticism in general, for, as Dean Inge reminds us, "in religion nothing fails like success";[1] prosperity usually brought laxness, and this in turn produced a wave of reform, resulting in new statutes or a new order, which prospered and grew lax in turn. At best, most monasteries led a humdrum existence, intellectually speaking. Thus the rich abbey of Troarn in Normandy, carefully studied by R. N. Sauvage, can show only one known writer, its first abbot, Durand (1059–88); its schools are barely cited in a document of 1169; its only library catalogue, dated 1446, is composed almost entirely of books of devotion. Few Norman abbeys or nunneries can show more.

For the Benedictine monasteries the twelfth century was a period of marked decline, if, indeed, the decline had not set in earlier, as at the ancient centres of Corbie,

[1] *Atlantic Monthly*, cxxxv. 190 (1925).

Luxeuil, St. Gall, and Bobbio. Only in the earlier half of the century do we still find Benedictine centres of intellectual importance. The oldest of all, Monte Cassino, has its most flourishing age in the eleventh and early twelfth centuries. Chief home of the peculiar South-Italian hand known as the Beneventan, it built up a great library of copies, of which the chronicler proudly records the titles to the number of seventy. The list "contains chiefly theological and liturgical works, but there are several histories: Josephus, Gregory of Tours, Paulus Diaconus, Erchempert, and others; there are also several classics: *De natura deorum* of Cicero, the *Institutiones* and *Novellae* of Justinian, the *Fasti* of Ovid, Virgil's *Eclogues*, Terence, Horace, Seneca, the grammatical works of Theodorus and Donatus." [1] Many of these codices are still preserved; indeed, without them the world would have lost Apuleius, what little we have of Varro, the *Histories* of Tacitus and probably the surviving parts of the *Annals*, as well as several texts and local records of the Middle Ages. That these books were read, as well as copied for a later age, we have abundant evidence. *Ca.* 1140, that precious forger, Peter the Deacon, drew up a long list of "the illustrious men of Monte Cassino," beginning with St. Benedict and ending with Peter himself, whose claims to authorship are displayed at length. These eminent men include two Popes, but most of them are authors: Constantine the African, that "new and

[1] E. A. Loew, *The Beneventan Script* (Oxford, 1914), p. 12.

shining Hippocrates," Alfano of Salerno, and Alberic the rhetorician, names which we have already met; also Leo of Ostia, the excellent chronicler of the monastery, and a long list of writers on religious subjects. In all, a roll of which any establishment might indeed be proud. But the catalogue is essentially an epitaph; the cloister had no great writers thereafter, and Peter himself is a symptom of its decline.

North of the Alps, but still under Italian influence, the most famous intellectual centre of the later eleventh century was Bec. Founded in 1034, it owed its intellectual eminence to Lanfranc, who entered the monastery in 1042 and became abbot soon thereafter, and to his successor, Anselm, abbot from 1079 to 1092. Canonist and perhaps civilian at Pavia, at Bec Lanfranc seems to have devoted himself chiefly to the trivium and theology, with much attention to the correct copying of biblical and patristic manuscripts. Anselm wrote his principal theological treatises at Bec, attacking the doctrines of Roscellinus as Lanfranc had withstood Berengar, so that in the two chief theological controversies of the century orthodoxy found its leader at Bec. By the early twelfth century this school at Bec was famous throughout Europe. It had trained one Pope, Alexander II, and great numbers of bishops and abbots. The immediate successors of Anselm, though of no great personal eminence, maintained the tradition, and Ordericus Vitalis could say that in his time "almost every monk of Bec seemed a phi-

losopher, and even the least learned there had something
to teach the frothy grammarians." In the early twelfth
century Bec had a library of one hundred and sixty-four
volumes, while it received one hundred and thirteen more
from the bishop of Bayeux in 1164.[1] Nevertheless, the
twelfth century soon becomes a period of decline, and by
the second half the decline is apparent. "The writers of
Bec are now only the anonyms of literary history, that is,
educated monks who are no doubt commendable for their
laborious life, but whose reputation does not go much beyond the walls of the monastery or the narrow circle of
their friends. . . . Studious youths no longer turn their
steps toward the abbey."[2]

Many monks of Bec rose to preferment in England, but
no English monastery occupied so high a position. The
Norman Conquest was followed by a wave of religious
reform: Norman abbots were set over English houses,
Norman monasteries received English lands and priories,
and Norman barons founded new establishments in England. This rapid development on the material side was
followed by a certain amount of intellectual activity, in
copying, in schools, and in literary composition. Yet the
literary output of the English Benedictines of the twelfth
century is disappointing, save in the field of history,
where it is redeemed by William of Malmesbury and the
Anglo-Saxon chronicler of Peterborough, as well as by

[1] For their contents, see my *Normans in European History* (Boston, 1915),
pp. 178–180.
[2] A. A. Porée, *Histoire de l'abbaye du Bec*, i. 539–540.

cathedral monks such as Florence of Worcester and
Simeon of Durham. In England, too, the movement dies
down as the century advances: the great efflorescence of
history under Henry II was connected with the court and
the cathedrals rather than with the monasteries. Yet
monastic historiography in England revives once more in
the thirteenth century, when it reaches its climax at St.
Albans in the writings of Matthew Paris.

If we take as a fair sample England's most famous
abbey, Westminster, it has only a modest share in the
intellectual life of our century. Its abbot from *ca.* 1085
to 1117, Gilbert Crispin, had been a monk of Bec,

Doctus quadrivio nec minus in trivio,

to whose authority as a theologian much weight was given
at the council of Rheims in 1148. Besides certain letters
to Anselm, he wrote an account of the foundation of Bec
and various theological and controversial treatises, of
which the most popular was a *Dispute between a Christian
and a Jew.* Westminster produced no annals of importance. Its historical interest centred about its patron,
King Edward the Confessor, of whom we have a biography written by the prior, Osbert of Clare (*ca.* 1138), and
another by Ailred of Rievaulx, which was dedicated to
Abbot Lawrence on the occasion of the translation of the
Confessor's body in 1163. Osbert also indited certain
verses to Henry II on the eve of his accession.

In Germany likewise the age is one of decay in the

monastic life. Old imperial abbeys like Fulda, Korvey, and Lorsch were almost bankrupt; the number of monks had shrunk; all intellectual leadership was gone. Germany became a fertile field for the newer movements of reform, Cistercian, Augustinian, and Premonstratensian, both in the older regions where discipline had declined and in the newer lands of missionary activity; but of these new orders none originated in Germany — all were Latin. Their extension did much for the spread of French agriculture and architecture to the East, less for books and learning. The newer libraries of the twelfth century are almost entirely limited to copies of the Fathers, though Tegernsee is still lending classical authors; and the new currents of thought start elsewhere. In law and medicine this is obvious; even in theology by "the second half of the century Germany is unmistakably behind the Romance countries." [1]

In Spain the natural development of monastic life had been broken by the Moorish invasion and the religious wars which followed, and in the revival of the eleventh century the lead had been taken by the Cluniacs rather than the Benedictines. These older foundations had passed their prime by the twelfth century: of the surviving codices of the library of Silos scarcely any betray the characteristic French hand of this age; Santa Maria de Ripoll reached its height under Abbot Oliva (1008–46), when we have a catalogue of its notable library of two

---

[1] A. Hauck, *Kirchengeschichte Deutschlands*, iv. (1903), p. 449.

hundred and forty-six titles, and by our period it has become a dependency of St. Victor of Marseilles. San Pedro de Cardeña was now chiefly remarkable for the tomb of the Cid. The new knowledge which Spain spread over Europe in this period had not found a place in her own monastic libraries; indeed, the whole number of twelfth-century manuscripts in Spain today is disappointingly small.

In the order of Cluni, also, the twelfth century was a period of decline. Founded in 910 as a protest against the secularization of monastic life, Cluni became the centre of the great movement of ecclesiastical reform which reached its height in the time of Gregory VII. Besides its efforts for freedom from lay and episcopal control, it replaced the manual labor of the Benedictines by a large extension of the office of the choir; and it substituted for their decentralized system of autonomous abbeys a monarchical regime in which a single abbot stood supreme, appointing the priors of all subordinate houses and visiting them in person or through deputies, while representatives of the whole order were later summoned to an annual chapter under the abbot. Such an organization was well devised for introducing and maintaining discipline in older monasteries which had fallen into decline; it was also excellent for colonization, so that Cluniac priories sprang up rapidly along the pilgrim routes that led to Spain, and spread in the Peninsula itself with the progress of the Reconquest, till the order came to number

twenty-six dependencies beyond the Pyrenees, some of
which counted seriously in the reëstablishment of Christian culture there. Sahagún, indeed, was called 'the
Spanish Cluni.' Moreover, in the Spain of the eleventh
century Cluni did notable work for Rome, supporting the
Roman against the Mozarabic liturgy, and securing
bishoprics for its *iuvenes dociles et litterati* who came from
France. The centralization of Cluni was also highly important in stimulating travel and communication, and
therewith doubtless the exchange of books and ideas and
types of art. The customs of Cluni provided for the copying of manuscripts, but looked askance at classical learning. If a monk wanted a book during the hours of silence,
he made a sign of turning the leaves; if he wanted a
classical book, he scratched his ear like a dog. Still the
classics were read, notably Virgil, Horace, and even Ovid
and Martial; indeed, there are many classical authors
among the five hundred and seventy volumes of the
twelfth-century catalogue of Cluni, a remarkably large
and complete collection for its time. The order of Cluni
had few famous schools, and its writers deal with subjects of devotion and ecclesiastical biography. History,
for example, was notably neglected. Of the seven great
abbots under whom Cluni flourished, the last died in
1156, Peter the Venerable, a worthy type, who has left
us in his correspondence records of his journeys to Spain
and Italy and of his labors against heresy and efforts to
combat Mohammedanism by securing translations of the

Koran and anti-Mohammedan tracts; also an inter-change of medical letters with a Salernitan Master Bartholomew, not to mention sermons, theological trea-tises, and poems showing acquaintance with the ancients. Already, however, Cluni is struggling against the *novi milites Christi* of Cîteaux, and its leadership goes down before the new asceticism of St. Bernard.

In new orders the twelfth century and the years just preceding were fruitful: the Carthusians, the Premon-stratensians, the Augustinian canons, the orders of Grammont, Fontevrault, and Camaldoli, and especially of Cîteaux. The purpose of these was, however, spiritual rather than intellectual, and their influence was exerted in the direction of missions or of a stricter observance of ascetic principles rather than in the advancement of learning. Specific obligations like the Carthusian rule of silence and contemplation worked, indeed, in the opposite direction, in spite of the explicit mention of copying in the cells. The best illustration of these ascetic ten-dencies is seen in the Cistercians and their great leader, St. Bernard; the proof of their popularity is found in the expansion of this order in forty years, until it comprised three hundred and forty-three communities at Bernard's death in 1153.

The Cistercians, exponents of the simple life, sought to restore the rule of St. Benedict in its most austere form. Manual labor in the fields was required; the office of the choir now occupies about six hours, including a service in the middle of the night. There were no hours of leisure. Everything was to be of the plainest, especially the churches. Copying of manuscripts there was, but illumination and ornament were forbidden. The purpose of the copying was principally to provide correct texts for the choir. In the Cistercian monasteries there must be the same text of "the Missal, the Epistolary, the Bible, the Collectarium, the Gradual, the Antiphonary, the Rule, the Hymnary, the Psalter, the Lectionary, and the Calendar." The library of Clairvaux has been reconstructed from what survives today; the codices of the twelfth century are almost wholly scriptural, patristic, and liturgical, with a little history, some textbooks, and a few classics. Law, medicine, philosophy, the scholastic theology, are almost entirely lacking. "Cîteaux was not a school of learning, not even of theological learning."[1] Its greatest leader, Bernard, was a mystic, not a scholar. At the best, the Cistercian libraries were theological, with little secular literature, as we may judge from the catalogues of Rievaulx and the Austrian cloisters. One could enter the order without being able to read.

The new orders had a further importance in intellectual history in that their European organizations counteracted the extreme localism of the individual monastery and required a certain amount of regular communication between different and often widely distant establishments, as contrasted with the irregular and casual rela-

[1] E. Vacandard, *Vie de Saint Bernard*, i. 54.

tions of earlier times. Monastic travel to and from Rome was also encouraged by the centralizing tendencies within the church in the matter of appeals and confirmations of possessions, and by the growth of papal protection of individual monasteries. On the other hand, both the individual exemption and the papal patronage of the new orders tended to loosen the local ties which bound the monastery to the diocesan, and thus to sharpen the contrast between regular and secular clergy. Nevertheless, even in this period of divergence, we must not think of a complete intellectual separation of regular and secular, particularly as regards adjacent groups. Thus, at Paris we may for many purposes associate in our minds the cathedral clergy, the secular canons of Sainte-Geneviève, the canons regular of Saint-Victor, and the monks of Saint-Germain-des-Prés and other cloisters of the vicinity. Nor must it be forgotten that many cathedrals had monastic chapters, notably in England, where Canterbury, Rochester, Winchester, Worcester, and Durham were conspicuous examples.

Then the intellectual connections of the monasteries with the lay world must not be overlooked, least of all after the convincing illustrations given by Bédier in his studies of the genesis of the French epic. If diffusion was slow from the monastery into the surrounding medium of field or forest, the case was very different in the towns and along the great highways, especially along the pilgrimage roads to Rome and Compostela. Stations of call and entertainment for every traveller, refuges of healing and consolation, shrines of devotion and even of miracles, these religious establishments collected distant fact and rumor for their local annals, spun their narratives of the wonders wrought by local saints and relics, and passed on rich material for the popular epics which grew up along these roads and about these shrines. They were the natural meeting-points of the world of the monk and the sacristan with the world of the pilgrim, the trader, and the jongleur, of sacred and profane, Latin and vernacular, till all become indistinguishable to our eye. Saint-Denis, Meaux, and Fécamp, Vézelay and Novalese, Gellone and Saint-Gilles, the Cluniac priories on the road to Spain, these and many others are now known as centres of creation and diffusion of the epics of the eleventh and twelfth centuries.

With the decline of the monasteries as intellectual centres, the cathedrals emerge for a time into a position for which they had long been preparing. By a reform which became general in the ninth century, the clergy attached to a cathedral had been subjected to the regime of a common, quasi-monastic life, according to a rule or *canon* which gave them what was henceforth their usual name. In course of time these canons acquired the function of choosing the bishop, from whom they insisted on receiving a definite share of the cathedral revenues, sooner or later parcelled out as prebends for the individual canons. They were organized into a chapter under a dean and with various lesser officers, such as the precentor, the *scolasticus*, and the treasurer. Sometimes the disintegrating chapter was reformed into a regular monastic community. In any case, the chapter likewise needed its books, its school, and its records; and we must also take account of those who more directly assisted the bishop in the administration of the diocese and formed the episcopal household, in which the canonistic and secretarial element was by this time considerable. For our purposes we may in the twelfth century consider the chapter and bishop together as an intellectual centre, rich, powerful, often well educated, and always established in an urban community rather than in the rural isolation of most of the monasteries. The cathedral library, the cathedral school, the cathedral archives, the *gesta* of its bishops, the writings of its canons, the bishop's jurisdiction, the bishop's patronage of learning, play a large part in this age, intermediate between the monastery on the one hand and the princely courts on the other.

Intellectually the most active body of cathedral centres in the twelfth century was those of Northern France. The importance of their schools we shall have occasion to examine when we come to study the origins of the French universities; their relation to the literature and philosophy of the age we shall need to discuss in still other connections. Here we can only stop to indicate the significance of Chartres and Orleans as seats of the classi-

cal revival, of Rheims and Laon as centres of scholastic
learning, of Paris as the home of the first Northern university, all of them drawing disciples from Germany and
England and even from beyond the Alps. A list of the
great writers of the age would include bishops like Hildebert at Le Mans (and Tours), Gilbert de la Porrée at
Poitiers, Peter Lombard at Paris, and John of Salisbury
at Chartres; chancellors like Anselm of Laon, Bernard of
Chartres, Peter Comestor and Peter of Poitiers at Paris;
canons like the profane poet Hugh of Orleans and the
scriptural versifier Peter Riga of Rheims; other cathedral
teachers like Robert of Melun, William of Conches,
Bernard Silvester, and Abaelard. Most of the great
names in poetry, theology, and education belong to the
cathedrals. Even prelates who did not themselves write
encouraged learning: William of the White Hands, bishop
of Chartres and archbishop of Sens and of Rheims (1176–
1202), cardinal, and regent of France during the Third
Crusade, received the dedications of the *Alexandreid* of
Walter of Châtillon, the *Microcosmographia* of an unknown William, the *Sentences* of Peter of Poitiers, and the
Historia scholastica of Peter Comestor. One is reminded
of the court of his brother and neighbor, Henry the
Liberal, count of Champagne.

In England Canterbury is the best example of such a
vigorous cathedral community; indeed, Stubbs goes so
far as to compare it as a literary centre to the Oxford
and Cambridge of our own day. Archbishop Theobald

(1138–61), who had been trained at Bec, gathered learned men about him at Canterbury. His secretary was John of Salisbury, "for thirty years the central figure of English learning," whose letters touch on literary as well as administrative subjects, and reflect relations with Continental scholars as well as his many journeys to France and Italy. His legal adviser was Master Vacarius, an Italian jurist who wrote on theology and on canon and civil law. Canterbury was already in close touch with the great schools of the Continent. The next archbishop was Thomas Becket, already trained under Theobald and in the royal curia; at Canterbury and in exile he drew about him the group of the *eruditi Sancti Thome* who did so much by their letters and biographies to keep his memory green. One of these, Peter of Blois, has left us this description of the archiepiscopal household:

This court in which I live is, I assure you, a camp of God, none other than the house of God and the gate of heaven. In the house of my lord the Archbishop are most scholarly men, with whom is found all the uprightness of justice, all the caution of providence, every form of learning. They, after prayers, and before meals, in reading, in disputing, in the decision of causes, constantly exercise themselves. All the knotty questions of the realm are referred to us, and, when they are discussed in the common hearing, each of us, without strife or objection, sharpens his wits to speak well upon them, and produces, from a more subtile vein, what he thinks the most prudent and sensible advice.[1]

Canterbury was a monastic chapter, and among the monks we find the historian Gervase, the poet Nigel

[1] W. Stubbs, *Seventeen Lectures on Mediaeval and Modern History* (1900), p. 164.

Wireker, author of a famous satire on the students of Paris, and the many correspondents of the *Epistolae Cantuarienses* toward the end of the century, one of whom has a fondness for quoting Ovid's *Art of Love*. The cathedral, too, had a famous library, which is now dispersed, but whose contents have been skilfully reconstructed through the patient labor of Dr. Montague James.

Though no other English cathedral could vie with Canterbury, there were many canons and archdeacons who distinguished themselves in the literature of the day, the canons often in history, the archdeacons in the law they had learned at Bologna while enjoying the fruits of their English livings and perhaps listening to the discussion of a stock problem of the day, "Can an archdeacon be saved?" [1] Bishop Henry of Winchester, brother of King Stephen, was eminent as a patron of art and letters. As the century wore on, St. Paul's was perhaps the most important of these centres; if a visitor came to town,

the venerable old dean, Ralph de Diceto, would show him the beautiful MS. of his *Ymagines*; from the canon Richard, the high treasurer, he might learn the history of the Exchequer, or even borrow the precious Tricolumnis before it was lost; Peter of Blois would be grumbling at the small profits of his archdeaconry, but wisely putting his pen to good interest; Roger Niger perhaps just flying from the wrath of the king, whom he has exasperated by savage invective; and the great Foliot himself, the able statesman who pitted all his skill, experience, and learning against the zeal of Becket and lost the game, at least in the opinion of his contemporaries.[2]

---

[1] *An archidiaconus possit salvus esse.*
[2] Stubbs, *Seventeen Lectures*, pp. 168–169.

Strangely enough, we hear comparatively little of the schools of these cathedrals, and as a matter of fact none of the English cathedral schools developed into a university.

In Spain the cathedral of Toledo was the most important, although mention should be made of the library of Barcelona, the translations of Arabic astrology directed by Bishop Michael of Tarazona (1119–51), and the *Codex Calixtinus* of the great pilgrim shrine, Santiago de Compostela, so important in the history of Carolingian romance. Restored to its ancient primacy by the Christian reconquest of 1085, Toledo was the natural place of exchange for Christian and Mohammedan learning. At this ancient centre of scientific teaching "were to be found a wealth of Arabic books and a number of masters of the two tongues, and with the help of these Mozarabs and resident Jews there arose a regular school for the translation of Arabic-Latin books and science, which drew from all lands those who thirsted for knowledge, . . . and left the signature of Toledo on many of the most famous versions of Arabic learning." [1] In all this Archbishop Raymond (1125–51) seems to have taken the initiative; the philosophical translations of his time were followed by works of medicine, mathematics, logic, and astronomy; and while there is no clear connection of the bishop with the greatest of these translators, Gerard of Cremona, a

[1] V. Rose, "Ptolemaeus und die Schule von Toledo," in *Hermes*, viii. 327 (1874).

medical version of Mark, canon of Toledo, his contemporary, shows some learning at the cathedral toward the close of the century. Gerard's name, however, is significant of the fact that most of the translators who worked in Spain were of foreign origin; but it is also noteworthy that they should seek "the wiser philosophers of the world" at Toledo, whether or not it had any formal cathedral school.

In Germany and Italy the story is different. The struggle over investiture had wrought lasting injury to the earlier centres of culture like Liége, and the twelfth century is a period of intellectual decline in Germany among the secular as well as among the regular clergy. The great prelates were in politics, most of them very deep in politics, as in the case of the Rhenish archbishops. Christian of Mainz was lieutenant of Frederick Barbarossa in Italy, whither Reinald of Cologne accompanied the emperor, taking the 'Archpoet' in his train and bringing back the bones of the Three Kings to enrich his cathedral treasury. The eminence of Freising under Bishop Otto was personal rather than institutional; indeed, Otto was a quite exceptional figure, trained in the new dialectic of France, which he was the first to introduce into Germany, monk as well as bishop, brother of Conrad III and uncle of Barbarossa, almost a court historian as he tells of their exploits which he personally witnessed at home, in Italy, and in the East.[1] In Italy,

[1] See Chapter VIII.

too, the higher clergy were likely to be in politics, municipal here as well as imperial, still more in politics as the struggle of Guelf and Ghibelline grew more intense, and they no longer show the intellectual leadership of the preceding age. It was rare to find a bishop-historian like Romuald II of Salerno (1153–81), author of a valuable universal chronicle which gives much first-hand information respecting the Sicilian kingdom; his cathedral is also remarkable for its imposing *Liber confratrum*, which could count nearly 12,000 names by the end of the twelfth century, but this is a monument of local nomenclature and palaeography rather than of intellectual activity, and such foreigners as appear in this 'Book of Life' were doubtless drawn to Salerno by its physicians rather than its cathedral clergy. So, at Milan, the Archbishop Chrysolanus, who disputes theology with the Greeks at Constantinople *ca.* 1112, is an isolated figure; his successors are less occupied with the Ambrosian tradition than with matters of administration and with the complications of Milanese and Lombard politics.

Concerning the court, feudal or royal, as an intellectual centre, ideas might vary. About 1155 a poet of Samarcand named Nizami declared that a properly constituted court should have four classes of educated men: secretaries of state, poets, astrologers, and physicians, for "the business of kings cannot be conducted without competent secretaries; their triumphs and victories will not be immortalized without eloquent poets; their enterprises will not succeed unless undertaken at seasons adjudged propitious by sagacious astrologers; while health, the basis of all happiness and activity, can only be secured by the services of able and trustworthy physicians." [1] A bit Oriental and elaborate all this sounds, though even in the West most courts had their astrologers by the thirteenth century — the earl of Chester even in the twelfth — and the other three might well be found still earlier, but in a less bureaucratic form. The small feudal court was only a rudimentary organism, intellectually speaking, particularly where the lord himself could neither read nor write. Still there was always a chaplain at least, to say mass in the chapel and write the necessary letters, in course of time a chancellor, or secretary, as the secretarial business grew and the archives needed attention. Indeed, a regular chancery becomes a sure test of administrative development. A tutor, as for the young Henry II at his father's or uncle's court, was rare, as was book learning for princes. The poet, or jongleur, could usually be found, if we are willing to stretch the word to include anything from a court jester, or fool, to the professional trouvère or troubadour, and to make of him in the lesser households not a permanence but an occasional visitor — "the way was long, the wind was cold, the minstrel was infirm and old"! Enough, in any case, to make the court a potential source

[1] E. G. Browne, *Arabian Medicine* (Cambridge, 1921), pp. 79–80.

of vernacular as well as of Latin literature. The sacred
and profane elements, however, might not always fuse
perfectly; whatever could be said for an archdeacon's
future, the clerical writers were quite clear respecting the
jongleurs, who 'have no use or virtue' and 'are beyond
hope of salvation.' So John of Salisbury, classical always, finds that the actors and buffoons of his day imitate the improprieties of Nero rather than the dignity of
Augustus and the ancient stage. Great festivals like a
coronation, a marriage, the knighting of a prince, or even
the three great yearly court days of the Anglo-Norman
kings, might bring together what the chroniclers would
call "an innumerable multitude of jongleurs and actors";
and the Provençal romance *Flamenca* (1234) enumerates
at length the tales which these might recount, from Troy,
Thebes, and Alexander to Goliath and Arthur and Charlemagne and the Old Man of the Mountain. The court was
always a potential centre of literary patronage, whether
permanent or occasional, also a potential centre of history, as we shall see in a later chapter. As regards literature, indeed, in the absence of a book market, courtly
patronage was a prime necessity for those who lacked
some assured ecclesiastical income, and was often the
best help toward securing a position in the church.

The process of feudal consolidation in this period
raised many of these courts to a higher power as administrative and intellectual centres. In the South, various
seats of Provençal poetry may serve as examples, not

forgetting prince-poets like William IX of Aquitaine and patrons like his granddaughter Eleanor. The counts of Champagne had a learned court, for which a copy of Valerius Maximus was made in 1167, and at least one of them, Thibaut IV, was himself a poet of importance. Even a relatively unimportant lord, like the count of Guines, might have his local historian, that priest of Ardres whom we shall meet later, and might cause French translations to be made of Solinus and other classics. In Saxony, Henry the Lion passes as a patron of culture — while he is in Saxony. In England, Earl Robert of Gloucester was a distinguished supporter of literature, receiving the dedication of the historical works of William of Malmesbury and encouraging Celtic romance in the person of his chaplain, Geoffrey of Monmouth, whose epoch-making *History of the British Kings* is likewise dedicated to this border prince. A little later, "every [English] baron kept his staff of clerks," though "that few of the barons who were not court officials knew any language besides Norman French is fairly certain." [1]

If the Anglo-Norman bureaucracy goes back to William the Conqueror, remembered for his Domesday Survey as well as for his minstrel Taillefer,

qui mult bien chantout,

it reaches its climax under Henry II (1154–89), master of an empire which extended from the Scottish border to the

[1] Mary Bateson, *Mediaeval England* (New York, 1904), p. 174.

Pyrenees, and probably the most powerful monarch of his day in Latin Christendom. While his realm had no single capital in the modern sense, finance and justice had certain fixed nuclei, like Westminster and Caen, to which the king constantly returned; and it had a well defined fiscal, judicial, and chancery procedure which required a vast number of officials, so vast that one contemporary likens them to an army of locusts. When the king held a great court day of his own, like the Christmas court at Caen in 1182, he could require his vassals to give up their own courts in order to attend. Moreover, Henry was a man of education, brought up in the household of his uncle, Robert of Gloucester, and acquainted with the languages of Europe from the Channel to the Jordan; his international relations were wide, his daughters being married to the rulers of Saxony, Sicily, and Castile; and the union of his own diverse lands in a single hand furthered the exchange of elements Germanic, Celtic, French, and Provençal. A patron of literature and of minstrelsy, he had an official chronicler, besides the fragments that fell from his table into the unofficial pages of Walter Map, and a mass of documentary records whose fulness and precision have been justly admired. Of the many books written by men of his court, a score or more were dedicated to him, including a little theology, some science and vernacular poetry, perhaps some medicine, much history both in Latin and French, and two works descriptive of his system of justice and finance, unique monuments to the high development of his administrative organization. There was still much confusion and 'grabbing for quarters' as the household moved about the country, but even such matters had been organized by Henry I in the *Constitutio domus regis*, the earliest of the many household ordinances of European royalty, where each of the many officers has his daily allowance of bread and wine and candle ends, department by department, beginning with the chancellor, the master of the *scriptorium*, and the chaplain. So the Exchequer of the same period combines the careful accounting of its clerks with a semi-annual public reckoning intelligible to the unlettered sheriffs who attended.

The Sicilian court is more clearly bureaucratic; indeed, it has a strongly Oriental flavor, Byzantine as well as Arabic, and its astrologers and poets, its Arab physicians and many-tongued secretaries come very near to reproducing the entourage described by the poet of Samarcand with whom we started. Its records, in Latin, Greek, and Arabic, required a large staff of expert clerks and a permanent depository at Palermo; its palaces suggest the pleasure dwellings of the Mohammedan East; its household has the seclusion of an Oriental harem. Its intellectual influence corresponds to its geographical position and opportunity. A meeting-point of North and South, East and West, it was a fertile source of translations from Greek and Arabic, even a place where works were written in these languages. Its first king, Roger, made a hobby of geography, and supervised the preparation of the great map of Edrisi with its accompanying Arabic text. Under his successor, William I, the chief translators, Aristippus and Eugene of Palermo, were officers of the royal administration. The reign of Frederick II (1198–1250) carries us into a later period, but it is in large degree the culmination of what precedes. The cradle of Italian poetry, Frederick's court also continues the Arabic traditions of its predecessors, while his cosmopolitan scientific and philosophic tastes are Sicilian as well as personal. All these matters we shall need to examine in later chapters.[1]

The less bureaucratic courts are less important for our purpose, for their more ambulatory character prevented them from acquiring so solid a nucleus of record, of historical writing, and of courtly literature in general. Among such centres the Empire comes first, in the person of Frederick Barbarossa and his son Henry VI, both men of intellectual tastes who encouraged particularly an official historiography in Latin verse, as we shall note in another connection; indeed such records are more abundant in their reigns than in that of their more brilliant successor Frederick II. The French monarchy is as yet insignificant as a patron of learning, while in Spain we must wait until the later thirteenth century for Alfonso the Wise.

The more highly organized centres bring into relief another matter of much cultural importance, namely the

[1] Chapters VIII, IX.

intercommunication of courts, which in these cases becomes more frequent and more easily traced. Henry II receives long visits from his son-in-law, the duke of Saxony, and sends a splendid escort with Princess Joanna to Sicily; he entertains a Norwegian archbishop for several months; his Assize of Arms is said to have been imitated by the less developed governments of his neighbors, the king of France and the count of Flanders; Peter of Blois makes himself useful at both the Norman and Sicilian courts; the Englishman Thomas Brown is welcomed with other foreigners to the household of Roger II, where he sits as judge and chaplain, and as Kaid Brûn certifies a fiscal record in Arabic, but he goes home to a position of dignity and responsibility at Henry's English Exchequer. Gervase of Tilbury, too, passes from the English to the Sicilian households, and later to the marshalship of the kingdom of Arles, picking up by the way the miscellanies of his *Otia imperialia*, which is dedicated to Otto IV. So, somewhat later, Frederick II and Henry III have the same Latin *versificator*, Henry of Avranches, who also writes for the Pope and various baronial patrons; while Frederick brings the poets of his *Magna Curia* into contact with the troubadours and Minnesinger of his Transalpine dominions, welcomes Theodore the philosopher from Antioch and Michael Scot from Spain, and maintains a learned correspondence with the scientists and philosophers of the various Mohammedan sovereigns of North Africa and the East.

The towns of the twelfth century have a larger place in the world of trade and politics than in the world of letters. There was not as yet a distinctive urban culture such as arose in the later Middle Ages, still less any urban patrons of art and literature like those who appear in the Italian Renaissance. The Maecenas of the twelfth century was still the prince, lay or ecclesiastical. At the same time, no merely academic or belletristic notion of culture can measure the importance of the towns of this period in the longer perspective of intellectual history. For Northern Europe, at least, the twelfth century saw in full course an economic and social revolution which marked the beginnings of a profound intellectual change. The wandering merchant "brought mobility to the midst of people attached to the soil; he revealed, to a world faithful to tradition and respectful of a hierarchy which fixed the role and the rank of each class, a shrewd and rationalist activity in which fortune, instead of being measured by social status, depended only on intelligence and energy." [1] To the traditional social classes of those who fight, those who farm, and those who pray, the towns added a fourth class of traders and manufacturers, the bourgeoisie of the future, which would even claim God as a bourgeois, *li premierz plus anchiiens et souverains bourgois de tous*, say the échevins of Douai in 1366. Sharply distinguished from the rural bondage round about it, the town was an area of freedom, a centre of capital, a focus

[1] H. Pirenne, *Medieval Cities* (Princeton, 1925), pp. 127–128.

of intense activity, a forum of discussion, with its own law and with at least some degree of self-government. Often its constitution was borrowed from that of another town, and that not always a neighbor. Many of its inhabitants travelled on business, sometimes long distances. On these journeys they met chiefly men from other towns, chancing upon them at the wayside shrines and markets where vernacular literature was in the making, gathering in larger groups at the great fairs whither men came from all parts of Europe, dusty-footed suitors in those pie-powder courts where their special law merchant was made and administered. They might in this way pick up strange and even forbidden ideas, like those dualistic heresies which had come a long way from the East along the lines of trade and were now spreading into the Northern towns, where weaver and heretic often became synonymous. Very mediaeval all this in its setting, very modern in its implications!

For all this development reading and writing were a convenience but not a necessity. Nevertheless, while the peasants did without these for many centuries to come, the townsmen of the North began to create lay schools where elementary education was given. For anything more we must as yet look to the older cities of the South, especially in Italy, where the traditions of lay education had survived among the notaries and scribes, and where, as in Venice, reading and writing had spread among the trading class. Already Italian cities had their local archives and their local chronicles, as well as their local schools of law. Moreover, the commercial republics of the Mediterranean were the chief means of communication with the East. Venice and Pisa each had a commercial quarter at Constantinople as well as in the principal Syrian cities; they sent out frequent diplomatic missions, and their citizens might even hold places at the Byzantine court. In 1136 we find at Constantinople James of Venice, who translated the *New Logic* of Aristotle; Moses of Bergamo, who has a valuable library of Greek manuscripts and writes a Latin poem on his native city; and Burgundio the Pisan, who passes back and forth to the East in the course of his long life, turning into Latin many works of Greek theology and medicine.[1] Somewhat earlier, an anonymous Pisan is celebrating in verse his city's victory over the Saracens of Majorca, and a fellow citizen named Stephen is translating Arabic medicine at Antioch. If the intercourse with the Mohammedan East is mainly concerned with the wares of commerce, we must remember that ever since the Greek and Phoenician traders it has been impossible to separate the interchange of wares from the interchange of knowledge and ideas. Unfortunately, such results of trade are likely to be intangible and to leave few immediate traces.

The university as a separate species of intellectual centre belongs rather to a later age than to that with which we are here concerned. It is true that the twelfth

[1] See Chapter IX.

century created the university type for the later world, and we shall see that at least five universities go back to the twelfth century: Salerno, Bologna, Paris, Montpellier, and Oxford. Nevertheless, these have not entirely emerged from the general group of schools: the name university is scarcely known in this sense; its distinctive organization is scarcely recognized; universities do not yet associate exclusively with other universities, nor has the Papacy laid its guiding hand upon them.

Of the communication within and even between these several sets of intellectual centres, the actual movement of ideas and knowledge and books from place to place, we know all too little. The roads we know, with their auxiliaries of river and sea, old Roman highways for the most part, connecting the ancient cities which were now the seats of bishops and cathedrals, and joining most of the newer towns as well, dotted with shrines and refuges and monastic establishments, the inevitable paths of all intellectual intercourse at long range. "In the beginning was the Road," says Bédier.[1] Lacking the security of the Roman peace and abandoned for their upkeep to the indifference of local authorities, the great highways still served the purpose of frequent and reasonably expeditious communication. The average itinerary for long journeys ran from twenty to thirty miles a day, but individual messengers might make forty miles. "A message from Rome might reach Canterbury in a little less than

[1] *Les légendes épiques*, second edition (Paris, 1914–21), iii. 367.

five weeks, and . . . a traveller, as distinguished from an express courier, was expected to spend about seven weeks on the journey." [1] The report of Frederick Barbarossa's death in Asia Minor required four months to reach Germany, whereas the news of Richard's capture in Austria reached England in about as many weeks. In 1191 the body of the archbishop of Cologne was carried home from Naples in six weeks. How fast did books travel?

The more specific facts of intellectual intercourse generally elude us; at best our knowledge is qualitative rather than quantitative. We know the routes of pilgrims and merchants, we do not know their number and the extent of their influence. We can trace the itineraries of the crusaders, but not the ideas which they carried with them. Few students can be followed on their journeyings, and even the classic accounts of Otto of Freising and John of Salisbury lack detail. The movements of the higher clergy can often be followed more closely and deserve further study. Thus the journeys of English ecclesiastics to Rome give the impression of a large amount of travel. Five bishops and four abbots from England attended the Lateran council of 1139. There was an English cardinal by 1144 and an English Pope, just returned from Scandinavia, in 1154. On the last of several visits to Rome, *ca.* 1150, Bishop Henry of Winchester bought ancient statues and came home by way of

---

[1] R. L. Poole, *The Early Correspondence of John of Salisbury* (British Academy, 1924), p. 6.

Spain and Compostela. Robert, prior of St. Frideswide's at Oxford, who dedicated an abridged Pliny to Henry II, visited Rome more than once and penetrated as far as Sicily. Two men of letters, Walter Map and Adam du Petit-Pont, stand out in the large British delegation that attended the council of 1179. The monks of St. Augustine's, Canterbury, sent thirty missions to Rome in the course of the century, those of Christ Church seventeen. Bishop Philip of Bayeux, a notable collector of books, made at least four visits to Rome. John of Salisbury visited Italy at least six times, consorting with the Sicilian chancellor, and serving for eight years at the papal court; he met the Pisan translator Burgundio and at least one other Greek interpreter. What did he carry back? All these examples are rich in intellectual possibilities, some of which may yield their secret to the diligent inquirer. For the most part, however, we have only tantalizing possibilities, and we must resign ourselves to the admission that many interesting and important facts concerning the twelfth century have been lost beyond recovery. We may try to console ourselves by remembering that this is true in some degree of all periods of history, and in an especial sense of those imponderable facts which make up the history of ideas.

BIBLIOGRAPHICAL NOTE

For the monasteries in general the chief sources are the *Consuetudines* of the several orders and the numerous biographies and chronicles of particular establishments; for the twelfth century we lack the concrete details given in the more systematic visitations and inquests of a later age. For a comprehensive bibliography, see *Cambridge Medieval History*, v, ch. 20. A good study of the monastery as an institution is that of F. Pijper, *De Kloosters* (The Hague, 1916). Favorable sketches by modern Benedictines are U. Berlière, *L'ordre monastique* (second edition, Paris, 1921), and F. A. Gasquet, *English Monastic Life* (London, 1904). For the intellectual life of the Cluniacs, see E. Sackur, *Die Cluniacenser* (Halle, 1892–94); for that of the Cistercians, H. d'Arbois de Jubainville, *Études sur l'état intérieur des abbayes cisterciennes au XIIᵉ et au XIIIᵉ siècle* (Paris, 1858); and E. Vacandard, *Vie de Saint Bernard* (fourth edition, Paris, 1910). Monte Cassino still awaits its historian; meanwhile see the excellent studies of E. A. Loew, *The Beneventan Script* (Oxford, 1914); and E. Caspar, *Petrus Diaconus* (Berlin, 1909). For Bec, see A. A. Porée, *Histoire de l'abbaye du Bec* (Évreux, 1901); for Saint-Évroul, Delisle's introduction to his *Ordericus Vitalis*, v (Paris, 1855); for Troarn, R. N. Sauvage, *L'abbaye de Saint-Martin de Troarn* (Caen, 1911). For Westminster, cf. J. A. Robinson, *Gilbert Crispin* (Cambridge, 1911); for English Cistercians, F. M. Powicke, *Ailred of Rievaulx* (Manchester, [1922]). There is little on the intellectual life in G. G. Coulton's *Five Centuries of English Religion*, i, 1000–1200 (Cambridge, 1923). For Germany, see A. Hauck, *Kirchengeschichte Deutschlands* (Leipzig, 1887–1911); for Spain, individual studies such as M. Férotin, *Histoire de l'abbaye de Silos* (Paris, 1897), and the monograph on Ripoll mentioned in the following chapter.

The cathedral as an institution is described in the manuals of canon law; as an intellectual centre it still awaits study. Meanwhile one may consult the biographies of eminent archbishops and bishops, as in the *Dictionary of National Biography*, or occasional monographs like V. Rose, "Ptolemaeus und die Schule von Toledo," in *Hermes*, viii. 327–349 (1874). The *Necrologio del Liber Confratrum di S. Matteo di Salerno* is admirably edited by C. A. Garufi (Rome, 1922). For cathedral schools, see below, Chapter XII.

The ordinary books on court and castle life have little to say of the court as an intellectual centre. See, instead, E. Faral, *Les jongleurs en France au moyen âge* (Paris, 1910); K. J. Holzknecht, *Liter-*

ary Patronage in the Middle Ages (University of Pennsylvania thesis, 1923); and the many books on the troubadours. On Henry the Lion, see F. Philippi, in *Historische Zeitschrift*, cxxvii. 50–65 (1922). For the court of Henry II, see Stubbs, *Seventeen Lectures on Mediaeval and Modern History* (third edition, Oxford, 1900), chs. 6, 7; Haskins, *Norman Institutions* (Cambridge, 1918), ch. 5; Haskins, "Henry II as a Patron of Literature," in *Essays in Mediaeval History Presented to Thomas Frederick Tout* (Manchester, 1925), pp. 71–77. For the Sicilian court, Haskins, *Studies in the History of Mediaeval Science* (Cambridge, 1924), chs. 9, 12–14, and "England and Sicily in the Twelfth Century," in *English Historical Review*, xxvi. 433–447, 641–665 (1911). There are unpublished doctoral theses in the Harvard University Library on "Englishmen in Italy in the Twelfth Century," by P. B. Schaeffer (1923), and on "Henry of Avranches," by J. C. Russell (1926).

The vast literature concerning mediaeval towns says little of their intellectual life in this period. For a brilliant sketch of the early history of the Northern towns, see H. Pirenne, *Medieval Cities* (Princeton, 1925); for the North-Italian translators, Haskins, *Mediaeval Science*, ch. 10.

On communication, see, besides such works as J. J. Jusserand's *English Wayfaring Life in the Middle Ages*, J. Bédier's *Légendes épiques*, and the general books on commerce, F. Ludwig, *Untersuchungen über die Reise- und Marschgeschwindigkeit im XII. und XIII. Jahrhundert* (Berlin, 1897); and Haskins, "The Spread of Ideas in the Middle Ages," in *Speculum*, i. 19–30 (1926).

On the subjects of this chapter, see also the later bibliographies, particularly that of Chapter VIII.

CHAPTER III

BOOKS AND LIBRARIES

ANY study of the mind of the twelfth century must keep in view the books which were then ordinarily available and the conditions which surrounded their manufacture and use. Indeed, it would be desirable, were it possible, to examine the intellectual background of each writer on the basis of his citations, his travels, and the books to which he had access. At the least, we must divest ourselves of modern prepossessions, not only in such obvious matters as editions and sales, but in the subtler assumptions of easy access to standard material. Without a realistic view of the libraries of an epoch, we easily run into misunderstandings. "Plato," says Coulton,[1] "might have shaken hands with Anselm"; but in any real sense this was impossible, because there were no Greek manuscripts in the West, because Anselm was ignorant of Greek, and because there were then no Latin translations of any work of Plato save a portion of the *Timaeus*. An admirable example of the proper approach to a writer of the twelfth century is seen in Léopold Delisle's introduction to the *History* of Ordericus Vitalis, where we find a catalogue of the library of his monastery of Saint-Évroul, a disquisition on the state of learning

[1] *Five Centuries of Religion*, i (Cambridge, 1923), p. 21. For mediaeval Platonism, see below, Chapter XI.

in the abbey, a summary of Orderic's reading, especially as seen in his citations, and an account of his rare travels as far as Cambrai and Worcester.

It is well to remember at the outset that when men spoke of a library in the Middle Ages they did not mean a special room, still less a special building. A common word for library was *armarium*, which means wardrobe or book-press, and that is what the 'library' was. This was ordinarily kept in the church, later often in an alcove of the cloister with shelves in the wall. In some cases there was a special place for schoolbooks. Such collections of books were perforce small, and the earliest monastic catalogues list but a few volumes, perhaps a score or so. Lanfranc's *Consuetudines* for English Benedictines at the end of the eleventh century assume that all the books of a monastery can be piled on a single rug, but they also assume that there will be enough copies to provide one for the annual reading of every monk. So much at least was necessary: a monastery without a library is like a castle without an armory, ran the saying of the time (*claustrum sine armario est quasi castrum sine armamentario*).

Such collections grew by gift, purchase, or manufacture on the spot. Purchase was in the twelfth century uncommon, for there was as yet no class of professional scribes and no general book market, though Bologna and Paris already appear as places where books were bought. Manuscripts were naturally dear, especially the large service books for the choir, and we hear of a great Bible bought for ten talents and of a missal exchanged for a vineyard. In 1043 the bishop of Barcelona bought two volumes of Priscian from a Jew for a house and a piece of land. Gifts to the libraries are often recorded, from monks on entering the monastery, from travellers who enjoyed its hospitality, and especially by bequest. Thus Rouen cathedral in the twelfth century enumerates as gifts: from Archbishop Rotrou (1165–83), Pliny's *Natural History*, Jerome's letters, Augustine's *City of God*, Isidore's *Etymologies*, Vitruvius, and two volumes of the works of his predecessor Archbishop Hugh; from Lawrence the archdeacon, half a Bible; from Master Galeran, a missal; from Master R. de Antan, nine volumes of the Bible, one of which has been lent to Saint-Georges de Bocherville in exchange for a glossed psalter, the borrowing of books being still common. In 1164 Bishop Philip of Bayeux bequeathed one hundred and forty volumes to the library of Bec, twenty-seven of which never arrived; in 1180 John of Salisbury left his small library to his cathedral of Chartres. The chief source, however, was manufacture in the monasteries, where the labor of the monks was unremunerated and the supplies of parchment could often be obtained from the lands of the establishment.

The monastic *scriptorium* is an institution by itself. Though copying is not prescribed specifically in the earliest rules, it soon became recognized as a meritorious form of labor, and "every revival of monastic discipline was accompanied by renewed zeal in writing." [1] The Cluniacs freed the copyists from service in the choir, and Abbot Peter the Venerable urges copying as superior to work in the fields. The Cistercians relieved their scribes from agricultural labor, save at harvest time, and permitted them access to the forbidden kitchen for the tasks necessary to their occupation. The Carthusians required copying from the monks in their several cells. Flagging zeal was stimulated by hope of eternal rewards: "for every letter, line, and point, a sin is forgiven me," writes a monk of Arras in the eleventh century; and Ordericus tells of an erring monk who gained salvation by copying, being finally saved from the Devil by a credit balance of a single letter over his many sins. Still it was not easy to keep monks at this work, and the hired copyist is heard of more and more. Even the monastic scribes might work for hire, as when Frederick Barbarossa orders a missal and epistolary from Tegernsee.

Writing books by hand was tedious business at best, and might be painful. Even an assiduous scribe like Ordericus was forced to lay aside this work when fingers grew numb with the cold of winter; and a Brother Leo of Novara, in the tenth century, complained that while three fingers write the back is bent, the ribs sink into the stomach, and the whole body suffers. Of the actual time

[1] W. Wattenbach, *Das Schriftwesen im Mittelalter*, third edition (1896), p. 441.

required, we have few exact indications before the late, and more careless, period. In 1004 Constantine of Luxeuil copied in eleven days the so-called *Geometry* of Boethius, about fifty-five ordinary pages of modern print. In the twelfth century the dean of Saint-Trond took a whole year to complete a gradual, from the preparation of the parchment to the final illumination and musical notation. In 1162 it is recorded as something remarkable that a Bible at Leon was copied in six months and illuminated in the seventh.[1] In 1220–21 a copyist of Novara spent a year and a quarter upon a Bible. If greater expedition were required, the volume was divided by quires among several scribes.

In any case the end was welcomed in very human fashion, as many signatures express. "Thank the Lord, that is done," is the most common sentiment, accompanied sometimes with the hope of heavenly reward, and sometimes with more earthly desires — wine, beer, a fat goose, a good dinner:

> Explicit, Deo gratias.
> Finito libro sit laus et gloria Christo.
> Hic liber est scriptus, qui scripsit sit benedictus.
> Propter Christum librum bene condidit istum.
> Qui scripsit scribat, semper cum Domino vivat.
> Qui scripsit scribat et bona vina bibat.
> Finito libro pinguis detur auca magistro.
> Detur pro penna scriptori pulchra puella.

The scribe goes to chant, or to play:

> Explicit expliceat, psallere scriptor eat.
> Explicit expliceat, ludere scriptor eat.

---

[1] R. Beer, *Handschriftenschätze Spaniens* (Vienna, 1894), p. 263.

Sometimes he takes a conscious pride in his work and its fame, like the Canterbury scribe Eadwin:

> Scriptorum princeps ego, nec obitura deinceps
> Laus mea nec fama: qui sim, mea littera clama.

In general, by the twelfth century the different services of a monastery had been assigned specific lands or revenues, and when the library was not cared for in this way it was likely to depend on casual gifts. Thus the librarian of Corbie now had a special endowment for the repair of old books and the making of new ones, while at St. Albans special tithes were set apart for hiring copyists, sufficient in amount to maintain at least one regular scribe. At Abingdon we have a detailed account of the upkeep of every service of the abbey except the making of books, but at Evesham by 1206 "the priory allotted the tithes of a village to provide parchment and the salaries of copyists," while "from a fund of rent and tithe the precentor found ink and colors for illuminating and materials for binding." [1] For the long list of edifying books which Otloh of St. Emmeram copied and gave to his friends there was available only the scanty leisure from his regular duties as schoolmaster.

In our period all books were of parchment, papyrus having passed out of general use in the earlier Middle Ages and paper not yet having been introduced into the West. Carefully prepared from sheepskin in its coarser form of parchment or its finer form of vellum (from young

---

[1] M. Bateson, *Mediaeval England*, p. 214.

lambs), the material was cut and folded into quires and lined with a rule.[1] The codices vary greatly in size: while there are many large Bibles and service books written in a large hand, the twelfth century has left us a great number of small volumes, 16mo or less, written clearly but often in a minute hand, and small enough to slip into the traveller's pocket. The early twelfth century is one of the golden periods in mediaeval chirography, for the hand still possesses the legibility of the Carolingian minuscule; later on we find the introduction of the Gothic strokes and ligatures and the numerous abbreviations which become common in the thirteenth century, when cursive writing also reappears.

The twelfth century was also a period of revival in the art of the illumination of manuscripts, for the Carolingian tradition had disappeared in most places by the eleventh, and the beautiful initials of the twelfth century usher in the great work of the succeeding age. So far this is chiefly confined to initials, in red and green and gold; but we learn that Peter Comestor introduced figures into his popular *Scholastic History*, and a famous example of the monastic art of the twelfth century once existed in the illustrated *Hortus deliciarum* of Abbess Herrad of Landsberg, burnt with the Strasbourg library in 1870. The growing mastery of design in this period is of much significance for the general development of art. Another manifestation of the careful work lavished on books is seen in

---

[1] See below, p. 134.

the fine stamping of the leather bindings which this century has left us.

What did these manuscripts of the twelfth century contain? Let the question be answered by that eminent authority, Dr. Montague R. James:[1]

> The strength and energy of Europe is now tremendous in every department, and not least in that with which we are concerned. Our libraries are crammed to-day with twelfth-century MSS. The Gregories, Augustines, Jeromes, Anselms, are numbered by the hundred. It is the age of great Bibles and of "glosses" — single books or groups of books of the Bible equipped with a marginal and interlinear comment (very many of which, by the way, seem to have been produced in North Italy). Immense, too, is the output of the writers of the time; Bernard, Hugh and Richard of St. Victor, Peter Comestor, Peter Lombard. The two last are the authors of two of the most popular of medieval textbooks — Peter Lombard of the *Sentences* (a body of doctrine), Peter Comestor of the *Historia Scholastica* (a manual of Scripture history). The Cistercian Order, now founding houses everywhere, is, I think, specially active in filling its libraries with fine but austerely plain copies of standard works, eschewing figured decoration in its books, as in its buildings, and caring little for secular learning.

We have not yet reached the many small Bibles, the *Sentences* and *Summae*, the multitudinous textbooks, the great theological and legal commentaries of the thirteenth century.

As for the contents of twelfth-century libraries as a whole, these included not only new copies but many older codices as well. They are known to us in part from contemporary catalogues, in part from later descriptions and from signs of ownership, pressmarks, or other char-

[1] *Wanderings and Homes of Manuscripts*, p. 38.

acteristic indications found in the volumes at the present time, though these marks have often disappeared in rebinding. The reconstruction of these libraries is not only a problem of much intrinsic interest, but a labor of great importance as giving us cross sections of the European mind at specific times. The catalogues,[1] some three score in number for the twelfth century, are not always of great help, being ordinarily nothing but rough check lists on the fly-leaves of manuscripts, without any indication of date and often with a very unsatisfactory account of contents, as when classical authors are lumped as 'schoolbooks' (*libri scholastici*). Later on in the Middle Ages, descriptions become fuller and more precise, often giving for each volume the first line of the second leaf and often a number or pressmark. These catalogues are almost never alphabetical, for the Middle Ages did not care much for alphabetical order, at least beyond the initial letter, and they would have faced a telephone directory with the consternation of an American office boy. The only catalogues which I have noted as even roughly alphabetical are those of Corbie and Saint-Bertin, but there is likely to be a loose arrangement by subjects, beginning with the Bible, service books, and the Fathers.

Every well appointed library of this period would thus have certain constant elements. First, the Bible, often

---

[1] For a good contemporary example, see the catalogue of the library of Saint-Évroul, in *Orderic Vital et l'abbaye de Saint-Évroul, notices et travaux* (Alençon, 1912), plate i.

in many duplicate copies, with St. Jerome's version frequently accompanied by the gloss and commentary which
supplemented the text with those interpretations, tropo-
logical, allegorical, and anagogical, which overlaid the
literal sense with a mass of conventional and universally
accepted exegesis. At any epoch the mediaeval mind was
full, not only of phrases and allusions drawn from the
text of Scripture, but of the overtones of allegory and
mysticism which each verse carried with it. Thus "the
little foxes that spoil the vines" in the *Song of Solomon*
(ii. 15) had so long been interpreted to mean the heretics
that this sense was taken over by the heretics themselves
in the early Waldensian commentaries. The Bible commonly filled several volumes, even without the gloss;
indeed, it was often called *bibliotheca*, a library — a library indeed to those who could understand! Naturally
certain parts of the Bible, psalter, gospels, epistles, would
often be separately preserved for liturgical use. Next
came the service books of the church — missal, antiphonary, lectionary, gradual, troper, etc. — an ecclesiastical calendar, and one or more monastic rules. Then
the Fathers: Ambrose, Jerome, Augustine, and Gregory,
always a considerable element even without reckoning
their biblical commentaries. Of the four, Ambrose and
Jerome occupied the least space, though Jerome was
especially popular for his letters in praise of the monastic
life and held a high place in the tradition of Christian
scholarship. The long list of Augustine's writings does

not appear as a whole in any mediaeval catalogue, but there is always a goodly proportion, including commonly some of the exegetical and theological works and the *De civitate Dei*. No writer had a more persistent influence on the higher ranges of mediaeval thought; his place in the twelfth century is seen particularly in the shaping of scholastic theology and in the philosophy of history as we shall see it illustrated in Otto of Freising. Gregory the Great was enormously popular in the Middle Ages, for he occupied a lower intellectual level than the severe and classical Augustine and made a wider appeal to credulity in his stories of the miraculous. To him Scripture had something for all minds, "pools and shallows where a lamb may wade and depths where the elephant may swim," and he remembered the needs of all in mediaeval rather than in Roman fashion. No ambitious library was considered complete without the six volumes of his *Moralia on Job*, that great "reservoir in the history of literature," his *Homilies on Ezekiel*, the stories and marvels of his *Dialogues*, and the exposition of a bishop's duties in his *Pastoral Care*. In 1133 the Icelandic Bishop Thorlak, on the outermost rim of Roman Christendom, asked to have the *Pastoral Care* read to him as he lay dying, "and men thought that he looked forward to his death with a better courage than before the reading began."[1]

Another group of essential books, 'without which no

[1] W. P. Ker, *The Dark Ages* (New York, 1904), p. 136.

gentleman's library is complete,' comprised the trans-
mitters — not transmuters! — of ancient learning: Martianus Capella, Priscian, Boethius, Isidore, and Bede.
Martianus, who has been called, with some exaggeration,
the most popular writer in the Middle Ages after the
Bible and Virgil, transmitted the conception of the seven
liberal arts, with an outline of each; Priscian stood for
Latin grammar, and through his examples for much of
Latin literature. Boethius was widely current in the
twelfth century: the humane *Consolation of Philosophy*,
the theological works now restored to him by modern
scholarship, above all his textbooks in logic, rhetoric,
arithmetic, and music, as well as a geometry which
wrongly bore his name. Isidore's *Etymologies* were still
the great mediaeval cyclopaedia, a children's cyclopaedia
it sometimes resembles, though many of its marvels go
back to the good Pliny; no one has counted the twelfth-
century manuscripts, but we know that by 850, something more than two centuries after its composition,
fifty-four complete copies and more than one hundred
manuscripts of extracts had passed from Seville beyond
the Pyrenees. Bede, too, had 'a good press' in the Irish
and Anglo-Saxon monks; apart from his great biblical
commentaries, his textbooks were still the standard in
chronology and astronomy.

There will be something of law, especially ecclesiastical
law. The Germanic codes and the Frankish capitularies
are now rarely copied, and the *Corpus Juris Civilis* is just

beginning to spread; but we regularly find collections of papal letters and of the canons of ecclesiastical councils, and often the new *Decretum* of Gratian. Poetry frequently appears in a Christian form, Prudentius, Fortunatus, Fulgentius, and perhaps some verse of the Carolingian period. Books in the vernacular are rare.

About this central core of standard works the remaining contents of libraries are grouped rather unevenly. In some places, as among the German Cistercians, the Fathers stand almost alone. The classics, as we shall see later, were likely to be represented, though in no fixed or regular fashion. There was frequently something from the pen of the Carolingian theologians and humanists: Alcuin, Rabanus Maurus, Paschasius Radbertus, Hincmar, Remigius, Smaragdus, the *Computus* of Helperic of Auxerre. Lives of saints are always found, but the particular saints vary greatly. There will be something of history: the general chronicles of the early Middle Ages, perhaps Gregory of Tours, and some local annals of the region or the church itself. Indeed, we shall regularly expect something peculiar to the individual monastery or cathedral, whether in the form of letters, biographies, or writings of its members, as well as material of an archival sort. The greater writers of the twelfth century itself, like St. Anselm, St. Ivo, St. Bernard, and Peter Lombard, soon find a place, but the lesser writers have no assured standing in the catalogues, and, if we are to judge by them, the new learning of logic, medicine, and natural science seems to spread very slowly.

Let us take a few specific illustrations from the catalogues, for, as Anatole France has reminded us, there is nothing so easy, so restful, or so seductive as a catalogue of manuscripts. In 1123 Arnold, abbot of Saint-Pierre-le-Vif at Sens, caused a list to be made of the twenty volumes which he had had copied during the twenty-seven years of his office to take the place of a library destroyed by fire: fourteen are biblical and liturgical, beginning with a Pentateuch made into a separate volume "so as to relieve the brethren of the weight of the whole Bible"; the Fathers are represented by Gregory, Augustine, and Origen, history by the *Lombard History* of Paul the Deacon, "the glorious wars of the Gentiles and Christians at Jerusalem and a description of the holy places," and bits of hagiography. Frederick, abbot of St. Godehard at Hildesheim (1136–51), gave it sixteen tomes 'of most solid parchment': namely, three of Gregory's *Moralia*, eight of homilies and collations, three of saints' lives, and two parts of a Bible. The forty-four codices of Poblet are nearly all liturgical. Fulda's eighty-five volumes are by this time all liturgical and patristic; much the same is true of S. Angelo in Formis, a dependency of Monte Cassino, the number of whose one hundred and forty-three volumes is swollen by twenty psalters, nine processionals, and nine antiphonaries, yet there are also four medical books, a lapidary, and a "book of fables." The larger libraries have greater variety. Before 1084 Toul has two hundred and seventy volumes, both ecclesiastical and classical, including a goodly representation of both 'divine' and gentile poets; and much the same distribution of topics meets us in the three hundred and forty-two volumes of Corbie *ca.* 1200. Michelsberg between 1112 and 1123 is sufficiently up to date to have among its two hundred and forty-two codices "a Saracen book on mathematics" and two Greek books on the same subject, as well as the autograph of Richer's *History*, which is still in Bamberg. Of Saint-Amand's one hundred and two volumes, many are medical, and medicine has a large place at Durham Cathedral, whose library of five hundred and forty-six titles must have been one of the largest of the late twelfth century.

We have spoken only of the corporate libraries of monasteries and cathedrals, for these were much the most important in the twelfth century. There was then no intrinsic reason why a student or a priest should not own books, but such instances are rarely recorded unless the book is later given to a monastery or cathedral. Princes had books for their chapels, and lettered princes might have others, too, as in the case of Henry of Champagne or the count of Guines who had a noteworthy library in the vernacular. Royal libraries also meet us. In England we hear of *libri Haroldi regis*, while Henry II, as we have seen, might have accumulated a considerable collection out of the books actually dedicated to him. His son John, certainly no bookworm, receives from the abbot of Reading the Old Testament in six volumes, Hugh of

St. Victor *On the Sacraments*, the *Sentences* of Peter
Lombard, Augustine's *City of God* (imagine John reading
this at Runnymede!), and certain other volumes. These
had apparently been lent to the abbot, like "our book
which is called Pliny," returned a few days later.[1] Frederick I had books at Hagenau and Aachen, while Frederick
II must have had a considerable library. St. Louis also
showed an interest in collecting books. Still, libraries for
kings and patrons were not yet fashionable; we must wait
till the fourteenth century and later for those princely
collections which were to form the nuclei of the Vatican,
the Laurentian, the British Museum, and the Bibliothèque Nationale.

Mediaeval libraries were, of course, not public libraries,
for there was no reading public, nor were they lending
libraries such as came into existence at the universities.
They were for the use of the owners, though there are
frequent examples of loans for the purpose of making
copies. Regular lists of borrowers belong to a later period.
In course of time a distinction would often be made between books kept in a chest under lock and key and others
which were placed outside for free use on the spot and
were often chained to the desk for safety, *cathenati ad
communem utilitatem*. 'The chained Bible' which has
been the object of so much virtuous indignation on the
part of Protestants was chained for the purpose of insur-
ing, not of restricting, its use.

---

[1] *Rotuli litterarum clausarum*, i (London, 1833), p. 108 (29 March, 4 April, 1208).

Not often does any library or part thereof continue today to occupy its twelfth-century site. The chief exceptions are certain of the older cathedrals of Spain, Italy, Germany, and England, and even these have often been rebuilt in a later age. Monastic examples are rare, like St. Gall or the Cistercian abbeys of Austria. Monte Cassino, it is true, still holds the incomparable mount whence Benedict "looked down and looked within"; but the buildings are modern, and much of the old library is scattered. When Boccaccio visited the room in the fourteenth century, he found the door gone, the windows grass-grown, the manuscripts deep with dust, while some of the finest volumes had been torn apart or had lost their margins, taken to manufacture little psalters and books of devotion for sale by the monks. Perhaps he exaggerates a bit for literary effect, as does Poggio when he rescued his famous copy of Quintilian from the damp and mould of a dark room at the bottom of a tower at St. Gall. In any case, the most careful monasteries sold duplicates freely in the fourteenth and fifteenth centuries. The dissolution of the English monasteries under Henry VIII dispersed their libraries far and wide, and the early modern period saw great dilapidations on the Continent. Much of the mischief had been done by the time the French Revolution and similar movements in other lands claimed monastic and other libraries for public depositories. By these measures of secularization the library of Mont-Saint-Michel found itself transported

to Avranches, those of Tegernsee and Benediktbeuern to
Munich, those of the Florentine cloisters to the Bibli-
oteca Nazionale Centrale in the Uffizi. But in many
cases the transfer came too late. The library of Fleury
went to Orleans, but much of it had been scattered by
the Protestants in 1562, and the fragments must now be
sought also at Bern, Rome, Leyden, London, and Paris.
Those of Bec and Bobbio were likewise widely dispersed.
So, too, individual codices were torn to pieces and scattered, sometimes to remote places, leaving only a couple
of fly-leaves to tell the tale. When once a volume left a
library, its danger was grave. It might fall into intelligent hands and ultimately reach some other library, but
it might also be used merely as so much parchment, for
the binding of books, to cover preserve-jars, or to make
cartridges. All this irrespective of contents, for in the
case of books the tooth of time is no respecter of persons.

Of archives, as distinguished from libraries, the early
Middle Ages knew little, save where the traditions of
Roman officialism still retained some hold, as in certain
Italian cities and notably at the papal curia. The distinction between manuscripts and official documents has
been so often disregarded in recent times that we are not
surprised at its slow recognition in the Middle Ages. A
single chest or press was often sufficient for both, and a
single official served as archivist and librarian, and often
in other capacities as well. Nevertheless, there is a dif-

ference, both in origin and in use, between official records and works of literature, and this difference asserts itself clearly with the development of organized administration in the twelfth century. It is due to accidents of destruction that the continuous series of papal registers and letter books now begins with Innocent III in 1198, for the Popes had their registers as early as the sixth century, and the Vatican archives are the oldest in Europe; but it is no accident that the long series of the English charter, patent, and close rolls date from the early years of King John. Indeed, the most developed department of the English government, the Exchequer, had its rolls before 1130, and the great and unique record of Domesday Book is of 1086. The Sicilian administration was as precocious as the English, though its early rolls have disappeared save for a register of military tenures; by the middle of the century it had its *scriniarius*, in charge of a mass of fiscal records and lists of lands and serfs which probably go back ultimately to Roman registers. Here the German emperors learned the first lessons of bureaucracy, for their rule had been essentially domanial and patriarchal, a migratory, rolling-stone sort of state which gathered no archives. The French archives were likewise ambulatory till 1194, when the loss of his baggage in battle taught Philip Augustus to leave his charters at Paris in the newly organized Trésor des Chartes. Monasteries and cathedrals had simpler problems, but they, too, are at work sorting and classifying and particularly copying their documents into great cartularies, so-called 'Black Books' and 'White Books' and 'Red Books,' for preservation and convenience of reference, like the fine cartulary of Mont-Saint-Michel drawn up by order of Robert of Torigni. Municipal archives also go back to this period, and in the South notarial registers, like that register of the Genoese notary, John the Scribe, which tells us much of Mediterranean commerce from 1155 to 1164. The archive, both local and national, has come to stay. Sometimes, too, it stays in the same place. If ecclesiastical archives have in general shared the fortunes of ecclesiastical libraries, there are city archives which preserve an unbroken tradition since the twelfth century, while the continuity of the Papacy and of the English government is most impressively illustrated by the archives of the Vatican and by the great collections of original rolls now gathered into the Public Record Office.

The growth of records, the increase of litigation, and the development of literary skill in the twelfth century carry another consequence in their train, namely, a large crop of forgeries. The literary conscience in such matters was less developed in the Middle Ages than later, and there was also something to be said for the monks who lost all their ancient title deeds in a raid by Northmen and had to face unscrupulous feudal adversaries with the best substitutes they could manufacture; but "forgery has always been a favorite occupation, and it has prevailed at all times when the literary skill required for its exercise was available." [1] The most famous of mediaeval forgeries are earlier, the Donation of Constantine in the eighth century and the Forged Decretals in the ninth, but the twelfth century has its full share. We learn from Walter Map that the seal of Henry II had been perfectly imitated, and Innocent III finds it necessary to multiply the precautions against counterfeiting papal bulls. No less a person than the great archbishop of Canterbury, Lanfranc, in support of Canterbury's superiority over York forged nine documents which were rejected by the papal curia in 1123 because they had no seals and "did not at all savor of the Roman style." A curious example of twelfth-century work is the so-called *Constitutio de expeditione Romana*, a decree respecting the duties of vassals on the Emperor's journey to Italy for the Roman crown, which purports to have been issued by Charlemagne in 790 "before our coronation," that is, ten years before the mediaeval Empire came into existence! Modern critics have had no trouble in unmasking the forgery and in tracking it to the imperial abbey of Reichenau on Lake Constance and to its archivist and schoolmaster, Udalric, whose hand and style reappear in many forged documents for the benefit of this abbey. The archivist betrays himself by clipping from Reichenau charters of Charles the Fat, the schoolmaster by the rhymed prose of this and other charters of this establish-

[1] R. L. Poole, *Lectures on the History of the Papal Chancery*, p. 151.

ment. Still more systematic are the comprehensive re-vamping of the documents of Fulda by a contemporary monk, Eberhard, and the work of Petrus Diaconus at Monte Cassino. On the other hand, the twelfth century is not responsible for the later fabrications which were given a twelfth-century date, such as the chronicle of Ingulph of Croyland, the false charters for the city of Messina, or the Austrian privileges resting upon supposed documents of Julius Caesar and Nero which were submitted by the Emperor Charles IV to the historical criticism of Petrarch. The work of Petrarch and Valla serves to remind us that an age of fabrication also produces critics, and some traces of historical criticism we shall also find in the twelfth century.[1]

BIBLIOGRAPHICAL NOTE

The best account of mediaeval books will be found in W. Watten-bach, *Das Schriftwesen im Mittelalter* (third edition, Leipzig, 1896). On handwriting, see E. M. Thompson, *Introduction to Greek and Latin Palaeography* (Oxford, 1912); and M. Prou, *Manuel de paléographie latine et française* (fourth edition, Paris, 1925). For libraries, see further J. W. Clark, *The Care of Books* (third edition, Cambridge, 1909). G. H. Putnam, *Books and their Makers during the Middle Ages* (New York, 1896–97), is more popular. M. R. James, *Wanderings and Homes of Manuscripts* (*Helps for Students*, no. 17), though brief, is full of first-hand information. Many observations of a great master of manuscript studies will be found in L. Traube, *Vorlesungen und Abhandlungen*, i (Munich, 1909).

The best guide to the contents of mediaeval libraries is the catalogues collected by G. Becker, *Catalogi bibliothecarum antiqui* (Bonn, 1885); see also T. Gottlieb, *Ueber mittelalterliche Bibliotheken* (Leip-

---

[1] See Chapter VIII.

zig, 1890); and the comprehensive series of mediaeval German catalogues in process of publication by P. Lehmann and others since 1918. Many interesting facts respecting the popularity of individual writers are brought together by J. de Ghellinck, "En marge des catalogues des bibliothèques médiévales," in *Miscellanea Francesco Ehrle* (Rome, 1924), v. 331–363. Types of illuminating special studies are M. R. James, *The Ancient Libraries of Canterbury and Dover* (Cambridge, 1903); L. Delisle, "Recherches sur l'ancienne bibliothèque de Corbie," in *Mémoires de l'Académie des Inscriptions*, xxiv, 1, pp. 266–342 (1861); H. Omont, "Recherches sur la bibliothèque de l'église cathédrale de Beauvais," *ibid.*, xl. 1–93 (1916); R. Beer, "Die Handschriften des Klosters Santa Maria de Ripoll," in *Sitzungsberichte* of the Vienna Academy, phil.-hist. Kl., clv, 3, clviii, 2 (1907, 1908); P. Batiffol, *L'abbaye de Rossano* (Paris, 1891). For the wanderings of a Fleury codex, see E. K. Rand in *University of Iowa Philological Quarterly*, i. 258–277 (1922). The formation of a great modern collection out of its mediaeval elements is set forth in masterly fashion by L. Delisle, *Le Cabinet des Manuscrits de la Bibliothèque Nationale* (Paris, 1868–81).

For mediaeval archives, see H. Bresslau, *Handbuch der Urkundenlehre* (second edition, Leipzig, 1912–15), chs. 4, 5. On forgeries, see A. Giry, *Manuel de diplomatique* (Paris, 1894), last chapter; R. L. Poole, *Lectures on the History of the Papal Chancery* (Cambridge, 1915), ch. 7. For the *Constitutio de expeditione Romana*, see P. Scheffer-Boichorst, *Zur Geschichte des XII. und XIII. Jahrhunderts* (Berlin, 1897), pp. 1–26; K. Brandi, *Die Reichenauer Urkundenälschungen* (Heidelberg, 1890).

CHAPTER IV

THE REVIVAL OF THE LATIN CLASSICS

FROM the fall of the Roman Empire down well into modern times the Latin classics furnished the best barometer of the culture of each period in Western Europe. Never wholly lost from sight, their study rose and fell in close relation to the general level of education and intellectual activity. In the stormy times of the early Middle Ages the classics suffered a temporary eclipse, but they reappeared with the revival of learning and education under Charlemagne and his successors. Then the 'iron age' of the tenth century pushed them once more into the background, to reëmerge in the renaissance of the later eleventh and the twelfth centuries. The thirteenth century is a partial exception, as an age of intense activity, but in philosophy and science more than in literature, fed by translations from the Greek and Arabic more than by direct appropriation of Latin texts. Then came the great Revival of Learning of the fourteenth and fifteenth centuries, a Latin revival in the first instance, which found its chief pioneer in the person of Petrarch, lover of Cicero and Virgil and eager searcher for manuscripts of Latin authors; the Latin side of humanism held its own after the recovery of Greek, and Latin long formed the basis of modern liberal education in the humanities.

The two earlier revivals of the classics were less permanent but none the less real so far as they went. That of the ninth century undoubtedly deserves well of the historian. Its copyists saved many of the ancients from destruction; it produced a considerable body of respectable Latin verse; and it raised the general level of Latin usage and Latin style for the age to come. Its centres, however, were relatively few and scattered, and humanists were rare of the type of Lupus of Ferrières, that "energetic borrower though somewhat wary lender of books," whose correspondence gives so engaging a picture of the scholar's life in the monastic age. Moreover, the Carolingian movement was confined to the Frankish lands, whereas by the twelfth century culture had spread far beyond and the number of cathedral and monastery centres had greatly increased; its field was Europe and not merely the Frankish empire. At the same time life became more varied as well as more intense, and this very activity raised up competitors and even enemies for the classics. Besides ignorance and barbarism, the ancients had always to contend with religion; they now found a new enemy in logic. The ups and downs of the classical curve of the Middle Ages must be plotted with reference to all these variables.

The conflict between Christianity and the Latin classics went back to Roman days, for Latin literature was part of the pagan environment into which the new faith was born and with which it waged fierce combat, and the

Latin language and literature were received by the Middle Ages as an integral part of their Roman inheritance. So long as Latin remained the language of the church, Roman literature was an open book, to be read by all who had the rudiments of an ecclesiastical education; and so long as the sacred books of the church, its creed and law and ritual, were in Latin, an acquaintance with the Latin language had to be required as an essential qualification for all ecclesiastics. This open book, however, was a pagan book, in the religion which it assumed if it did not directly teach, and still more in its view of life, with its frank acceptance of the world that is and all its joys and pleasures. So the contradiction was handed on unresolved from age to age, inherent in the tradition of culture and in the ecclesiastical system. In the view of the stricter party, the study of Latin ought to be narrowly limited to the essentials of grammar which gave a practical command of the language; any further study of the ancients was at the best a waste of time, and at the worst a peril to the soul. The mere beauty of Latin style might itself be a danger for men who turned their backs on this world. St. Jerome gives an oft cited account of a vision in which an angel rebuked him for being a Ciceronian rather than a Christian. The fourth council of Carthage in 398 forbade bishops to read the books of the gentiles. "The representatives of St. Peter and his disciples," said the legate Leo in the tenth century, "will not have Plato or Virgil or Terence as their masters nor the rest of the philosophic cattle." Even a small amount of grammatical study was opposed by Gregory the Great, who wrote, "I do not shun at all the confusion of barbarians. I despise the proper constructions and cases, because I think it very unfitting that the words of the celestial oracle should be restricted by the rules of Donatus." Priscian and Donatus were criticised for omitting the name of God — an omission for which the Constitution of the United States and the multiplication table have likewise been blamed! — and Smaragdus in the ninth century wrote a grammar with the examples taken from the Vulgate instead of from the dangerous pagan authors.

The twelfth century had the same difficulties. The so-called Honorius of Autun asks, "How is the soul profited by the strife of Hector, the arguments of Plato, the poems of Virgil, or the elegies of Ovid, who, with others like them, are now gnashing their teeth in the prison of the infernal Babylon, under the cruel tyranny of Pluto?" Even Abaelard inquires 'why the bishops and doctors of the Christian religion do not expel from the City of God those poets whom Plato forbade to enter into his city of the world'; "while Nicholas, the secretary of Bernard of Clairvaux, sighs over the charm he had once found in Cicero and the poets, and in the golden sayings of the philosophers and the 'songs of the Sirens.' " [1]

[1] J. E. Sandys, *History of Classical Scholarship*, i, 3d ed. (Cambridge, 1920), p. 618.

Guibert de Nogent regrets the Latin poets of his youth. The poets were regarded with special disfavor, being sometimes classified with magicians. Thus in the illustrations in the *Hortus deliciarum* of Herrad of Landsberg four 'poets or magicians,' each with an evil spirit prompting him, are placed outside the circle of the seven liberal arts. When Gratian, *ca.* 1140, prepared his *Concord of Discordant Canons*, one of the major differences which he seeks to reconcile is this very question, "Shall priests be acquainted with profane literature or no?" Authorities are marshalled on both sides, as we see from this turning-point of the argument:

From all which instances it is gathered that knowledge of profane literature is not to be sought after by churchmen.

But, on the other hand, we read that Moses and Daniel were learned in *all* the wisdom of the Egyptians and Chaldeans. We read also that the Lord ordered the children of Israel to spoil the Egyptians of their gold and silver; the moral interpretation of this teaches that should we find in the poets either the gold of wisdom or the silver of eloquence, we should turn it to the profit of salutary learning. In Leviticus also we are ordered to offer up to the Lord the first fruits of honey, that is, the sweetness of human eloquence. The Magi, too, offered the Lord three gifts, by which some would have us understand the three parts of philosophy.[1]

Pope Clement and others are quoted to the effect that the knowledge of profane writings is necessary for the understanding of sacred scriptures, and Gratian draws the rather colorless conclusion that priests must not be ignorant. Plainly the problem was too much for the

[1] Dist. 37, c. 7, the whole translated at greater length by A. O. Norton, *Readings in the History of Education* (Cambridge, 1909), pp. 64–66.

canonists, and it was never wholly solved, for there was a strong current of sheer paganism in the Italian Renaissance of the Quattrocento.

Yet, in point of fact, it was not religion but logic and practical interests that proved the most dangerous enemies of the classics and finally killed the classical renaissance of the twelfth century. The reception of Aristotle's *New Logic* toward the middle of this century threw a heavy weight on the side of dialectic in the balance of the liberal arts, and the disparity grew with the further recovery of the Aristotelian *corpus*. With so much logic and philosophy to master, there is little time and less inclination for the leisurely study of letters. Logic is in the saddle, and literature must give way. The new generation of teachers, such as the so-called Cornificians, pride themselves on short cuts, with a minimum of grammar, just as the Bolognese rhetoricians teach a practical rhetoric without wasting time on Cicero. The classical authors (*auctores*) retreat before the arts (*artes*). Whereas the cathedral schools of Chartres and Orleans had made a large place for the authors, these disappear from the curriculum of the new universities. Already in 1215 they are conspicuously absent from the arts course at Paris, and the fuller curriculum of 1255, while prescribing only Donatus and Priscian among Latin writers, throws all its emphasis upon the new versions of Aristotle. Paris represents the triumph of logic, while grammar and the authors endeavor to maintain themselves at Orleans.

The last phase of the struggle is sketched in the poem of Henri d'Andeli, *ca.* 1250, on *The Battle of the Seven Arts*, a battle of the books in which Grammar represents Orleans and Logic Paris. In the conflict Priscian and Donatus are aided by the principal Latin poets as well as by the sympathy of the author of the poem, and Logic is for the moment driven back to her citadel only to triumph at the end:

> Paris and Orleans are at odds,
> It is a great loss and a great sorrow
> That the two do not agree.
> Do you know the reason for the discord?
> It is because they differ about learning;
> For Logic, who is always wrangling,
> Calls the authors authorlings
> And the students of Orleans mere grammar-boys.
> . . . .
> However, Logic has the students,
> Whereas Grammar is reduced in numbers.

While it lasted, the classical revival of the twelfth century manifested itself in the wide reading of Latin authors, especially the poets, and in commentaries thereon; in the active study and practice of grammar and rhetoric; and in the production of a large amount of excellent Latin prose and verse, some of which has the antique quality and feeling. At its best it stood for a harmonious and balanced type of culture in which literature and logic both had their place, but which was hostile to the professional and technical spirit that triumphed in the new universities. In this sense its highest representative was

John of Salisbury, trained by long years of leisurely study of philosophy and literature in the North of France. He favored the scholarly methods of Bernard of Chartres, whom he calls "the most abounding spring of letters in Gaul in modern times," and whose mode of teaching we shall have occasion to consider in describing the study of grammar.[1] Well read in the great Latin writers then accessible, John quotes them freely and to the point, and although he was ignorant of Greek, no writer of the Middle Ages, says Poole, can be placed beside him in extent and depth of classical reading. Stubbs compares his reading and power of quotation to those of Burton, the author of *The Anatomy of Melancholy*. Especially was John steeped in Cicero, whom he regarded as the greatest Latin, and he maintains something of the Ciceronian attitude toward philosophy and the humanities. His remarkably pure and flexible style shows strong Ciceronian influence, and the variety of his writings — letters, history, verse, philosophical reflections on life, learning, and the state — has a Ciceronian many-sidedness. Who doubts, he asks, "that the poets, historians, orators, mathematicians should be read, especially since without these men cannot be lettered? For those who are ignorant of these writers must be called illiterate even if they know their letters. . . . Yet abundance of reading does not make a philosopher," wisdom comes only from truth.[2] If John knew his classics, he also knew his Bible

[1] Chapter V.   [2] *Policraticus*, vii, c. 9.

and his Latin Fathers and quotes them side by side. To him the classics were not a mere training for theology, they were worthy of study for their own sake and for moral profit. There is no sense of antagonism between Roman and Christian, but the two are fused in a well rounded Christian humanism. John of Salisbury was the ripest product of the school of Chartres, where he studied in his youth and where he died bishop in 1180, bequeathing to the cathedral his patristic and classical manuscripts.

The school of Chartres, whose tradition went back to Bishop Fulbert and his predecessors, was the most eminent of the cathedral schools of the early twelfth century, and its eminence was primarily as a school of letters. Its most famous teachers were the Breton brothers, Bernard and Thierry, and the Norman William of Conches. Bernard was the principal source of inspiration, for literature at least, a grammarian first and foremost but in a large and liberal sense, full of Virgil and Lucan, commenting on the ancients from every side and glorifying in verse the quiet life of study and meditation. For him the men of his own time were dwarfs on the shoulders of the giants of a greater past. Thierry, who also taught at Paris, is called by John of Salisbury "a most diligent investigator of the arts," a judgment confirmed by his *Eptatheuchon*, or *Book of the Seven Arts*, which summarizes the liberal culture of his age in two huge volumes of *ca.* 1150 still preserved at Chartres. Rhetoric has a large place in this work, and is further elucidated in a commentary on the *Ad Herennium*, while a treatise on the Creation is a daring piece of Platonism. His influence is further shown by the dedication to him of books on cosmology and logic and the first Latin translation of Ptolemy's *Planisphere* (1143). William of Conches, best known as a philosopher, John of Salisbury also praises as a grammarian, placing him next after Bernard; his humane interests are seen in a commentary on that last product of the antique mind, the *Consolation of Philosophy* of Boethius, and perhaps in a treatise *De honesto et utili* which he is supposed to have dedicated to the future Henry II of England, with whom he was otherwise connected. Whoever the author may be, this compilation is thoroughly characteristic of our age, made up as it is of a patchwork of quotations from a variety of gentile philosophers and moralists, particularly Cicero, Seneca, and the Roman satirists. Such a combination of philosophy and letters would well represent the school of Chartres, whose main peculiarity is just "this reverent dependence on the ancients." [1]

Orleans as a literary centre is rather later than Chartres, and makes a less reverent or at least a more pagan impression upon us; nor can it boast any master like Bernard or any pupil equal to John of Salisbury. Perhaps its methods of study were less thorough than those which

[1] R. L. Poole, *Illustrations of the History of Mediaeval Thought* (1920), p. 102.

John describes. Nevertheless, Virgil, Ovid, and Lucan were there held in high esteem, and the glosses of a certain Master Arnold on Lucan and Ovid have come down to us, while the letter-writers of the time speak of the superiority of Orleans for the study of the authors. The principal French school of rhetorical composition, or *dictamen*, was connected with Orleans and the neighboring monastery of Fleury, and many letters reflect the life of the Orleanese students and their literary preoccupations toward the end of the century. These letters are full of mythological allusions — Pyramus and Thisbe, Paris and Helen, Thais and Hebe and Ganymede — indeed a grammarian of 1199 declares that Orleans with its glorification of the pagan gods will lose the way to Paradise unless it changes its tone. In the field of Goliardic poetry Orleans can claim one of the cleverest writers, the so-called Primate, canon and teacher at Orleans, whose fame lasted throughout Europe until the fourteenth century, and whose brilliant and often disreputable verse has a strongly pagan quality.

No other school had the eminence of Chartres and Orleans as a centre of classical study. Indeed, such cathedral schools as Laon and Rheims are distinguished rather for dialectic and theology, and the school of rhetoric and poetry at Tours is little more than a name to us. There is, however, abundant evidence of wide acquaintance with Latin authors in many writers of the period, while their letters and poems are deeply influenced by ancient models. The Latin poetry of the age, whether in classical metre or mediaeval rhyme, often achieves a real distinction, as we shall see more fully in another chapter. Such verse is widely diffused throughout Northern France and neighboring lands, though much of the best of it comes from the valley of the Loire. Names of special eminence as Latinists are Marbod of Angers and Hildebert of Le Mans and Tours at the beginning of the century, Bernard Silvester of Tours about 1150, followed by his pupil Matthew of Vendôme, and toward the century's close by Peter of Blois, pupil of John of Salisbury and defender of the same tradition of humanism. *Ca.* 1142 the author of the *Metamorphosis Golie Episcopi* sees in a dream the ancient divinities, followed by the poets and philosophers of antiquity, "all of whom discourse in polished diction without rusticity," though the famous masters of his own time whom he celebrates are chiefly logicians. Even a man trained at Paris later in the century, like Alexander Neckam, can show extensive classical reading and a preference for the authors rather than the arts alone. We shall have occasion more than once to cite the long list of ancient writers whom he recommends for the perusal of youth.

The body of Latin classics potentially available to the twelfth century was much the same as that available today, for nothing of importance has since been lost, so far as we know, and little has been transmitted to us by other means than the manuscripts then in the libraries of Western Europe. Potential access does not, however, mean actual use, for many codices lay unknown and neglected, and some texts, like the *Germania* of Tacitus and the poems of Catullus, hung by the thread of a single manuscript then overlooked or disregarded. Moreover, many of the larger Roman works, such as Livy's *History*, had been pushed aside by the more convenient compends of the later empire, and others, like Lucretius, which make a strong appeal to the modern age, were then little known. The literary perspective of the twelfth century was not that of the Roman Empire or of our own time, and the difference was one of taste as well as one of accessibility.

Of the individual Latin authors known to the Middle Ages, the chief was of course Virgil, Dante's "courteous soul of Mantua, whose fame shall last so long as the world endures." "As supreme centre of the literary inheritance left by the Romans, as representative of classical learning, as interpreter of that Roman sentiment which survived the downfall of the Empire, the name of Vergil acquired in Europe a significance well nigh equivalent to that of civilization itself." [1] In the Middle Ages Virgil retained the position which he had held in later Roman days, the supreme poet, the model of style, the heart of school instruction, the ever ready source of examples to the makers of grammars. With the revival of

[1] D. Comparetti, *Vergil in the Middle Ages* (London, 1895), p. 74.

the imperial tradition he becomes the poet of Roman imperialism, who best celebrates the glories and greatness of eternal Rome, while the supposed prediction of Christ's coming in the Fourth Eclogue gave him at times the quality of a prophet, as on a twelfth-century stall in the cathedral of Zamora, where he is represented among the seers of the Old Testament. Virgil is copied, cited, admired, imitated in the twelfth century, as indeed throughout the Middle Ages. Bernard Silvester wrote a commentary on the first six books of the *Aeneid* — the same six books so familiar to the modern schoolboy — but it is a moral as well as a grammatical commentary, in which Virgil is made to describe the life of the human spirit during its temporary imprisonment in the body. Virgil, like the Bible, was allegorized and given hidden meanings in an allegorical age. Even John of Salisbury, that finished classical scholar, tells us that Virgil expresses the truth of philosophy under the guise of fables, and that the *Aeneid* unfolds, book by book, the story of human life from infancy to old age. On the heels of allegory treads romance, and Virgil in the twelfth century is a source of the stories of Troy and Aeneas and Brutus which then make their appearance in the vernacular. Thus Wace begins his *Brut*, or *geste* of the British kings, with a summary of the *Aeneid*, and Chrétien de Troyes describes an ivory saddle-bow on which was carved

> Comant Eneas vint de Troie,
> Comant a Cartage a grant joie
> Dido an son lit le reçut,
> Comant Eneas la deçut,
> Comant ele por lui s'ocist,
> Comant Eneas puis conquist
> Laurente et tote Lonbardie,
> Dont il fu rois tote sa vie.[1]

A source of legend, Virgil also becomes the subject of legend, and it is precisely in our twelfth century that we first hear of him as a magician in the stories of his miraculous tomb and other wondrous works at Naples which are widely diffused throughout Europe in the succeeding period. The fame of the mediaeval Virgil, poet, prophet, magician, master of the black art, Dante's model and guide through the realm of shades, would fill many books, but the twelfth century sketches the outline of the whole.

Next to Virgil in the Middle Ages came Ovid; indeed, one suspects that with the more carnally minded Ovid often came first. First he seems to have been in the twelfth century, that 'age of Ovid' which followed the Carolingian 'age of Virgil.' Any one who still believes that the Latin classics were a sealed book to the men of the Middle Ages, who cared only for the next world and had no appreciation of the beauties of literary art and the joys of the realm of sense, should ponder the popularity of Ovid and grow wiser. The vogue of the poet of Sulmona was continuous down to Boccaccio and Chaucer and the later writers of the Italian Renaissance. There

---

[1] *Erec*, ed. W. Foerster (second edition, Halle, 1909), lines 5339–46.

was the usual attempt to allegorize and point a moral —
Ovid furnishes a rich harvest of *flores morales* to Vincent
of Beauvais — but this must ordinarily have been the
rationalizing effort to find justification for what men were
reading for other reasons. All of his writings were read,
but especially the *Metamorphoses*, the *Art of Love*, and the
Remedies of Love. The last named was regularly considered a moral treatise, and efforts were even made to
discover hidden truths in the *Metamorphoses*, but to most
readers this 'poet's Bible,' 'the Golden Legend of antiquity,' seems to have been a source of poetry and delight, as well as the chief medium for their acquaintance
with classical mythology. In the twelfth century the
wide diffusion of Ovid is one of the surest indications of
the classical revival. His poems were freely copied, even
in severe Cluni; they were cited and much imitated by
the Goliardi, one of whose rhymes is entitled the *Metamorphosis Golie*; they furnished many a theme to the
masters of rhetoric and *dictamen*, and more than one quotation to those immortal lovers, Abaelard and Heloise.
The monks of Canterbury quote Ovid in their correspondence, and the *Art of Love*, that *art d'aimer sans
amour*, is allegorized for the benefit of nuns. Then, too,
Ovid had his influence on the poets of the vernacular,
especially the troubadours and Minnesinger, to whom this
amorigraphus was the highest authority in matters per-
taining to love. The Ovidian Pyramus and Thisbe run
throughout the Provençal poets, and meet us in enduring

stone on a contemporary capital of the cathedral of Basel;
the *Art of Love* inspires the *Rota Veneris* of Boncompagno,
and begins its long course in the vernacular with a version by Chrétien de Troyes, who also translates the
Remedies of Love. Even the stricter party has its Ovid.
A writer toward the close of the century, probably Alexander Neckam, monk of St. Albans and abbot of Cirencester, says, "Let the student hear the elegies of Naso
and the *Metamorphoses* of Ovid, but let him be especially
familiar with the book *De remedio amoris*. Yet it has
seemed right to men of authority that love poems and
satires should be kept from the hands of the young, as if
they were told:

> Ye lads who stoop for flowers and strawberries,
> Beware! a cold snake coils in yonder green.

Some hold that the book of the *Fasti* should not be read,"
doubtless because of its paganism.

Such doubts respecting satirists conclude a passage in
which Neckam advises the student to keep "the moral
precepts of Juvenal in his innermost heart and avoid
wholly the nature of Horace" while reading his works.
The Middle Ages were nothing if not moral and didactic.
John of Salisbury, who frequently cites these poets and
Persius, calls them all *ethici*, and many a tag of Horace is
valued for its worldly wisdom. The *Satires* and *Epistles*
of Horace were, it would seem, more highly regarded and
more frequently quoted than the *Odes* and *Epodes*,
though one wonders just how much moral edification was

derived from certain satires. The *Odes* were imitated
by Metellus of Tegernsee in his poems in honor of St.
Quirinus. At best, however, Horace had no such popularity as he has enjoyed in modern times, while Juvenal
and Persius followed behind him in spite of the vogue of
their ethical precepts. Lucan and Statius, on the other
hand, were mediaeval favorites, as readers of Dante will
recall, contributing not only much of the popular knowledge of Caesar and the tale of Thebes, but a mass of
citations and excerpts to the collectors and copyists.
Lucan, indeed, the *poeta doctissimus* of John of Salisbury,
was considered an historian as well as a poet — as indeed
he himself claimed to be — and he affected writers of
history in the twelfth century both as a model for historical poems like the *Ligurinus* of Gunther of Strasbourg
and as an influence upon their prose style.

Martial is frequently cited and is imitated in the pious
tituli of the monastic poets. Apart from Ovid and Horace,
the lyric poets are almost unknown. Of the later poets
Claudian was the most popular, being frequently mentioned by the writers of the period and furnishing the
obvious inspiration for one of its principal poems, the
Anticlaudianus of Alain de Lille. Neckam has heard of
the tragedies of Seneca. Plautus seems known only at
second hand, and many of the quotations from Terence
are culled from Priscian, indeed Terence was often considered a prose writer. Yet John of Salisbury quotes
Terence frequently, using all of the plays except the

Hecyra; but even he has been thought capable of making two authors out of Suetonius Tranquillus.

Of prose writers, Cicero naturally came first, revered, if for nothing else, as the 'king of eloquence' and the chief representative of one of the seven arts, rhetoric. So voluminous an author had, however, to take his chances amidst the accidents of manuscript transmission, and his works were not all known in the same degree. Indeed, when one of his admirers, Wibald of Korvey (d. 1158), expresses the natural wish to put all his writings into a single volume, we may well believe that Cicero was 'more admired than read.' The rhetorical and philosophical treatises meet us most frequently, then certain of the *Orations*, and least of all the *Letters*. A great library such as Cluni might have them all, or nearly all; its catalogue from our period records three manuscripts of the *Letters*, four of the *Orations*, five of the rhetorical, and seven of the philosophical works. It is characteristic of the age that Abbot Ailred of Rievaulx, who loved the *De amicitia* as a boy, should emphasize spiritual friendship in a dialogue which he wrote late in life. Even John of Salisbury cannot be shown to have had direct acquaintance with the *Orations* and *Letters*, though he left his copies of the *De officiis* and the *De oratore* to Chartres. The *De officiis* is highly commended by Neckam, who registers a doubt respecting the *De natura deorum*. The last named, however, is listed among other philosophical works of Cicero in the library of Bec,

where Étienne de Rouen copied long examples of style
from Cicero and Seneca and prepared an abridgment of
Quintilian's *Institutes of Oratory*. Quintilian also came
under the wing of rhetoric and meets us in the catalogues
and writers of the century, though only an incomplete
text of his *Institutes* was then in circulation, along with
the *Declamations* which went under his name. As we
shall see later, the new rhetoric of the twelfth century
had scant respect for any Roman models.

The 'moral Seneca' is often cited in this period for his
Natural Questions as well as his *Letters* and ethical works;
he had a further claim on the age as the supposed author
of the correspondence with St. Paul which gave him a
fictitious standing as a Christian. His proverbs and
apothegms also circulated freely, and St. Bernard even
quotes a sentence of Seneca to urge the crusade on a re-
luctant Pope. Pliny the Elder appealed powerfully to
the mediaeval love of the marvellous, but the *Natural
History* was a big book to copy, and complete manuscripts are not numerous. Men turned rather to the
Collectanea of Solinus, which were translated into French
before 1206, or to such an abridgment as the *Deflora-
tiones Plinii* which Robert of Cricklade prepared for
Henry II of England, omitting names of many places
"from which tribute could no longer be collected." Such
writers as Frontinus, Aulus Gellius, and Macrobius
appear with considerable frequency. How little the larger
works of the Roman historians were then read, we shall
see in the chapter on historical writing.

In any estimate of the influence of classical authors in our period, full account must be taken of the large body of quotations which came at second hand, through the Fathers, the Latin grammars and glossaries, and the various collections of extracts. Chief among such sources was the Latin grammar of Priscian, whose ten thousand lines of quotations from the ancients include a large amount of Cicero, Sallust, and the poets, quotations to which many readers were indebted for whatever acquaintance they possessed with these authors. There were also anthologies (*florilegia*), a literary *genre* which goes back to Carolingian days, and other books of elegant extracts. Among such collections of the fuller sort two manuscripts of our period may serve as illustrations. One, in the Vatican,[1] of the later twelfth century, begins with fragments of the *Saturnalia* of Macrobius, 'verses of Cicero,' and proverbs and sentences of the philosophers, followed by extracts from the letters of St. Jerome and Pliny, Apuleius, Cicero's *Orations* and *Tusculan Disputations*, Seneca's *Letters* and *De beneficiis*, Aulus Gellius, and Ennodius, with some miscellaneous matter at the end. The other, at the Bibliothèque Nationale,[2] belongs a generation or so later and contains more poetry, comprising extracts from Prudentius, Claudian, Virgil, Statius (much), Valerius Flaccus, Lucan, Ovid (especially full), Horace (considerable), Juvenal, Persius, Martial, Petronius, Calpurnius, Terence (phrases only, as prose),

[1] MS. Pal. Lat. 957, ff. 97–184 v.   [2] MS. Lat. 7647, ff. 34–185 v.

Sallust, Boethius, a bit of Plato, Macrobius, Cicero *De officiis* and *De amicitia*, Quintilian, much Seneca, the *Aulularia* of Plautus, Sidonius Apollinaris, Cassiodorus, and Suetonius.

Another measure of the classical interests of this epoch may be found in the considerable number of commentaries and analyses of Latin authors. The writing of brief glosses or *scholia* on ancient works was a favorite form of literary instruction in the schools. Such glossed manuscripts of Horace meet us in this period, while the loan of glosses on Virgil and Lucan is a theme of correspondence between students at Orleans. "We have made little glosses, we owe money," is the terse summary of school life which comes from two students at Chartres. The glosses of Master Arnold of Orleans on Lucan and on several poems of Ovid have already been mentioned, and similar notes on Lucan, Juvenal, and Persius come somewhat earlier from the region of Liége. So we have seen that Bernard Silvester of Tours was the author of a commentary on the first six books of the *Aeneid*, influenced like many commentaries of the period by that of Macrobius on the *Dream of Scipio*, and that Thierry of Chartres wrote on the *Rhetorica ad Herennium*. A survival of these glossarial habits of the older humanists is found in the thirteenth century, when William the Breton cites passages from the pagan poets to explain the more difficult words of the Bible.

Still another measure of the classical revival must be

mentioned, though it cannot be discussed as it deserves, namely its influence upon vernacular poetry. We are here in the formative period of French and Provençal poetry, and thus indirectly of the other literatures which they affected, and all of these were profoundly influenced by the classical tastes of this age. The Latin poets furnished classical mythology and ancient matter of romance, models and themes for imitation, even opportunities for direct translation; and their position in Dante's *Divine Comedy* and Chaucer's *House of Fame* is founded upon two centuries of use by vernacular writers. The twelfth century gives us long poems on Troy and Thebes, upon Aeneas and Alexander, in French as well as in Latin; it gives us shorter poems on Pelops, Philomela, Narcissus, Phyllis, Pyramus and Thisbe, and other episodes from that great story-teller, Ovid, whose precepts did much to form its code of courtly love. And if all the matter of 'Rome la grant' is no longer Roman, if Aeneas and Alexander are, like Charlemagne, made over into knights of a new age, that is the penalty of all literary revivals. Even so have men of our own time done unto King Arthur and St. Joan and Helen of Troy.

From a modern point of view, the acceptance of the ancients *en bloc* by the men of the twelfth century was lacking in critical discrimination. To them ancients were ancients — unless like Plautus their speech was too ancient — and few distinctions were drawn. Horace was lumped with Statius, the authors of the Ciceronian and

Augustan age with those of the later Empire. Indeed, there was rather a preference for late writers who were brief, like Florus and Solinus, or didactic like Martianus Capella, while Christian poets such as Prudentius and Arator were highly regarded. Nor was the line drawn sharply so as to exclude those of a still later age: the *Eclogue* of the Carolingian Theodulus was a favorite book for elementary reading, and the *Tobias* of Matthew of Vendôme, written in the twelfth century, was prescribed by at least one university of the later Middle Ages. The author of the *Battle of the Seven Arts* brackets Seneca with another twelfth-century work, the *Anticlaudianus* of Alain de Lille, while he calls to the aid of Grammar other books of the same age such as the *Alexandreid* of Walter of Châtillon and the *Aurora*, or versified Bible, of Peter Riga. The *Laborintus* groups these later writers with Homer and the great Romans. Even in the fifteenth century the sense of style did not jump at once to full perfection, just as its prose did not attain forthwith the height of Ciceronian elegance. As late as the Cinquecento men might strive for Tully only to achieve "Ulpian at the best."

The truth is that, while they could make certain literary distinctions, neither group of humanists was equipped to see the Roman writers in their individual setting of time and place, for their historical sense was defective, lacking in both cases the notion of development and change, and dulled by an almost superstitious veneration for the ancients. So in the twelfth century this reverence extended to the whole body of Latin writers, while the glamour of a distant past and 'the grandeur that was Rome' magnified them all into giants. The ancients were Romans, as well as ancients. Back of Roman literature and the Latin language lay Rome itself, 'the shadow of the Roman name' across the ages.

To the men of the Middle Ages Rome was the great fact in their immediate past, for the Roman Empire had for several centuries been conterminous with the civilized world and had handed on conceptions of unity, universality, order, and authority from which Latin Europe could not escape. Rome was their common memory, Rome not fallen, Rome eternal. Wherever they looked back they saw Rome and heard its voice, "the voice of the murmuring of Rome." By the twelfth century the murmur had become confused with legend and invention, as in the mass of material which went to make the *Gesta Romanorum* and all the "matter of Rome the great," but it is still a theme in literature: Rome the lion, Rome the eagle, Rome the store of untold wealth, Rome the unconquerable citadel, Rome the founder of cities in Germany and Gaul, like that Rouen (*Rotoma*) which would become Rome by losing two letters.

> Roma caput mundi regit orbis frena rotundi,

ran the old line. Amatus of Monte Cassino writes:

> Orbis honor, Roma splendens decorata corona.

Alexander Neckam says:

> Roma stat, orbis apex, gloria, gemma, decus.

To the apprehension of the Middle Ages Rome was an empire, not a republic; indeed many a chronicle jumps directly from the Tarquins to Caesar. Not only did the empire as the latest period overshadow all that went before, but it was reflected in Latin poetry, in the Roman law, and in Christian literature. The appeal of Rome as a republic belongs chiefly to modern times, to the Revolutionary days in France "when the learning of the classroom foamed out into the street," and to the tribunes and Brutuses and Publicolas of the American eighteenth century. "Caesar had his Brutus," shouted Patrick Henry; "twelve Roman proconsuls and several citizens" Daniel Webster found it expedient to delete from President Harrison's inaugural address. Already in Shakespeare Brutus is a hero; yet as late as Dante he is a traitor, crunched with Judas in Satan's jaws in the lowest hell. In the twelfth century Rome is of course an empire still, with imperial prerogatives fed by the revival of Roman law till they blossomed out in the pretensions of Frederick Barbarossa, who ordered his decrees inserted in the *Corpus Juris* and referred to his "predecessors the divine Emperors, Constantine the Great, Valentinian, and Justinian." Yet, curiously enough, this same age, like that of Rienzi and Petrarch, witnesses a brief revival of the republican tradition under the leadership of Arnold of Brescia, when the Senate strikes coins bearing the ancient emblem *Senatus Populusque Romanus* and dreams of a Roman capital at the head of the world, its people the ultimate source of power, dictating to Pope and Emperor alike. Otto of Freising, an eyewitness, brings the two theories face to face in the bombastic speech which he puts into the mouth of the Roman envoys, and in the red-bearded Emperor's curt and haughty reply as the lawful possessor who dares them to take the club from Hercules. The club was his for the moment, but the Holy Roman Empire was almost as much a dream as the Roman Republic, both glorified memories of a vanished past.

The city of Rome by the twelfth century was no longer ancient Rome, even outwardly. "The Goth, the Christian, time, war, flood, and fire" had long been at their work of destruction — especially the Christian. Rome had just been sacked and burnt by Robert Guiscard and his Normans in 1084, a blow from which whole quarters like the Aventine and the Caelian were never to recover. More gradual but more deadly was the destruction wrought by the marble cutters and limeburners who made lime of ancient statues and did a thriving business in the export of Roman marbles and mosaics. These went to adorn Italian cathedrals like Pisa, Lucca, and Salerno; the abbey church of Monte Cassino, for which Desiderius purchased "columns, bases, capitals, and marbles of various colors"; even distant Westminster Abbey, where in the thirteenth century "Petrus Romanus civis" engraved his name on the shrine of Edward the Confessor, and Abbot Richard of Ware brought home slabs of porphyry and serpentine for his tomb, as the inscription neatly tells us:

Hic portat lapides quos huc portavit ab Urbe.

Suger, mighty builder of St. Denis, regrets that he could not transport thither columns which he often admired in the baths of Diocletian. His contemporary, Bishop Henry of Winchester, actually did bring statuary from Italy. Rome is already a hunting-ground for the antiquarian.

Being now a ruin, Rome has tourists and guidebooks for 'seeing Rome.' The tourists are chiefly pilgrims, intent on the shrines of the Holy City rather than on its pagan remains. At least they were not archaeologists. Gibbon boasts in the *Autobiography* that when he entered on his Italian journey in 1764 "few travellers more completely armed and instructed have ever followed the footsteps of Hannibal"; and there is no one in the twelfth century who could gainsay him. Rabbi Benjamin of Tudela, who journeyed through Italy and the East in 1160–73, is interested chiefly in the Ghetto. *Ca.* 1195 Conrad of Querfurt, bishop elect of Hildesheim, is at some pains to show his classical training in describing places which at school he had seen in a glass darkly but now face to face—Mantua, Modena, and Ovid's Sulmona, the insignificant stream of the Rubicon, Virgil's tomb and the

Virgilian legends of its neighborhood, Etna and the fount of Arethusa — but he does not pass through Rome. The only Northern writer of the time who has much to say of Rome is William of Malmesbury, who contrasts its feeble state with its ancient greatness as mistress of the world. Most travellers approached the city in the spirit of that great song which the preceding age had produced somewhere in the North of Italy:

> O Roma nobilis, orbis et domina,
> Cunctarum urbium excellentissima,
> Roseo martyrum sanguine rubea,
> Albis et virginum liliis candida:
> Salutem dicimus tibi per omnia,
> Te benedicimus: salve per secula.

It is for such visitors that the chief guidebook of the period was produced, the *Mirabilia Urbis Rome*. This extraordinary combination of fact and fable, pagan and Christian, falls into three parts. The first, after describing the foundation of Rome on the Janiculum by Janus, son of Noah, lists its gates and arches, its baths, palaces, theatres, and bridges, its Christian cemeteries, and the places where the saints suffered martyrdom. The second comprises various legends of emperors and saints, especially legends of statues, including the popular *Salvatio Rome*, a set of bells attached to the statues of the several provinces on the Capitol so as to give the alarm whenever the province revolted; the philosophers Phidias and Praxiteles in the time of Tiberius; the passion of the martyrs under Decius; and the foundation of the three great churches by Constantine. The third part takes the reader through the various quarters of the city and points out the striking monuments and the ancient traditions connected with them, concluding:

> These and many more temples and palaces of emperors, consuls, senators, and prefects were in the time of the heathen within this Roman city, even as we have read in old chronicles, and have seen with our eyes, and have heard tell of ancient men. And moreover, how great was their beauty in gold, and silver, and brass, and ivory, and in precious stones, we have endeavored us in writing, as well as we could, to bring back to the remembrance of mankind.[1]

Another guidebook, only recently printed, seems to belong to the same period, "Master Gregory on the Marvels of Rome whether made by magic art or by human labor." This account is chiefly devoted to the ancient remains, many of which have since disappeared, rather than to the saints and martyrs. Yet the author is no archaeologist. None, he says, can enumerate Rome's towers and palaces, soon to go the way of all things earthly. His own description groups the ruins by classes rather than topographically: bronze beasts, marble statues (nearly all destroyed by Gregory the Great), palaces, triumphal arches, and pyramids. The fate of ancient buildings is illustrated by the temple of Pallas, torn down with much labor by the Christians and much injured by time, leaving only the portion which serves as a granary for the cardinals, and surrounded by heaps of broken statues, among them the headless image of the

---

[1] As translated by F. M. Nichols, *Mirabilia Urbis Romae*, p. 117.

goddess before which Christians had once been brought to test their faith. Already we see that neglect of ancient ruins which Poggio was to lament in the fifteenth century; the Rome, once golden, now mellow with the decay etched by Piranesi, which led Gibbon to plan his *Decline and Fall* as he sat "musing in the Church of the Zoccolanti or Franciscan fryars, while they were singing Vespers in the Temple of Jupiter on the ruins of the Capitol."

It was a distorted memory at best that the Rome of the twelfth century preserved of its ancient past, scarcely less distorted than the legends of Charlemagne which were localized in the Roman ruins along the great highways of the empire. The Rome of the Caesars has plainly become the Rome of the Popes, as we find illustrated in a document of 1199 by which Innocent III grants to the church of SS. Sergius and Bacchus one-half of the arch of Septimius Severus, with the rooms attached thereto and the tower which then surmounted it. The *Ordo Romanus* shows us that when the Popes went about on their official processions within the city they purposely made their way through the ancient triumphal arches of paganism: a "new Via Sacra had arisen for Christian pomps." [1] We are far from the humanist Popes of the fifteenth century, yet it is something to see efforts to preserve ancient monuments, as when the urban senate in 1162 decreed that Trajan's column "should never be mutilated or destroyed,

---

[1] F. Gregorovius, *History of the City of Rome in the Middle Ages*, tr. Hamilton, iv. 659.

but should remain as it stands to the honor of the Roman people, as long as the world endures."[1] And this same age preserves a precious piece of humanism in the noble lines written by its best Latin poet, Hildebert of Le Mans, after his visit to Rome in 1106, beginning:

> Par tibi, Roma, nihil, cum sis prope tota ruina;
>   Quam magni fueris integra fracta doces.
> Longa tuos fastos aetas destruxit, et arces
>   Caesaris et superum templa palude iacent.

[1] *Ibid.*, iv. 686.

BIBLIOGRAPHICAL NOTE

The best guide to the history of classical studies in the Middle Ages is J. E. Sandys, *A History of Classical Scholarship*, i (third edition, Cambridge, 1920). Latin authors are treated, as part of the general Roman tradition, in A. Graf, *Roma nella memoria e nelle immaginazioni del medio evo* (Turin, 1882–83). See also E. Norden, *Die antike Kunstprosa* (Leipzig, 1898), pp. 689–731; D. C. Munro, "The Attitude of the Western Church towards the Study of the Latin Classics in the Early Middle Ages," in the *Papers of the American Society of Church History*, viii. 181–194; L. J. Paetow, *The Arts Course at Medieval Universities* (Urbana, 1910); and his edition of *The Battle of the Seven Arts* (Berkeley, 1914).

For the external history of the several Latin authors, the material has been collected by M. Manitius, in *Philologus*, xlvii–lvi, and Supplement, vii. 721–767; and *Rheinisches Museum*, Neue Folge, xlvii, Erg.-Heft (1892). Their literary influence has been insufficiently studied: see D. Comparetti, *Vergil in the Middle Ages* (London, 1895), which is useful chiefly for the Virgilian legend; M. Manitius, *Analekten zur Geschichte des Horaz im Mittelalter* (Göttingen, 1893); L. Sudre, *Publii Ovidii Nasonis Metamorphoseon libros quomodo nostrates medii aevi poetae imitati interpretatique sint* (Paris thesis, 1893); H. Unger, *De Ovidiana in Carminibus Buranis quae dicuntur imitatione* (Berlin diss., 1914); C. Landi, "Stazio nel medio evo," in *Atti* of the Padua Academy, xxxvii. 201–232 (1921). E. K. Rand, *Ovid and his Influence* (Boston, 1925), is admirable within its compass; the author knows not only Ovid but the Middle Ages.

On *florilegia*, see Miss E. M. Sanford, "The Use of Classical Latin Authors in the *Libri Manuales*," in *Transactions of the American Philological Association*, lv. 190–248 (1924); for commentaries, *Histoire littéraire de la France*, xxix. 568–583.

On John of Salisbury, see R. L. Poole, in *Dictionary of National Biography*, and his many recent studies. On Neckam, see my *Mediaeval Science*, ch. 18. For Chartres, A. Clerval, *Les écoles de Chartres au moyen-âge* (Chartres, 1895); for Orleans, L. Delisle, "Les écoles d'Orléans," in *Annuaire-Bulletin de la Société de l'Histoire de France*, 1869, pp. 139–154. For examples of the use made of the classics by individual prose writers of the period, see C. C. J. Webb, *Ioannis Saresberiensis Policratici Libri VIII* (Oxford, 1909), i, pp. xxi ff.; Walter Map, *De nugis curialium*, ed. M. R. James (Oxford, 1914), p. xxiii; A. Hofmeister, "Studien über Otto von Freising," in

Neues Archiv, xxxvii. 727–747 (1912); E. Boutaric, "Vincent de Beauvais et la connaissance de l'antiquité classique au treizième siècle," in *Revue des questions historiques*, xvii. 5–57 (1875). On classical reminiscences in the Latin poets, cf. K. Francke, *Zur Geschichte der lateinischen Schulpoesie des XII. und XIII. Jahrhunderts* (Munich, 1879), pp. 22–55.

On Rome in the twelfth century, see Graf, as above; and F. Gregorovius, *History of the City of Rome in the Middle Ages*, tr. by Annie Hamilton, iv (London, 1896). The *Mirabilia*, edited by Parthey (Berlin, 1869), is translated by F. M. Nichols (London, 1889). Master Gregory is edited by M. R. James in *English Historical Review*, xxxii. 531–554 (1917); and by G. McN. Rushforth in *Journal of Roman Studies*, ix. 14–58 (1919). F. Schneider, *Rom und Romgedanke im Mittelalter* (Munich, 1926), treats chiefly of the earlier period.

CHAPTER V

THE LATIN LANGUAGE

IN the twelfth century the common language of Western Europe was Latin. The vernacular idioms were only in process of formation for literary purposes out of the various local dialects; while French was spoken in England, and somewhat in Italy, its European vogue, as the "language most delectable and common to all," dates from the following century. To say that Latin was the international language is, however, to give a very inadequate impression; it was not only the language of international intercourse, but for many purposes the language of the several peoples at home. As the speech of the universal church it was the vehicle of communication between the clergy of distant regions, but it was also the language of ecclesiastical and religious life. Men prayed in Latin, sang in Latin, preached in Latin in every part of Western Christendom. It was the language of learning and education everywhere: the textbooks were in Latin, and boys were taught everything through the Latin, and taught to speak Latin in school, so that it became the speech of educated men even in their lighter and more popular writings. It was the language of law or at least of all treatises on law, not only of the Roman law and the canons of the church, but of Glanvill and the Norman customal, of the Lombard *Libri feudorum* and the *Usages* of Barcelona, of the assizes of Henry of England and Roger of Sicily; the language, too, of administrative and business records, as represented by the rolls of the Anglo-Norman exchequer, the registers of Italian notaries, and the enormous body of accounts and charters and legal instruments throughout Europe. The merchant and the lawyer, the bailiff's clerk and the physician, needed their Latin as well as the scholar and the priest.

With so wide an extension in space and so wide a variety of application, no language could be uniform and unchanging, and we are quite prepared to find that the Latin of the Middle Ages differs according to place and subject, developing new usages to express new meanings and shades of meaning, and adopting many local terms and even the order of words and habit of thought from the vernacular. Thus the Latin of Magna Carta has taken over words like *vicecomes* (sheriff) and *sergenteria* (serjeanty) from the Norman-French of the period, and its style and sequence are those of Anglo-Norman law, not those of Cicero or a contemporary papal bull. Its most famous clauses are full of mediaeval and technical terms, thus (c. 39):

> Nullus liber homo capiatur, vel imprisonetur, aut dissaisiatur, aut utlagetur, aut exuletur, aut aliquo modo destruatur, nec super eum ibimus, nec super eum mittemus, nisi per legale iudicium parium suorum vel per legem terre.

The vocabulary, especially, varies from one country to another, so that we really need separate Latin dictionaries for each of the great regions of Europe. Indeed it is this very adaptability and power of absorbing new elements which kept Latin a living language until it was killed by the revival of antique standards in the fifteenth century. Mediaeval Latin has its ups and downs from age to age, depending upon the general level of education and culture and the greater or less influence of the vernacular, as well as upon the education of the particular individual who is writing; but it always tries to keep within hailing distance of the standard Latin grammars. The twelfth century, as a time of classical revival, is a period of relatively good Latin, at least in the centres of culture, however much the local notary or scribe might deviate from classical or even the best contemporary standards. Says Bishop Stubbs:

The Latin of the twelfth century is fairly good and grammatical Latin; adjective agrees with substantive and verb with its nominative case; *ut* governs the subjunctive, and the dependent sentence follows the mood and tense prescribed by the principal sentence. There is a great fertility of vocabulary, there are frequent and consistent uses of words which in classical Latin are somewhat rare, as if the writer prided himself on knowing how to use *dumtaxat* and *quippe* and *utpote*, and brought them in at every turn: but even here there is nothing that is labored; the Latin, if too free, is scarcely ever unnatural. It is Latin written as by men who on literary matters talked and thought in Latin; is it not dead but a living language, senescent, perhaps, but in a green old age.[1]

So close an approach to classical Latinity implies thorough drill in Latin grammar, and the twelfth century saw the culmination of the mediaeval study of grammar,

[1] *Seventeen Lectures*, p. 175.

both in the narrow sense of formal accidence and syntax and in the wider sense of the scholarly appreciation of literature. The standard textbook was the *Institutiones* of Priscian of Caesarea, composed early in the sixth century, whose popularity throughout the Middle Ages is attested by the thousand manuscript copies and extracts still surviving. Solid, substantial, fortified by copious citations from Roman authors, its eighteen books carry on the traditions of Latin literature as well as of grammar. One who knew his Priscian had learned many excellent passages from Cicero, Sallust, Virgil, Terence, and other poets, indeed it is likely that for many a man these extracts constituted the principal medium of acquaintance with these classical authors. An age of classical revival was inevitably an age of Priscian, and it was natural that he should be chosen to represent grammar among the figures of the seven liberal arts which adorn the façade of Chartres cathedral, in whose school Thierry copies the whole of Priscian into his *Eptatheuchon*, or library of the seven liberal arts. A full century earlier Fulbert of Chartres lends "one of our Priscians" to a bishop in Hungary; in 1147 a canon of Halberstadt bequeathes his Priscian to his cathedral as he passes into eternal rest at distant Troyes. About the same time Priscian was the subject of an elaborate grammatical commentary by Pierre Élie, who taught at Paris. Priscian's *Institutiones*, however, is a big book, filling two stout volumes of the modern printed edition, and beginners turned rather to the briefer manuals. There were the *Ars maior* of his predecessor Donatus, and the briefer and more common *Ars minor*, often learned by heart, discussing in the form of question and answer the eight parts of speech within the compass of ten printed pages. Catechetical, too, was the short work of Priscian in which the first twelve lines of Virgil's *Aeneid* served as the *corpus vile* for dissection, with three pages on the first word *arma* — its character as a noun, gender, case, number, syntax, and especially its derivatives.

The usual introductory readers of the twelfth century had the sanction of long use: the *Distichs* of the so-called Cato, the *Fables* of Avianus, and the *Eclogue* of Theodulus, all three often meeting us in the same volume. The *Disticha* of Cato, now placed in the later Empire, gained added authority from their association with Cato the Elder; while they contained no specifically Christian matter, their moral tone was unexceptionable, and they were universally valued for their moral teaching, as in the opening lines:

> If God a spirit is as poets sing,
> With mind kept pure make thou thy offering.
>
> Be oft awake: from too much sleep abstain,
> For vice from sloth doth ever nurture gain.

"Wisest of men since Solomon," as Walter Map considered him, 'Cato' was the primer of virtue and of Latin in the twelfth century, as for many generations later;

indeed, he became a synonym for elementary education in Chaucer's line on the carpenter who

> knew nat Catoun, for his wit was rude.

Avianus (*ca.* 400) was the author of the most popular of the many collections of Latin fables, preferred because of its poetical form and well suited to beginners, while the *Eclogue* of Theodulus, a Carolingian production, was likewise treated as a classic. All three were repeatedly copied and paraphrased. We have a gloss of Theodulus by Bernard of Utrecht in the eleventh century, and a paraphrase of Avianus by Alexander Neckam a hundred and fifty years later. Indeed, Theodulus was considered to be a book of such value that it required a threefold interpretation, literal, allegorical, and moral, like Holy Scripture itself.

For the most part the twelfth century made its own dictionaries, if we include in this period the work of the Italian lexicographer Papias, who flourished about 1050. The lexicon of Papias, variously known as *Alphabetum*, *Breviarium*, *Mater verborum*, and *Elementarium doctrine rudimentum*, was a combined dictionary and cyclopaedia, drawn from the older grammars and glossaries, but containing many recent examples and evidently composed in close relation to the subjects of school instruction. Here, as throughout the Middle Ages, an alphabetical order holds only for the first letter of the word and is further affected by the current mediaeval spelling. Although Papias survived into several printed editions, he did not wholly satisfy the immediately succeeding generations. The Englishman Osbern wrote a great *Panormia* in the early twelfth century; and toward 1200 the Pisan canonist Hugutio, professor at Bologna and bishop of Ferrara, compiled from Papias and Osbern a book of *Derivations* which earned him a place beside Priscian in the century of Petrarch. All three writers pay much attention to etymology, and particularly to Greek roots; yet none of them knows Greek, and their mistakes and corruptions are often ludicrous. Some acquaintance with this language was claimed by William of Corbeil, who in the early twelfth century dedicated his *Differentie* to Gilbert de la Porrée. These lexicographers were also great sticklers for quantity, Hugutio even threatening that one who shortened the penult of *sincerus* should have his name stricken from the Book of Life. Another type of dictionary was the descriptive vocabulary, which took away the bareness of the older glossarial lists by putting words into connected sentences explanatory of their meaning. This series begins, for our epoch, with Adam du Petit-Pont, master at Paris in the early twelfth century, and continues with another Paris teacher, Alexander Neckam, toward its close. Their treatises tell of household utensils, court life, the implements of learning, etc.; a century later John of Garland will take his readers on a walk through the streets of Paris, discoursing on the wares of the several trades as he goes. The temptation in such works is to display acquaintance with rare and strange terms, and they offer wide scope for the pedantry of the thirteenth century. For an example of the simpler style let us take Neckam's account of the materials of the *scriptorium*:

> The copyist (*librarius*), who is commonly called the scribe, shall have a chair with projecting arms for holding the board upon which the quire of parchment is to be placed. The board must be covered with felt on which a deerskin is fastened, in order that the super-fluities of the parchment or membrane may be more easily scraped away by a razor or *novacula*. Then the skin of which the quire is to be formed shall be cleaned with a mordant pumice and its surface smoothed with a light plane. The sheets shall be joined above and below by the aid of an *appendix* wrapped round them. The margins of the quire shall be marked on either side with an awl in even measure so that by the aid of a rule the lines may more surely be drawn without mistake. If in writing any erasure or crossing out occurs, the writing shall not be cancelled but scraped off. . . .[1]

Neckam (1157–1217) was at the same time more than a lexicographer. Student at Paris, teacher at Dunstable, canon and abbot of Cirencester, he tells us he had "faithfully learned and taught the arts, then turned to the study of Scripture, heard lectures on canon law and on Hippocrates and Galen, and did not find the civil law distasteful." His voluminous writings in prose and verse included Aesopic fables and popular science, theology, and scriptural commentary, as well as many doubtful attributions. One of the most characteristic is a treatise on the *Natures of Things* which consists of two books of moralized science and three of commentary on Ecclesi-

[1] Haskins, *Mediaeval Science*, p. 361.

astes. Though receptive toward the new Aristotle, he is to be reckoned with the humanists of the age, a writer of respectable Latin verse, quoting widely from the ancient writers, but interested especially in words and their meanings.

At its best the study of grammar in the twelfth century carried with it the serious study of literature, as it is described by John of Salisbury at Chartres:

> Bernard of Chartres, the most abounding spring of letters in Gaul in modern times, followed this method, and in the reading of authors showed what was simple and fell under the ordinary rules; the figures of grammar, the adornments of rhetoric, the quibbles of sophistries; and where the subject of his own lesson had reference to other disciplines, these matters he brought out clearly, yet in such wise that he did not teach everything about each topic, but in proportion to the capacity of his audience dispensed to them in time the due measure of the subject. And because the brilliancy of discourse depends either on propriety (that is, the proper joining of adjective or verb with the substantive) or on metathesis (that is, the transfer of an expression for a worthy reason to another signification), these were the things he took every opportunity to inculcate in the minds of his hearers.
>
> And since the memory is strengthened and the wits are sharpened by exercise, he urged some by warnings and some by floggings and punishments to the constant practice of imitating what they heard. Every one was required on the following day to reproduce some part of what he had heard the day before, some more, some less, for with them the morrow was the disciple of yesterday. Evening drill, which was called declension, was packed with so much grammar that one who gave a whole year to it would have at his command, unless unusually dull, a method of speaking and writing and could not be ignorant of the meaning of expressions which are in common use. [The material, however, of the evening lesson was chosen for moral and religious edification, closing with the sixth penitential psalm and the Lord's prayer.]
>
> Before those for whom the preliminary exercises of boys in imitating prose or poetry were prescribed, he held up the poets or ora-

tors, and bade them follow in their footsteps, pointing out their combinations of words and the elegance of their phrasing. But if any one had sewed on another's raiment to make his own work brilliant, he detected and exposed the theft, though very often he inflicted no punishment. But if the poorness of the work had so merited, with indulgent mildness he ordered the culprit to embark on the task of fashioning a real likeness of the ancient authors; and he brought it about that he who imitated his predecessors became worthy of imitation by his successors.

The following matters, too, he taught among the first rudiments and fixed them in the students' minds: the value of order; what is praiseworthy in embellishment and in the choice of words; where there is tenuity and, as it were, emaciation of speech; where a pleasing abundance; where excess; and where the limit due in all things. History and poetry, too, he taught, should be diligently read, without the spur of compulsion; and he insistently required that each pupil should commit something to memory every day; but he taught them to avoid superfluity and be content with what they found in famous writers. . . . And since in the entire preliminary training of pupils there is nothing more useful than to grow accustomed to that which must needs be done with skill, they wrote prose and poetry daily, and trained themselves by mutual comparisons.[1]

Such patient and prolonged devotion to classical authors, which enjoyed "the sole privilege of making one lettered," had its opponents in John of Salisbury's time, and by the thirteenth-century grammar had fallen back into the position of being merely one of the seven liberal arts, confined to its elementary task of teaching the Latin language for practical purposes. The *artes* have vanquished the *auctores*. In the *Battle of the Seven Liberal Arts* (*ca.* 1250) Donatus and Priscian still represent grammar in the sense of literary studies, but they fight a losing battle. Logic, indeed, has now encroached upon the

[1] *Metalogicus*, i, c. 24: cf. A. O. Norton, *Readings in the History of Education*, pp. 31–33.

method as well as the sphere of grammar: not only is less time given to grammar, but it must be studied in a logical rather than a literary fashion. Already in the twelfth century William FitzStephen describes the interscholastic debates of the London boys, "quarrelling in verse or disputing concerning the principles of the grammatical art and the rules of preterites and supines." [1] Literary form came to be despised; indeed, logic professed to be able to supply defects in one's grammatical studies. By the thirteenth century grammar becomes a speculative science. The texts of the new age are the *Doctrinale* of Alexander de Villedieu (1199) and the *Grecismus* of Évrard de Bethune (1212). Both treatises are in verse for aid in memorizing. The *Doctrinale*, in 2645 leonine hexameters, aims to take the place of Priscian and the reading-books. Thus the rules for the first declension begin (lines 29-31),

> Rectis *as es a* dat declinatio prima,
> Atque per *am* propria quaedam ponuntur Hebraea,
> Dans *ae* diphthongon genetivis atque dativis.

So the *Grecismus*, which gets its name from a chapter on Greek derivations but is conspicuously ignorant of Greek, begins its chapter on euphonic change as follows (v, 1, 2):

> Ecce quod usus habet, cedunt sibi saepe sonantes,
> *B* mutatur in *f* in sexque *c g p m s r*.

Such a system is obviously aimed at immediate results rather than at literary perfection. These representatives

---

[1] *Materials for the History of Thomas Becket*, edited by J. C. Robertson for the Rolls Series, iii (London, 1877), pp. 4-5.

of a 'barbarous Latin' held the field until driven out by the humanists, and even then their slow retreat is indicated by the fact that two hundred and sixty-seven editions of the *Doctrinale* were published between the invention of printing and 1588.

Rhetoric, grammar's sister art, had a different history in the Middle Ages, since in its Roman form it was less adapted to mediaeval conditions, and the modifications which it underwent carried it far from classical models. Ancient rhetoric was concerned with oratory, mediaeval rhetoric chiefly with letter-writing. The fundamentally oratorical character of the Roman rhetoric is illustrated by the titles of the principal treatises, the *Orator, De oratore,* and *Brutus (De claris oratoribus)* of Cicero, and the *Institutes of Oratory* of Quintilian, all devoted to the art of effective oral discourse before courts or public assemblies. The whole basis of such forensic oratory disappeared with the Roman political and judicial system; the word *oratio* itself came ordinarily to mean the most private sort of discourse, the prayer of man to his Maker, and it is rare to find a treatise on the rhetoric of prayer, such as an unknown author of our period has left in a manuscript of the Vatican.[1] Even the less forensic rhetoric of the later Empire failed to adjust itself to Christian conditions; Martianus Capella perpetuated the Ciceronian tradition, and the teaching of the professional

[1] Vatican, MS. Reg. Lat. 1222, ff. 37 v–39 v.

rhetoricians became more and more formal and empty. For the Middle Ages rhetoric could no longer be the centre and goal of liberal education.

Nor did rhetoric possess a simple and convenient manual like Priscian or Donatus to carry it through the rough wear of the Dark Ages. There was something in Martianus and the later Roman compends, something less in Bede and Isidore (who still gives it the forensic definition), but in the nature of things these lacked the hard core of a grammatical textbook and could not keep alive a subject which was dying for other reasons. The better scholars of the twelfth century stretched their minds on Cicero and Quintilian and held these up before their pupils as the ideal texts of the art, as in Neckam's list of standard authors, but this is rather a counsel of perfection, and, in any case, these Roman works were read as models of rhetorical style rather than as textbooks. How little Cicero and Quintilian were actually used appears from the number of surviving copies, respectable for a classic but insignificant for a standard text. For a time they received lip service from the newer generation, but students turned steadily toward the up-to-date manuals which concentrated attention upon the practical subject of epistolary composition or *dictamen*. At first these works will be labelled 'according to Tully,' but by the thirteenth century the popular professors of rhetoric pride themselves on their ignorance of Cicero and their ability to get practical results. The final absurdity of the

Tullian school appears in the unpublished treatise of a certain John, which is thrown into the form of a dialogue between Cicero and his son, and contains a wealth of classical quotation and rhetorical discussion, but ends with instructions from the elder Cicero concerning the proper forms of salutation to be observed between Pope and Emperor, Frederick Barbarossa and Henry II of England![1]

The earliest known exponent of the new epistolary style — 'sweet new style' we cannot call it — was Alberic of Monte Cassino, who lived in the fruitful reign of Abbot Desiderius (1058–86). The art of drafting official letters or documents — for the official documents of the Middle Ages inherited the Roman epistolary form — had, it is true, not disappeared in the early Middle Ages, being kept alive by notaries and royal clerks; but it was a rigorously practical art, taught by the imitation of standard types and collections of forms, and with no freedom or spontaneity of expression. Indeed such collections remained highly popular throughout the Middle Ages both for public and private correspondence, since in an illiterate age the easiest way to write a letter was to imitate one already written, much as in the complete letter-writers which are still used by those of small education. The innovation of the late eleventh and the twelfth centuries consisted in the preparation of brief manuals of the art of letter-writing, suited to the new

[1] Bruges, MS. 549, f. 1.

conditions, and accompanied by illustrations, whether in the way of scattered examples or a more systematic appendix of forms. Alberic, grammarian and author of lives of saints and verse and controversial pamphlets, was apparently not the first to compose such treatises, but he was the first whose works have reached us. His *Breviarium de dictamine* still contains a good deal of what we should call grammar, and its examples are few, but it fixes the type. Its author, whose *Flores dictaminum* show some classical reading, also seems to have been responsible for the revival of the ancient rhythmical prose, or *cursus*, in the new or accentual form which it was to retain until the Italian humanists; certainly one of his pupils, John of Gaeta, chancellor of the Roman curia and later Pope Gelasius II (1118–19), introduced this into the papal chancery, where as the *cursus Romane curie* it became a test of genuineness for the documents of the Holy See.

The future of the *ars dictaminis* in Italy was, however, bound up neither with Rome nor with Monte Cassino, but with Bologna, whither it was transplanted at the beginning of the twelfth century. Having been kept alive in the earlier Middle Ages as an adjunct to legal drafting, it was natural that *dictamen* should be closely associated with legal teaching after the full establishment of law as an independent subject of professional study, and that it should flourish most at the greatest of mediaeval law schools. In such an environment the practical side of the art was more and more emphasized, and by the thirteenth century it developed into a special *ars notaria* for the drafting of notarial acts, with special degrees and a special faculty whose professors are apt to express great scorn of the humanistic rhetoric and all its works. In the pages of the amusing and grandiloquent Bolognese professor Boncompagno, in the early thirteenth century, we see that the study of rhetoric has become a short business course, whose professors well understand the business art of advertising. Boncompagno's *Antiqua rhetorica* was publicly read and crowned with laurel at Bologna in 1215 and at Padua in 1226, while he seized every other opportunity for self-advertisement. We are far from the gentler humanism of Orleans and Chartres.

Meanwhile *dictamen* had been transplanted to France, where it struck root in the congenial soil of Orleans and grew in close relations with the classical studies of this school, which, indeed, trained secretaries for the papal curia. The manuals written at Orleans and Tours did not revert to Cicero and Quintilian, but they emphasized Latin composition in prose and verse, and their letters are the prose parallel to the Goliardic poetry of this age. Such collections of letters are especially numerous in the reign of Philip Augustus (1180–1223), when they constitute perhaps our best evidence for the vitality of the literary tradition of Orleans. Notably is this true of the more frankly imaginative compositions which meet us in these manuscripts — correspondence between Paris and

Helen, Ulysses and Penelope, Winter and Spring, the Soul and the Body, Life and Death, Man and the Devil, and letters describing delicate situations not usually treated in writing — topics handled with skill and freedom and at times in the antique spirit. In all such compilations there are likely to be several letters in praise of rhetoric and the attainments of particular teachers of this art. Many of them treat of the commonplaces of student existence, as we shall see in another connection; indeed, where so much is conscious invention, the chief historical value of such collections lies in their reflection of the general conditions of the age rather than in preserving specific detail, for the compiler aimed to give a set of forms for all possible occasions, and, if he did not have an actual document at hand, he made one up or took the best exercises of his. pupils. At one extreme we have collections of archival documents, at the other, collections of invented models.

The theoretical expositions of epistolary composition commonly divided a letter into five parts: the salutation, a point on which mediaeval etiquette was very severe, the form of address being elaborately fixed for each dignity and station in society; the exordium, or *captatio benevolentie*, designed to put the reader in the right frame of mind and often consisting of a proverb or scriptural quotation; the narrative or exposition; the petition, for a request was always expected and was likely to take the form of a logical deduction from the major and minor premises already laid down in the exordium and narration; and finally the conclusion. Here is a simple analysis of a theme without the developments and variations with which it is accompanied in the original: [1]

To his father H., C. sends due affection. *This is the salutation.* I am much obliged to you for the money you sent me. *This is the captatio benivolentie.* But I would have you know that I am still poor, having spent in the schools what I had, and that which recently arrived is of little help since I used it to pay some of my debts and my greater obligations still remain. *This is the narration.* Whence I beg you to send me something more. *This is the petition.* If you do not, I shall lose the books which I have pledged to the Jews and shall be compelled to return home with my work incomplete. *This is the conclusion.*

A similar conclusion is reached in more distinctive fashion in the following letter:

To their very dear and respected parents M. Martre, knight, and M. his wife, M. and S. their sons send greetings and filial obedience. This is to inform you that, by divine mercy, we are living in good health in the city of Orleans and are devoting ourselves wholly to study, mindful of the words of Cato, "To know anything is praiseworthy," etc. We occupy a good and comely dwelling, next door but one to the schools and market place, so that we can go to school every day without wetting our feet. We have also good companions in the house with us, well advanced in their studies and of excellent habits — an advantage which we well appreciate, for as the Psalmist says, "With an upright man thou wilt show thyself upright," etc. Wherefore lest production cease from lack of material, we beg your paternity to send us by the bearer, B., money for buying parchment, ink, a desk, and the other things which we need, in sufficient amount that we may suffer no want on your account (God forbid!) but finish our studies and return home with honor. The bearer will also take charge of the shoes and stockings which you have to send us, and any news as well.[2]

---

[1] L. von Rockinger, *Ueber Briefsteller und Formelbücher* (Munich, 1861), p. 40.

[2] Ed. L. Delisle, in *Annuaire-Bulletin de la Société de l'Histoire de France*, 1869, pp. 149–150.

The more fanciful compositions of the Orleanese *dicta-tores* show some imagination and often treat classical or contemporary themes in a manner that suggests the Latin poets of the time. Thus, a group of such letters in one manuscript [1] begins with a complaint of the Soul to the Creator on account of its constant struggle with the grossness of the Body; the Creator exhorts the Body to mend its ways, but the Body replies that nothing better can be expected of its earthy origin and the flimsy stuff of which it is made. The fall of Jerusalem in 1187 is adumbrated in a letter from the Church, Christ's Spouse, to the Mother of God. Job complains to Fortune of his pitiful estate, and Fortune replies that she is wont to humble the proud and exalt the humble with the turning of her wheel. Meat and Fish dispute their respective claims to the month of April; the Pygmies beg the king of Spain for aid against the cranes and are promised an army of falcons; a Norman urges a friend to help fight the great beast tortoise (*testudo*). Finally Adrastus consoles Polynices over the fate of Tydeus, and with a father's letter urging his son to study we are back once more in the schoolroom.

Besides the formal treatises on rhetoric and their accompanying models, we must take account of the letters of the best Latinists of the age, copied and recopied as examples of good epistolary style in this and succeeding periods. This was true particularly of the correspondence

[1] Bibliothèque Nationale, MS. Lat. 1093, ff. 68–69.

of Hildebert of Le Mans and John of Salisbury, and the letters which pass under the name of John's pupil, Peter of Blois, but still require critical sifting. The letters of Hildebert were even committed to memory in the schools. In general, such collections provided excellent models of Latin style until they were thrust aside by the more turgid manner of the Capuan *dictatores* of the thirteenth century, and they are spoken of with respect by that finished secretary of a later age, Coluccio Salutati.

No single manual of composition or collection of forms would remain long in use, for the fashions kept changing and new circumstances kept arising, while the proper names or initials were subject to constant revision. Still each *dictator* built upon the work of his predecessor, so that there is a continuous tradition, with adaptation to time and place, throughout the whole of the later Middle Ages in all parts of Europe. The systematic treatises reach their climax in the thirteenth century, and the later period was satisfied with formularies for particular chanceries and with complete letter-writers.

The rhetorical manuals are silent respecting another species of prose composition, namely the structure and style of sermons. Not that the twelfth century lacked sermons, for several hundred have been preserved from this period and some thousands from the century following, so that two volumes have been written on French society as illustrated by the sermons of this epoch. Nor were there lacking discussions of the art of preaching, as a brief treatise of Alain de Lille testifies, but if these are not entirely independent of the ancient rhetorical tradition, they add nothing to our knowledge of the general intellectual life of the time. Moreover, as we come into the thirteenth century, the formal style declines before a more popular preaching full of stories and anecdotes, until Dante complains of those "who go forth with jests and buffoonery to preach" and swell with pride if they can raise a laugh. We are now well out of Latin and into the vernacular. In one respect there is parallelism between sermons and letters, namely in the matter of copying. Many preachers had no scruples in appropriating sermons of others, and for the lazy or uneducated there were complete series of sermons for the ecclesiastical year, like the popular *Dormi secure* which insured a morning's sleep to priests otherwise unprepared for the day's demands in the pulpit. Indeed, this serviceable collection passed through many editions and was reprinted as late as 1612 with a title page which praises "its singular piety and multifarious utility."

One form of copying has been countenanced by the public oratory of all ages, namely the anecdote. The stories, or *exempla*, with which the sermons were embellished comprise the greatest variety of legends and miracles and contemporary tales, so that they afford a most valuable insight into the popular religion and superstitions of their day, besides preserving a considerable mass of varied information concerning the manners and customs of the time. This material was collected into convenient manuals for current use, and while most of these belong to the thirteenth century, they are foreshadowed in the twelfth in the Oriental tales of the *Disciplina clericalis* of Petrus Alphonsi and in the *Verbum abbreviatum* of Petrus Cantor, while the famous collections of Jacques de Vitry and Caesar of Heisterbach belong to the early years of the new century. Here again we are unable to distinguish the subject matter of learned and popular, Latin and vernacular. Collections of stories were also made for, or in, royal courts. Thus Gervase of Tilbury began his literary career with a *Liber facetiarum* for Henry II's son, the Young King, and ended it with the *Otia imperialia* designed to while away the imperial leisure of Otto IV; and the delightful miscellany of Walter Map's *Courtiers' Trifles* was noted down hurriedly in the midst of the busy court of Henry II.

The mention of Walter Map brings us back to rhetoric, from which it would be pleasant to wander still further amid examples of informal narrative and popular tales. Map has not only the wide reading and keen wit of a humanist, but, it has recently been shown, he has also a clear idea of the ancient distinction between the simple and the ornate style, according as he is dealing with plain narrative or with more declamatory matter. A similar contrast appears in the writings of his voluble contemporary, Giraldus Cambrensis, while even the sober William of Malmesbury has his purple patches. Other historians of the twelfth century betray fondness for poetical usage, with reminiscences particularly of Lucan; and in general the historical style of this age shows an attention to literary form which is lacking in the great compilations of the following century. As the most flourishing period of mediaeval rhetorical studies, the twelfth century left its mark on most forms of prose style.

While it is true that mediaeval rhetoricians concentrated themselves on letter-writing, they accorded at least theoretical recognition to poetical composition. Often they begin by dividing *dictamen* into three sorts, prose, metrical, and rhythmical, thus recognizing and distinguishing both the ancient quantitative metre and the new accentual rhythm, even when the treatise goes on to concern itself with prose composition alone. With the exception of the so-called Bernard, poetical composition comes off rather badly in the manuals, most of which content themselves with lifting bodily some simple rules of prosody from the Latin grammars where they primarily belonged. Nor is the great fertility of the twelfth century in new rhythmical forms reflected in special manuals; these must be examined inductively in the poems themselves. Toward the end of the century begins a series of more systematic treatises on the art of poetry, based upon the *De inventione* of Cicero, the *Rhetorica ad Herennium*, and the *Ars poetica* of Horace, as well as upon more or less independent study of ancient types and of certain contemporaries like Alain de Lille.

Poets as well as critics, these writers introduce examples of their own make as well as gems from the ancients. Their chief works are the *Ars versificatoria* of Matthew of Vendôme (*ca.* 1175) and the *Doctrina de arte versificandi* and versified *Poetria nova* of Geoffrey de Vinesauf (*ca.* 1200). The centre of dispersion of these doctrines seems to have been first Orleans and later Paris. Devoted to rhetoric rather than poetics, their interest is greater for the student of literary workmanship than for the lover of poetry. The best poetry of this period had already been written before the critics came to show how it should be done, and to this poetry itself we must now turn our attention.

BIBLIOGRAPHICAL NOTE

The history of the Latin language in the Middle Ages still remains to be written, nor have we as yet even a preliminary sketch. The individual authors of the twelfth century still require investigation, and there is much to be done with its grammarians and lexicographers. For some general remarks on the peculiarities of mediaeval Latin, see L. Traube, *Vorlesungen und Abhandlungen*, ii (Munich, 1911), pp. 31–121; and C. H. Beeson, *A Primer of Medieval Latin* (Chicago, 1925). For other anthologies of mediaeval Latin, see *Speculum*, i. 110–114 (1926).

The indispensable basis of study of the language and technical terms of the period is C. Du Fresne Du Cange, *Glossarium mediae et infimae Latinitatis* (best edition in seven volumes, Paris, 1840–50; also in ten volumes, Niort, 1883–87); the new dictionary in preparation by the International Union of Academies stops *ca.* 1000. There is no satisfactory brief dictionary. Of the lexicographers of the eleventh and twelfth centuries only Papias, Osbern, and Hugutio are discussed by G. Goetz, *Corpus glossariorum Latinorum*, i (Leipzig, 1923). For Adam du Petit-Pont and Alexander Neckam, see T. Wright, *A Volume of Vocabularies* (London, 1857); and A. Scheler, in *Jahrbuch für romanische und englische Literatur*, vi–viii (1865–67); for Neckam, also Haskins, *Mediaeval Science*, ch. 18; and M. Esposito, in *English Historical Review*, xxx. 450–471 (1915). Cf. my paper on the *Summa derivationum* of Walter of Ascoli, *ca.* 1228, in the *Mélanges Ferdinand Lot* (Paris, 1926), pp. 245-257.

Donatus and Priscian are edited in H. Keil, *Grammatici Latini* (Leipzig, 1855–80), ii–iv; Alexander's *Doctrinale* by D. Reichling (Berlin, 1893); the *Grecismus* by J. Wrobel (Breslau, 1887). The *Ars minor* of Donatus is translated by W. J. Chase (Madison, 1926), who has also translated and discussed Cato's *Disticha* (Madison, 1922). On Theodulus, see the edition of J. Osternacher (Linz, 1902); and the article of G. L. Hamilton, in *Modern Philology*, vii. 169–185 (1909). On the grammatical doctrines of the period, see the full and excellent discussion of C. Thurot, in *Notices et extraits des manuscrits*, xxii, 2 (1868), and G. Manacorda, *Storia della scuola in Italia* (Milan, [1915]), i, 2, ch. 5; on catechetical grammars, Manacorda, "Un testo scolastico di grammatica del sec. XII in uso nel basso Piemonte," in *Giornale storico e letterario della Liguria*, viii. 241–282 (1907); on punctuation, F. Novati, in *Rendiconti dell' Istituto lombardo*, xlii. 83–118 (1909). For the curriculum in grammar and rhetoric, see L. J. Paetow, *The Arts Course at Medieval Universities* (Urbana, 1910).

The best guide to the bibliography of the *ars dictaminis* is H. Bresslau, *Handbuch der Urkundenlehre* (second edition), ii, 1, pp. 225 ff.; cf. A. Bütow, *Die Entwicklung der mittelalterlichen Briefsteller bis zur Mitte des 12. Jahrhunderts* (Greifswald diss., 1908); and the bibliography in Paetow's *Guide*. I have discussed the student letters in the *American Historical Review*, iii. 203–229 (1898), and certain Italian treatises of the twelfth century in the *Mélanges H. Pirenne* (Brussels, 1926), pp. 101–110, and the *Essays Presented to Reginald Lane Poole* (Oxford, 1927). For examples of thirteenth-century papal formularies, cf. my discussion of a MS. now in Philadelphia, *Miscellanea Ehrle*, iv. 275–286. On the papal *cursus*, see the excellent summary in R. L. Poole, *Lectures on the History of the Papal Chancery* (Cambridge, 1915), ch. 4, and the treatment of the whole subject in K. Polheim, *Die lateinische Reimprosa* (Berlin, 1925); on fictitious letters, W. Wattenbach, in *Sitzungsberichte* of the Berlin Academy, 1892, pp. 91–123. The fullest collection of rhetorical treatises is still that of L. von Rockinger, in *Quellen und Erörter-ungen zur bayerischen und deutschen Geschichte*, ix (1863–64).

On mediaeval Latin style, see M. B. Ogle, in *Speculum*, i. 170–189 (1926). Walter Map's *De nugis curialium* is edited by M. R. James (Oxford, 1914), and translated by James (London, 1924), and by F. Tupper and M. B. Ogle (London, 1924). Its plan and composition are discussed by James Hinton in the *Publications of the Modern Language Association of America*, xxxii. 81–132 (1917). For treatises on poetry, see E. Faral, *Les arts poétiques du XIIᵉ et XIIIᵉ siècle* (Paris, 1924); for rhythmics, W. Meyer, *Gesammelte Abhandlungen zur mittellateinischen Rythmik* (Berlin, 1905). On the sermons of the period, see L. Bourgain, *La chaire française au XIIᵉ siècle* (Paris, 1879); and cf. my article on the Paris sermons of the thirteenth century in the *American Historical Review*, x. 1–27 (1904).

CHAPTER VI

LATIN POETRY

EACH of the three important classical revivals of the Middle Ages was accompanied by a notable revival in the writing of Latin poetry; indeed, this is perhaps the best test of the vitality of such a renaissance of Latin letters. Of the three movements, the Carolingian was the most limited, both in bulk of product and in range of interests. The four thick volumes of the *Poetae Latini Aevi Carolini* bear witness to a marked improvement in Latin style and treat a considerable variety of themes, historical, hagiographical, occasional, and miscellaneous, both in ancient metre and mediaeval rhyme; but they show little contact with popular life, and the best of this poetry has an academic quality which gives it a higher place in the history of culture than in the general perspective of European poetry. In the resolute assimilation of the antique spirit as well as in cleverness and technical finish, the Italian Renaissance is preëminent; but by this time Latin verse was engaged in a hopeless competition with the vernacular, and the broad current of poetry now flowed in new channels. Already in the fourteenth century Petrarch is remembered for his Italian sonnets and not for the Latin epic *Africa* on which he expected his lasting fame to rest. The Latin verse of the twelfth century stands between that of these other periods in character as well as in time. It is much more abundant and more varied than that of the Carolingian age, but it has not yet been crowded out by the vernacular. Indeed, while vernacular poetry is springing up rapidly in this epoch, it preserves many intimate relations with the Latin. At most points the two run parallel, and there are constant mutual influences both in subject matter and in form. Latin is still the natural medium of expression of most poets; Latin poetry appeals to a wide public, and it reflects every aspect of contemporary life. Not only is there a widespread and often successful imitation of ancient models, but there is much verse of a new type, and a wealth of new metrical forms, seen especially in the free lyrics of the Goliardi and the new religious drama, both owing more to the new conditions of this age than to ancient tradition. Thus the Latin poetry of the twelfth century was far more than a mere revival of ancient modes and subjects; it was a manifold expression of the vigorous and many-sided life of the age, an age of romance as well as an age of religion. This very variety, however, is a sign of the impending decline of Latin: the numerous vernacular tongues become the more natural vehicles of literature, and the twelfth century is the last great age of international poetry.

The first impression made by this body of Latin poetry is its bewildering profusion. No collection or *corpus* has been attempted, and if one were to be made it would fill many times the four volumes of the Carolingian poets. Every subject is represented: epic, history, and legend; biblical story and ancient fable; dedications, epitaphs, and occasional verse; hymns, sequences, tropes, and other liturgical pieces; didactic, moral, and contemplative poems; lyrics, sacred and profane; parodies of every sort; drinking songs and love songs, dialogues and debates, useful and mnemonic rhymes and proverbs; professors' exercises and texts and school compositions; and many lesser or miscellaneous types. There are long poems of many thousand lines and short poems of one or two couplets. There is poetry mixed with prose, and there are even macaronic rhymes of mixed Latin and vernacular.

This material defies systematic classification. We may use the traditional terms epic, lyric, and dramatic, but these are so broad and their subdivisions so numerous that they are of little help. Geography fails us, for the same speech prevailed throughout the whole of Western Europe and much poetry had a European circulation. While Northern France was the most active centre of production in this period, there is a singular absence of the local and provincial note; save as it deals with particular individuals or places, this poetry cannot be divided by geographical lines. Chronology, too, is of little use as a guide in so short a space of time, beyond the general fact that the late eleventh and early twelfth centuries confine themselves more closely to the older type of religious and occasional composition, and that the greater variety of lyric and epic and of the more popular rhymes develops in the course of the twelfth century and reaches its climax somewhere about 1200.

Nor is there a fundamental distinction of metre, though here again chronology manifests itself in the increased variety and vogue of new forms as the century advances. "Poetical *dictamen* is either metrical or rhythmical," say the books on rhetoric, but they do not go on to define the appropriate subject matter of each. The classical hexameter and pentameter were employed freely throughout the century, and occasionally some one like Alfano of Salerno could use more complex and difficult forms. So Alain de Lille could handle sapphics, and he and others used a mixture of prose and verse such as had come down in Martianus Capella and the *Consolation* of Boethius. Naturally those most imbued with the antique spirit were most likely to keep alive the ancient forms of verse, which thus remained the set tradition of the epic, whereas those whose themes ran closest to the vernacular favored the new forms of rhyme; but there was no fixed rule. Some writers would treat classical themes in the elegiac distich, others in the freer rhymes of the Goliardi. The last named group, as we shall see later, employed a great variety of verse forms for their fresh and unacademic compositions. Religious poetry had already given up the ancient metres by the tenth century, and its two forms of rhythmic verse and prose sequence had practically coalesced in the rhymed verse which reached its climax in the twelfth century. New forms, and many of them, were almost a necessity of Christian poetry, for, as Mr. Henry Osborn Taylor puts it:[1]

Christian emotion quivers differently from any movement of the spirit in classic measures. The new quiver, the new shudder, the utter terror, and the utter love appear in mediaeval rhymed accentual poetry: —

Desidero te millies,
Mî Jesu; quando venies?
Me laetum quando facies,
Ut vultu tuo saties?

Quo dolore
Quo moerore
Deprimuntur miseri,
Qui abyssis
Pro commissis
Submergentur inferi.

Recordare, Jesu pie,
Quod sum causa tuae viae:
Ne me perdas illa die.

.   .   .   .

Lacrymosa dies illa
Quâ resurget ex favillâ,
Judicandus homo reus;
Huic ergo parce, Deus!
Pie Jesu, Domine,
Dona eos requie!

Let any one feel the emotion of these verses and then turn to some piece of classic poetry, a passage from Homer or Virgil, an elegiac couplet or a strophe from Sappho or Pindar or Catullus, and he will realize the difference, and the impossibility of setting the emotion of a mediaeval hymn in a classic metre.

---

[1] *The Classical Heritage of the Middle Ages* (New York, 1901), pp. 246–247.

One apparently easy criterion of classification we must also in large measure give up, namely, the distinction between sacred and profane. Time was when men divided sharply the intellectual life of the Middle Ages into the clerical, or Latin, and the lay, or vernacular, two watertight compartments, one of which was wholly religious and the other wholly secular in life and in literary expression. Further study of the actual conditions has broken down this separation at many points all along the line. There was from comparatively early times a religious literature in the vernacular, as illustrated by the Anglo-Saxon homilies, the *Heliand*, the Old French poems on saints, and other works of edification; and, what is more to our purpose, there was an enormous secular literature in Latin. Not only were there laymen who knew Latin, like the Italian notaries and physicians, but there were many clerks who were essentially laymen at a time when the habit and tonsure were easily taken and secured many profitable exemptions, even for those who did not proceed to holy orders. University students were *ipso facto* clerks, and students have been much the same in all ages. Even those who embraced the monastic or sacerdotal career did not lose all touch with the world. That very carnal poet, the Primate, was a canon of Orleans, and Ovid's lines were imitated in many a cloister. There was a colossal amount of parody, very sacred in form and very secular in spirit, which refuses to be placed on either side of an arbitrary line. We now know that many of the vernacular epics were closely connected with pilgrimage roads and pilgrimage shrines, and were often founded upon materials furnished by particular churches and cloisters, the result being neither wholly sacred nor wholly profane.

"The collections which contain religious songs," says Dreves,[1] "offer material of every sort in many-colored confusion: liturgical and non-liturgical, sacred and profane, edifying and unedifying, not to say scandalous." The most famous body of Goliardic poems, some of them very earthy, the *Carmina Burana*, has many a sacred piece as well, all copied by the monastic scribes of Benediktbeuern. Another great collection of mediaeval verse shows the same confusion, the splendid manuscript of the Laurentian called the *Antiphonary* of Piero de' Medici, which was copied with the musical notation and illuminated somewhere in France *ca.* 1300. The first half of the volume is properly an antiphonary; the second half consists of some hundreds of poems, chiefly of the later twelfth and early thirteenth centuries: hymns and commemorations of the saints, interspersed with much occasional verse and eulogy and with much that is clearly secular or sharply critical of Rome and the ecclesiastical system. The principle of arrangement is not religious but musical. Thus a group of hymns and sacred verse for the Christmas season is immediately preceded by a poem on the capture of La Rochelle in 1224, which closes with the

[1] *Analecta hymnica*, xx. 7.

praise of good French wine in contrast to the beer and water of England,

> Terra Bachi Francia,
> Moysis est Anglia.

Another poem exhorts youth to pay its debt to Venus. Where shall we place this volume whose compiler recognized differences between quartets and solos but not between sacred and profane? How shall we classify the compositions of one of its authors?

> Frater, en Jordanus,
> Vester veteranus,
> Quondam publicanus,
> Modo doctor sanus,
> Monet, cum sit vanus
> Splendor hic mundanus,
> Ne sit parca manus.

For a different example let us turn to the poems of a single poet, Baudri, abbot of Bourgueil from 1089 to 1107 and then bishop of Dol until 1130, as these are preserved to the number of two hundred and fifty-five in a contemporary codex of the Vatican, respectable verse on the whole, chiefly in the ancient elegiac metre, as befitted a pupil of Fleury, and dealing with all kinds of subjects. First comes a hymn, then a dedication of verse, then poems on the Incarnation and Passion, a "Go, little book" which praises the copyist and the illuminator and is paralleled by poems on the author's *stylus* and tablets; answers to invitations and exchanges of verse with other poets; a long poem from Paris to Helen and a still longer reply; Ovid to Florus, and Florus to Ovid; verses on the death of Cicero; many eulogies and obituaries both lay and ecclesiastical; poems to noble ladies within and without the cloister, the longest of all one addressed to Adela, countess of Blois, and descriptive of an apartment and its adornments, which is supposed to give an account of the Bayeux tapestry. Part of the material is classical, most is contemporary, concerning both persons and places; some is grave, some is trivial, what in another age would be called *vers de société* — indeed the author finds it necessary to explain why he writes so much on love and borrows so much from the ancients. The religious side is not stressed nor does it go very deep. Again classification is impossible.

A further source of confusion lies in the fact that much of the poetry of this period is anonymous, much of it pseudonymous, and many problems of identification still await the labor of the critic. For the anonymous material we often have only the dates of manuscripts and the general criteria of style. Style may be deceptive; while the signature of the twelfth century can often be recognized by the expert, his tests are not infallible. If the works of this age are less learned and less labored than those of the thirteenth century, they are not so easy to distinguish from those of the preceding epoch, likewise marked by a straining after allegory and antithesis and an effort to attain a classical quality which few achieve. Indeed the critic may have to disentangle the ancient from the mediaeval when a scribe puts Ovid and Ausonius under the name of Hildebert and Hildebert under the aegis of the ancients. Poetic form is also a guide, for the twelfth century develops many new types, such as the common use of the pure two-syllabled rhyme. Manuscript investigation is often surer: an eleventh-century codex would suffice to remove a poem from the list of St. Bonaventura's writings and thus from the documents by whose aid the attempt has been made to reconstruct his inner life. False attributions also have their snares, for many a poem soon lost its tag and became attached, by the mediaeval scribe or a modern editor, to the train of well known figures like Hildebert or St. Bernard. The criticism of Hauréau stripped St. Bernard and Walter Map of their fictitious adornments; the researches of others have restored to us the lost personalities of the Primate and the Archpoet.

If we take up first the more immediately classical aspects of twelfth-century poetry, we are prepared to find much direct imitation of Roman models in a period when the classical poets were so freely read. Geoffrey of Winchester (d. 1095) wrote epigrams in the style of Martial. Ralph Tortarius a little later composed a book of *Memorabilia* after the manner of Valerius Maximus. Horace we have seen imitated by Metellus of Tegern-

see. Virgil, model of all epics, was copied often by lesser
poets, as by the anonymous Pisan chronicler of the
Majorcan expedition of 1114 who begins, in one text,

> Arma, rates, populum, vindictam celitus actam.

Ovid has his imitators everywhere. The poetry of the age
is full of classical reminiscences.

The fullest assimilation of the spirit as well as the form
of Latin poetry is seen in Hildebert, born at Lavardin
ca. 1055, bishop of Le Mans 1097–1125, and archbishop
of Tours until his death in 1133 or 1134. Best known of
the poets of his century, he is called 'the divine Hildebert,' *egregius versificator*, a second Homer; but naturally
his works were soon confused with those of others, and it
was not until 1882 that Hauréau introduced order into
the mass of writings ascribed to him. For the most part
his themes are the usual ones of the time, epitaphs, epigrams, the mysteries of theology, moral disquisitions,
praise of contemporaries. A more personal note is struck
in a poem on his exile from his see, regretting the gardens
and the wealth which he has lost, and turning at the end
from pagan fortune to the Christian God who rules over
all:

> Ille potens, mitis, tenor et concordia rerum,
> Quidquid vult in me digerat, eius ero.

Christian in its conclusion, this has a large serenity which
suggests the ancient philosophers. Still more of the antique spirit permeates his two poems on Rome, the ancient and the modern, full of real feeling for the eternal

city expressed in a style which long secured him a place in the Latin *Anthology* and still seems to some too classical to be wholly Hildebert's. Conscious of the importance of the new Rome of the Popes, which can scarcely remember its remoter past —

> Vix scio que fuerim, vix Rome Roma recordor —

Hildebert can still celebrate the glories of the older Rome in an elegy which we may quote in full as representing the high-water mark of twelfth-century classicism:[1]

> Par tibi, Roma, nihil, cum sis prope tota ruina;
>   Quam magni fueris integra fracta doces.
> Longa tuos fastus aetas destruxit, et arces
>   Caesaris et superum templa palude jacent.
> Ille labor, labor ille ruit quem dirus Araxes
>   Et stantem tremuit et cecidisse dolet;
> Quem gladii regum, quem provida cura senatus,
>   Quem superi rerum constituere caput;
> Quem magis optavit cum crimine solus habere
>   Caesar, quam socius et pius esse socer,
> Qui, crescens studiis tribus, hostes, crimen, amicos
>   Vi domuit, secuit legibus, emit ope;
> In quem, dum fieret, vigilavit cura priorum:
>   Juvit opus pietas hospitis, unda, locus.
> Materiem, fabros, expensas axis uterque
>   Misit, se muris obtulit ipse locus.
> Expendere duces thesauros, fata favorem,
>   Artifices studium, totus et orbis opes.
> Urbs cecidit de qua si quicquam dicere dignum
>   Moliar, hoc potero dicere: Roma fuit!
> Non tamen annorum series, non flamma, nec ensis
>   Ad plenum potuit hoc abolere decus.
> Cura hominum potuit tantam componere Roman
>   Quantam non potuit solvere cura deum.

---

[1] Text from Hauréau, *Les mélanges poétiques d'Hildebert de Lavardin* (Paris, 1882), pp. 60–61.

Confer opes marmorque novum superumque favorem,
    Artificum vigilent in nova facta manus,
Non tamen aut fieri par stanti machina muro,
    Aut restaurari sola ruina potest.
Tantum restat adhuc, tantum ruit, ut neque pars stans
    Aequari possit, diruta nec refici.
Hic superum formas superi mirantur et ipsi,
    Et cupiunt fictis vultibus esse pares.
Non potuit natura deos hoc ore creare
    Quo miranda deum signa creavit homo.
Vultus adest his numinibus, potiusque coluntur
    Artificum studio quam deitate sua.
Urbs felix, si vel dominis urbs illa careret,
    Vel dominis esset turpe carere fide!

Such poetic heights were rarely reached in the Middle Ages, when the classical impulse was apt to lose itself in the didacticism and allegory of the longer poems which begin to meet us in the later part of our century. Of such works the most successful was the *Anticlaudianus* of the Universal Doctor, Alain de Lille. Its nine books of metrical hexameters show much classical learning and a poetic imagination which carries the author beyond such ancient models as Claudian and Martianus Capella. Allegory dominates, its keener "subtilty sharpening the finished intellect" beyond the merely material and moral senses, as the labored preface says; and the allegory is intricate, comprising the seven liberal arts and their ancient masters as well as the Virtues who triumph over the Vices in the end. There is much descriptive writing by the way and much classical lore. The poem is philosophical as well as moral: "its subject is man; its philosophic or religious purpose is to expound the functions of

God, of Nature, of Fortune, of Virtue and Vice, in making man and shaping his career." [1]   Still more mediaeval is the *Architrenius*, or *Archweeper*, of John of Hauteville, also in nine books, a long dirge upon the evils of the world through which the author journeys, with much classical allegory, ending finally with the content which comes with moderation. The stream of classical epic runs thin in the *Troy* of Joseph of Exeter and the *Alexandreid* ascribed to Walter of Châtillon, though no thinner than in the interminable *Troie* of their French contemporary Benoît. At the close of the century a canon of Rheims, Peter Riga, also wrote elegies which became confused with those of Hildebert, but his great work was a versified Bible, *Aurora*, and while this was enormously popular and was strongly recommended for its style in Alexander's *Doctrinale*, it takes us definitely out of the classical and into the religious field.

The twelfth century was a great age, probably the culminating age, of religious poetry. Being strikingly active both in religion and in literature, it naturally produced a very large amount of religious literature, but not so much by the creation of new types as by the development of older forms in quite extraordinary number and variety. The material is so vast, and so much of it is characteristic of the Middle Ages as a whole rather than

[1] H. O. Taylor, *The Mediaeval Mind* (1925), ii. 121, where the poem is analyzed at length.

specifically of the twelfth century, that we must pass over it rapidly. Some of this poetry was religious in the wider sense of dealing with religious subjects — biblical stories, lives of saints, virtues of ecclesiastics, sin and repentance, death and judgment, and all that touched the religious life. Much was religious in the more special sense of association with religious worship: the prose sequence, pivoted on the final *a* of the alleluia which is so common a termination in Latin, and now taking on the more usual forms of rhythm; the formal rhythmic poems which had come down from Carolingian times and developed new metrical types under the influence of the sequence; the tropes which produced the liturgical drama; and complete offices of the saints. The greater part of this poetry is anonymous, but much bears definite names such as Abaelard and Adam of St. Victor. Occasionally the anonymous verse can be dated and localized, as in the case of the mortuary rolls carried about from church to church soliciting prayers on behalf of a recently deceased abbot or abbess, for insertion in which each establishment set its best stylist to compose its 'title' of praise in prose or verse, the most successful pieces of verse being often copied by the chroniclers. Thus we still have the curious original of the roll of Vitalis, founder of the order of Savigny, who died in 1122, made up by two hundred and eight monasteries and churches in France and England, a monument of local calligraphy as well as of poetry.

It is often forgotten that Abaelard was a poet, not only

an incomparable dialectician and brilliant teacher but the author of famous love songs which have perished, of a poem of advice to his son Astrolabe, and of a group of beautiful hymns composed for the abbess and nuns of the Paraclete. These show the greatest variety of form, from the more complicated metres to the simplicity of Rachel weeping for her children:

> Est in Rama
> Vox audita
> Rachel flentis,
> Super natos
> Interfectos
> Eiulantis.

The same variety appears in his *planctus*, such as the laments of David for Saul and Jonathan or of the daughters of Israel for the daughter of Jephthah the Gileadite; indeed, Wilhelm Meyer considers Abaelard one of the great creative spirits of that golden age in the creation of new forms of verse, the twelfth and thirteenth centuries.

Adam of St. Victor was likewise a Breton, though he was not a logician but a mystic, like the other Victorines, full of a complicated symbolism which must be studied in detail to be appreciated or even understood. He was also a gifted poet, who developed the older sequence form into golden verse. His simpler style may be illustrated from the opening stanzas of his hymn for St. Stephen's day (26 December), the first of which tells of Christmas just past while the second introduces the first martyr:[1]

---

[1] *The Liturgical Poetry of Adam of St. Victor*, translated by D. S. Wrangham, i. 176 f.

Heri mundus exultavit
Et exultans celebravit
  Christi natalitia;
Heri chorus angelorum
Prosecutus est coelorum
  Regem cum laetitia.

Protomartyr et Levita,
Clarus fide, clarus vita,
  Clarus et miraculis,
Sub hac luce triumphavit,
Et triumphans insultavit
  Stephanus incredulis.

Yesterday the world, elated,
Joyed, and, joying, celebrated
  Christ the Saviour's natal day:
Yesterday, heaven's King surrounding,
Angel-choirs, his welcome sounding,
  Sang to him with joyful lay.

Protomartyr and a deacon,
Faith's clear light and life's bright beacon,
  For his wonder-works well known,
Stephen on this day all-glorious
Won the victory, and, victorious,
  Trod the unbelievers down.

Of the so-called 'seven great hymns' of the mediaeval church, only one belongs with certainty to the twelfth century, and that is no hymn at all, but has been quarried by modern hands out of the vast *De contemptu mundi* of the Cluniac monk, Bernard de Morlas, thus transformed into a series of hymns which have acquired a profound place in the worship of the English-speaking world. The original poem has nearly three thousand hexameter lines, for whose intricate triple rhyme the author believed he had received special divine aid. Diffi-

cult the rhyme certainly is, and the more rapid English
version, good as it is and hallowed by devout association,
lacks the compactness of the original and at times sounds
a bit thin and reedy beside the rolling organ tones of the
Latin:

> Hora novissima, tempora pessima sunt, vigilemus.
> Ecce minaciter imminet arbiter ille supremus.

> > The world is very evil;
> >   The times are waxing late:
> > Be sober and keep vigil;
> >   The Judge is at the gate.

> > .   .   .   .

> Hic breve vivitur, hic breve plangitur, hic breve fletur;
> Non breve vivere, non breve plangere, retribuetur.

> > Brief life is here our portion;
> >   Brief sorrow, short-liv'd care;
> > The life that knows no ending,
> >   The tearless life, is *There*.

> > .   .   .   .

> Urbs Syon aurea, patria lactea, cive decora,
> Omne cor obruis, omnibus obstruis, et cor et ora.
> Nescio, nescio, que iubilatio, lux tibi qualis,
> Quam socialia gaudia, gloria quam specialis.

> > Jerusalem the Golden,
> >   With milk and honey blest,
> > Beneath thy contemplation
> >   Sink heart and voice oppressed:
> > I know not, O I know not,
> >   What social joys are there;
> > What radiancy of glory,
> >   What light beyond compare!

Religious poetry, as we have seen, easily runs into
secular. Not only are religious and secular pieces found
side by side, set to the same music, in the same books,

but they often had the same author who sang the joys of earth and the joys of heaven to the same tune and in almost the same breath. Under these circumstances, the influence of ecclesiastical poetry and music upon secular poetry and music must have been very great, though in the nature of the case it is not easy to trace in specific instances, and much further investigation is required. The Roman liturgy was a fruitful parent and grandparent of new literary forms, for as it gave birth to the sequence and the trope, these in turn created other poetry and drama, religious and, at least ultimately, secular. Of these, the greatest historical interest attaches to the religious drama as the source of the secular drama of the later Middle Ages and of modern times.

In the field of dramatic art the break with classical antiquity was complete, and mediaeval drama was built up anew out of mediaeval and specifically Christian elements. The Roman theatres disappeared with the Roman empire, to the great satisfaction of the leaders of the Christian church, and the plays of the Latin dramatists survived only in books which were little read, even at times of revived interest in the classics. So when Terence was imitated by Hrotswitha and Plautus indirectly by Vitalis, their compositions were not meant to be acted, and the so-called elegiac comedies of the twelfth century, the *Alda* of William of Blois and the anonymous *Pamphilus*, show the influence of Ovid rather than of Terence and have no discoverable relation to contempo-

rary or subsequent drama. The drama of the Middle
Ages grew out of the liturgy of the church and long remained under ecclesiastical tutelage. It was, however,
directly affected by the intellectual and social conditions
of its time; indeed, its three chief types have been brought
into relation with the three principal intellectual revivals
of the Middle Ages: the mystery or liturgical Scripture
plays with the Carolingian renaissance, the miracle play
with the intellectual movement of the eleventh and
twelfth centuries, the morality with "the fourteenth
century renaissance of France and England." [1]

The dramatic possibilities of Christian worship have
often been remarked. The great cathedral or monastery
church, the richly vestured clergy, the awed congregation
of worshippers, furnished the setting; the succession of
ceremonies gave scope for action; the liturgy offered the
dramatic material, in the central sacrifice of the mass, in
the processions of Palm Sunday and various saints' days,
in the rich store of biblical narrative and saintly legend,
and in the culminating observances of those chief seasons
of the ecclesiastical year, Christmas and Easter. Anti-
phonal response was early provided by the two halves of
the choir, it needed only to be developed into imper-
sonation and action. Scholars are agreed in finding the
earliest germ of the religious drama in a trope added in
the ninth century, probably at St. Gall, to the *Introit* of
Easter, a dialogue of four lines based upon the gospel

---

[1] J. M. Manly, in *Modern Philology*, iv. 594.

narrative of the visit of the Maries to the tomb of their risen Lord:

"Whom seek ye in the tomb, O followers of Christ," sing the angels.
"Jesus of Nazareth the crucified, O dwellers in Heaven," answer
    the women.
"He is not here, he is risen as he foretold;
Go, announce that he is risen from the tomb."
"I am risen," begins the *Introit*.

So long as these are chanted responsively by the two halves of the choir we have only dialogue; when the two angels and the three Maries are individualized and impersonated, drama begins.

By the twelfth century these simple beginnings have grown into elaborate liturgical plays for Easter, often localized about a sepulchre within the church, and a rudimentary play of the Passion; while an analogous development for the Christmastide comes to comprise a play of the Shepherds and a play of the Prophets for Christmas day, and for Epiphany a play of the Three Kings and one called *Rachel* concerning the Slaughter of the Innocents. Texts from many parts of Europe bear witness to the wide diffusion of the new art; and the great festivals of the Christian year have become an occasion for drama as well as for popular merrymaking, a drama still within the folds of the church but capable ultimately of standing by itself and taking on a secular character. Indeed, this secularization has already begun in the twelfth century in the use of French and in the change of scene to the more spacious quarters of the churchyard and the market place.

Religious still, but less specifically liturgical, are the miracle plays which arise in our period, dealing with the life and miracles of a saint. They originate somewhere about 1050, and *ca.* 1190 FitzStephen in his description of the city of London contrasts with the spectacles of ancient Rome the sacred plays of his London, "representing the miracles wrought by the holy confessors and the sufferings by which the constancy of the martyrs shone forth." The lives of the saints abound in dramatic matter: romantic, rich in action and color, lived usually in close contact with the people, whom these higher beings continued to help by fresh miracles, they were the religious and popular parallel to the *chansons de gestes* of the feudal world. And if the feudal epics took shape in connection with particular shrines and cults on the pilgrimage roads, the saints had likewise their local attachments to individual churches and monasteries throughout Europe which, though severed often by wide stretches of space, were united in the veneration of the same saintly patron. Just when and how these *gestes* of saints were turned into plays we cannot be quite sure, but it is clear that St. Nicholas and St. Catharine were early examples, for we have two plays of St. Nicholas in a Hildesheim manuscript of the eleventh century, and a play of St. Catharine was performed at Dunstable before 1119. Indeed, as St. Nicholas and St. Catharine early became the patron saints of scholars, these plays have an academic as well as a popular side. Students have a hand in the early plays as regards composition, performance, and diffusion, for this is the age of monastery and cathedral schools and of the wandering scholars who have so large a place in lyric poetry. About 1119 we hear of dramatic exhibitions by the clergy in the refectory of Augsburg cathedral, joyous celebrations of which Gerhoh of Reichersberg repented in his later and more pious years; about 1140 the students of Beauvais have produced the words and music of a play called *Daniel*. Daniel is likewise the theme of their contemporary, the poet Hilary, pupil of Abaelard, who also wrote plays on St. Nicholas and on the resurrection of Lazarus and is the first of these dramatic writers whose name has survived. St. Nicholas, who brought to life his three clerks slain by an innkeeper in a foreign country, was particularly dear to scholars, and his festival, 6 December, just before the Christmas season, became a special time of merriment in the schools, to a degree which scandalized the preachers of Paris. The world of the miracle plays lies close to the world of the Goliardi.

The drama might also thus early approach the world of contemporary politics. Somewhere about 1160, when relations were strained between the Emperor Frederick I and the Pope and also between the Emperor and the king of France, when the Saracens were threatening Jerusalem, and when many of the clergy were bitter against reformers whom they considered hypocrites, a German clerk wrote the play of *Antichrist*, which has reached us in a unique codex of the cloister of Tegernsee in the Bavarian Alps. In the first part of the play the Emperor receives the homage of the kings of Greece, Jerusalem, and, after a military victory, France; he then overcomes the king of Babylon and lays aside his crown in the Temple at Jerusalem. Then comes the turn of Antichrist, who is in more or less friendly relations with the French king, and, by raising a man from the dead, deceives even the Emperor. With the aid of the Hypocrites he is on the point of deceiving the Synagogue as well, and kills the prophets Enoch and Elijah who rise up to warn the Jews. All the kings bow before the enthroned figure of Antichrist till it is destroyed by a clap of thunder, when all return to the faith of the church in the glory of Christ's Advent. This is a spectacle as well as a drama, with something of the majesty of the Signorelli frescoes at Orvieto, requiring a great scene with a temple and seven royal thrones and room for processions and battles and many symbolic figures. The stage directions are minute, as may be seen from the opening of the second part:

Then while the Church and the Gentiles and the Synagogue sing in turn as above, let the Hypocrites come forward silently, bowing in every direction with a show of humility and seeking the favor of the Laity, till at last they assemble before the Church and the throne of the king of Jerusalem, who shall receive them honorably and submit himself wholly to their counsel.

Thereupon Antichrist enters, with a coat of mail under his robes, accompanied by Hypocrisy on his right and Heresy on his left, to whom he sings:

> Mei regni venit hora.
> Per vos ergo sine mora
> Fiat, ut conscendam regni solium,

Me mundus adoret et non alium.
   Vos ad hoc aptas cognovi,
   Vos ad hoc hucusque fovi.

As these lines indicate, this play is also poetry, skilfully written in a great variety of verse but always in strict rhythmical form, and often suggesting the Goliardic rhymes preserved at the neighboring monastery of Benediktbeuern.

The twelfth century, *ca.* 1125–1230, is the great age of Goliardic poetry, as the secular lyric poetry in Latin is generally called. The name has come down to us from the time itself, the authors speaking of themselves as Golias or disciples of Golias, without stopping to explain who he was. Probably he was Goliath the Philistine, who appears in the Fathers and later as a name for the Devil, leader of the evil ones of the earth, whose followers were identified especially with the vagrant and ribald clerks. As early as the tenth century a decree is ascribed to Archbishop Walter of Sens fulminating against the 'family of Golias'; a council of 1227 condemns more specifically the wandering scholars or Goliardi who scandalized the faithful by singing "verses on the *Sanctus* and the *Agnus Dei* in the divine offices," evidently verses of their own which borrowed the music and often parodied the themes of the liturgy. *Vagantes*, loose-living, disreputable clerks, lewd fellows of the baser sort the church authorities evidently considered them, and such many undoubtedly were; but they also comprised older and well established ecclesiastics, authors of some of the best of the Goliardic rhymes. "The jongleurs of the clerical world," they may well have included as varied elements as the vernacular rhymesters. We may not, however, think of them as an organized body or order any more than were the jongleurs; when they speak of the worshipful order of Goliardi, they are merely satirizing the other orders of their time:

> We the laws of charity
>   Found, nor let them crumble;
> For into our order we
>   Take both high and humble;
> Rich and poor men we receive,
>   In our bosom cherish;
> Welcome those the shavelings leave
>   At their doors to perish.
>
> We receive the tonsured monk,
>   Let him take his pittance;
> And the parson with his punk,
>   If he craves admittance;
> Masters with their bands of boys,
>   Priests with high dominion;
> But the scholar who enjoys
>   Just one coat's our minion! [1]

This and other verse seemed so 'unmediaeval,' so contrary to the conventional view of the Middle Ages which long prevailed, that the first impulse was to ascribe such writings to some isolated genius, some sport of nature born out of due time into an age not his own. Indeed, a candidate for the place of Golias long existed in the person of an English clerk of the twelfth century, Walter

---

[1] Translation by J. A. Symonds, *Wine, Women, and Song* (Portland, 1899), p. 49.

Map, whose name was attached to many Goliardic pieces by late copyists and early editors. Now Walter Map is a well known man,[1] student at Paris, chancellor of Lincoln, archdeacon of Oxford, clerk and itinerant justice of Henry II, at whose court he wrote in odd moments a most entertaining set of reminiscences entitled *Courtiers' Trifles*, discursive, scrappy, but full of verve and wit, with something of the daring use of Scripture which we find in the Goliardic poetry, but none of the other characteristics of the 'jovial toper' who wrote the drinking songs once attributed to him. Map may very well have written some of the Goliardic poetry, but there is no contemporary evidence that he wrote any of it, and it is quite impossible that he should have written all. This poetry stretches over a full century of time and a good deal of space, and shows great variety of theme and treatment all the way from poetry of the schools to the popular ballad or folk song — even a syndicate could not have written the whole of it. Its chief centre was Northern France and especially the student class of the cathedral schools and the earliest universities, but it can be traced elsewhere, as in Germany, and in course of time it acquired a European circulation. Golias was a school, if you like, or an epoch, but not an individual.

Nevertheless, modern research has succeeded in recovering certain lost members of this shadowy group, most notably the two who pass by the name of the Pri-

[1] Cf. p. 148.

mate and the Archpoet. The Primate was one of the
most famous of mediaeval poets down to the time of
Boccaccio. In the thirteenth century he joins with Ovid
to guard the rear of Grammar in the mimic battle before
Orleans, and Salimbene calls him "a most amusing rogue
and a great versifier and extemporizer, who, if he had but
turned his heart to the love of God, would have had a
great place in divine letters and have proved most useful
to God's church." He becomes an almost mythical figure,
author of all sorts of clever verse, who sings with his
mouth half open because he has only half a prebend, and
throws off in a competition two intricate lines which sum
up the whole of the Old and the New Testament:

> Quos anguis tristi virus mulcedine pavit,
> Hos sanguis Christi mirus dulcedine lavit.

We now know that his name was Hugh and that he was
canon of Orleans *ca.* 1140, having studied and taught at
Paris and travelled about much of Northern France.
Small and deformed, the loss of wealth and position embittered him while it sharpened his biting wit. A careful
student of the classics, he had a remarkable command of
poetic rhythm and diction, and while much of his work
has perished, enough survives to give him a definite place
among mediaeval poets. "A creature of contrasts:
master of smooth hexameters and flawless rhythms,
author of mordacious and rough verses mixed of French
and Latin; now a conscious poet of elegant diction, now
spewing forth nastiness that would shame a gamin of the

streets — such Wilhelm Meyer shows him to be, with every shading that combined erudition, acumen, and intuition can disclose." [1]

Of the personality of the Archpoet, it was once said by John Addington Symonds "we know as little as we do of that of Homer," but this is no longer true. If his name still escapes us, we at least know that he was a follower of Reinald, archbishop of Cologne and archchancellor of Frederick Barbarossa, and that his poems were written for these patrons in Germany, Provence, and Italy, *ca.* 1161–65. Of knightly origin and classical education, he was dependent upon the archbishop's bounty, which he solicits openly, especially in the autumn when his money is spent and he must have shirt and cloak for the winter. When he is bidden to write in a week an epic on the Emperor's Italian campaigns, he complains that he cannot write on an empty stomach: the quality of his verse varies with the quality of his wine —

> Tales versus facio quale vinum bibo.

He was no mere penny-a-liner, however, but a poet of real merit, greatest perhaps of the Goliardic school and author of its masterpiece, the *Confession of Golias*, also dedicated to the archbishop, which describes the temptations of youth in Pavia and contains the familiar stanzas on the tavern's joys, beginning: [2]

---

[1] P. S. Allen, in *Modern Philology*, vi. 19 (1908).
[2] Text in M. Manitius, *Die Gedichte des Archipoeta* (Munich, 1913), pp. 24–29; translated by Symonds, *loc. cit.*, pp. 61–68.

Meum est propositum in taberna mori,
Ut sint vina proxima morientis ori.
Tunc cantabunt letius angelorum chori:
"Sit Deus propitius huic potatori."

In the public-house to die
Is my resolution;
Let wine to my lips be nigh
At life's dissolution:
That will make the angels cry,
With glad elocution,
"Grant this toper, God on high,
Grace and absolution!"

Wine, women, and song, these are the perennial themes of much of the Goliardic poetry, as they form the title of the best volume of English translations, that of John Addington Symonds. These rhymes glorify the joys of the tavern in rollicking drinking-songs which belong to no epoch in particular, indeed many of them have been reprinted for the use of modern German students: *Carmina clericorum . . . Supplement zu jedem Commersbuch.* "Let us drink deeply, then drink once more," is the favorite refrain. Venus appears even more frequently than Bacchus, a pagan Venus, who does not, and for clerks and monks cannot, crown her love with marriage, but is celebrated in fervid appeals of sensuous passion. There is little of the formal sentiment of the vernacular poems of courtly love, but occasionally the more poignant note of the deserted, as in the Byronic lament which begins:

Humor letalis
Crebro me vulnerat,
Meisque malis
Dolores aggregat.

A mortal anguish
  How often woundeth me;
Grieving I languish,
  Weighed down with misery.

In another song the bald realism of the consequences of betrayal is prefaced by an apostrophe to love and spring:

Tempus instat floridum,
Cantus crescit avium,
Tellus dat solatium.
  Eia, qualia
  Sunt amoris gaudia!

The pleasures of love and youth and spring, the joys of the open road and a wandering, carefree life, an intense delight in mere living — this spirit runs throughout the Goliardic poetry. Its view of life is frankly pagan, full of enjoyment of this world rather than ascetic anticipation of the next; and it is this even more than their borrowed mythology and their abundant citations of Ovid which links the Goliardi with the ancient poets. If their classical robes are often worn thin, their clerical disguise is even thinner, and the natural man shows through. Whether he be a man of the people or a man of the schools, we need not here stop to decide. Non-religious at the least, the Goliardic poetry easily becomes irreligious or sacrilegious.

The Middle Ages were a golden age of parody, and many of the best parodies belong to the twelfth century. Given a common fund of material, the requisite literary skill, and an adequate absence of reverence, and any period can produce good parodies; but these conditions

were combined to an unusual degree in the twelfth century. There was one common medium of communication
in prose and verse, universal familiarity with a limited
body of serious matter available for burlesque — the
Vulgate, the words and music of the liturgy, the canon
law, the textbooks of the liberal arts — and also a degree
of irreverence for which the modern reader is unprepared.
Nowhere is the uncanny cleverness and sheer naughtiness
of the Goliardi more clearly exhibited. One of the stock
accusations against them was their disturbance of church
services by the ribald words they sang at mass. Is not the
Goliardic masterpiece a 'confession,' closing with a play
on the prayer for divine mercy on a sinner? Does not one
of their most fervent songs of earthly love begin with the
Apostle's glorification of heavenly love, Though I speak
with the tongues of men and of angels? One of their
begging songs opens,

> Ecce homo
> Sine domo.

For that matter, the whole conception of the order of
Golias is a burlesque on the regular orders of monks.
Nothing was so sacred as to be exempt — neither the
Gospels nor the canon of the mass nor the most solemn
hymns, not even the creeds or the Lord's Prayer. The
Verbum bonum et suave of the hymn to the Virgin becomes
Vinum bonum et suave. Another bibulous piece was made
by changing the second and following lines of the hymn
of the office of prime, so as to read,

Iam lucis orto sidere
Statim oportet bibere,
Bibamus nunc egregie
Et rebibamus hodie.

There was a Drinkers' Mass with *potatores* substituted
for the *pastores* of the gospel, and a long Office of Gam-
blers. There was an erotic summary of Latin grammar.
We have the versified minutes of a council at Remiremont
ca. 1150 where nuns meet under the presidency of a
'cardinaless' to listen to the gospel according to Ovid.
The same spirit of mockery meets us in the festivals of
students and in the grotesques which adorn church edi-
fices. One of the cleverest of the parodies, whose language is heavy with scriptural reminiscences, is the
Gospel according to Mark-s of Silver, the oldest form of
which belongs to this period:[1]

Here beginneth the Holy Gospel according to Marks of Silver.
At that time the Pope said unto the Romans, "When the Son of
Man shall come to the throne of our Majesty, say unto him first,
'Friend, wherefore art thou come?' But if he shall continue knock-
ing without giving you anything, cast him out into outer darkness." And it came to pass that a certain poor clerk came to the
court of the Lord Pope and cried out, saying, "Have pity upon me,
O doorkeepers of the Pope, for the hand of poverty hath touched
me. I am poor and needy, and therefore I beseech you to succor my
misfortune and my misery." But when they heard him they were
filled with indignation and said, "Friend, thy poverty perish with
thee! Get thee behind me, Satan, because thou savorest not what
the pieces of money savor. Verily, verily, I say unto thee, thou shalt
not enter into the joy of thy Lord till thou hast paid the uttermost
farthing."

So the poor man departed and sold his cloak and his tunic and all
that he had, and gave unto the cardinals and the doorkeepers and

---

[1] P. Lehmann, *Parodistische Texte* (Munich, 1923), no. 1a; cf. E. Emerton,
Mediaeval Europe (Boston, 1894), p. 475.

the chamberlains. But they said, "What is this among so many?"
and they cast him out, and he went out and wept bitterly and would
not be comforted.

Then there came unto the curia a certain rich clerk, who had
waxed fat and grown thick, and had committed murder in the in-
surrection. He gave, first to the doorkeeper, then to the chamberlain, then to the cardinals. But they thought among themselves that
they should have received more. Then the Lord Pope, hearing that
the cardinals and servants had received many gifts from the clergy-
man, fell sick nigh unto death; but the rich man sent him a medicine
of gold and silver, and straightway he was healed. Then the Lord
Pope called unto him the cardinals and the servants and said to
them, "Brethren, see to it that no man deceive you with vain words;
for, lo! I give you an example that even as I receive, so receive ye
also."

Such a piece is quite as much satire as parody, and the
Latin poetry of this epoch is full of satire. Some of this is
directed against those common objects of mediaeval
vituperation, women and villeins, or against particular
orders of monks, but the most virulent attacks are levelled
against the ecclesiastical system, especially the Roman
curia and the higher clergy. Something of this abuse goes
back to the pamphlets of the controversy over investiture, much of it goes on uninterruptedly, though with
varying intensity, to the Protestant revolt. Indeed so
abundant and so violent was such criticism in the Middle
Ages that a Protestant of the sixteenth century, one
Flacius Illyricus, alias Matthias Vlacich, thought to
prove the corruption of the mediaeval clergy out of their
own mouths by publishing the earliest printed collection
of such poems: *Varia doctorum piorumque virorum de
corrupto ecclesiae statu poemata*. The authors were not all
learned and many of them were far from pious, least of

all were they reformers before the Reformation, but they knew whereof they spoke, subject always to the allowances to be made for satire in every age. Most of them are anonymous, spokesmen of the poorer class of clerks, often also the looser and wandering element, who missed the wealth and ease that came with promotion and willingly turned against their ecclesiastical superiors; but now and then an author can perhaps be identified, like Philip de Grève, chancellor of Paris (d. 1236), to whom has been ascribed a poem on the Roman church, *Bulla fulminante*, quite as bitter as the Goliardic

> Propter Sion non tacebo
> Sed ruinam Rome flebo.

So Walter Map, the real Walter this time, makes the following acrostic out of the verse, The love of money is the root of all evil,

> Radix
> Omnium
> Malorum
> Avaricia.

Rome is portrayed as the head and front of offence, *caput quia capit*:

> Roma caput mundi est sed nihil capit mundum.

The word Pope, *papa*, is derived from *pay, pay*. The higher clergy are pictured as proud, hard, and greedy for gain, ready to use their power for their own ends, as in the *Excommunication of Golias*, which thunders sentence of death against him who steals a cap,

> Raptor mei pilei morte moriatur.

Perhaps the most popular and most pungent of these satires is the *Apocalypse of Golias*, or *Revelation of Golias the Bishop*, of which the English version goes back to *ca.* 1600. The four beasts of the vision are the Pope, the bishop, the archdeacon, and the dean:

> The lion is the Pope, that useth to devoure,
>   And laiethe his bookes to pledge, and thirsteth aftir gold,
> And dothe regard the marke, but sainct Marke dishonor,
>   And while he sailes alofte on coyne takes anker holde.
>
> And to the Bisshoppe in the caulfe that we did se,
>   For he dothe runne before in pasture, feild, and fenne,
> And gnawes and chewes on that where he list best to be,
>   And thus he filles himselfe with goodes of other men.
>
> Th' Archedeacon is likewise the egell that dothe flie,
>   A robber rightlie cald, and sees a-farre his praie,
> And aftir it with speed dothe follow by and by,
>   And so by theft and spoile he leades his life awaie.
>
> The Deane is he that hathe the face and shape of man,
>   Withe fraude, deceipt, and guile fraught full as he may be,
> And yet dothe hide and cloke the same as he best can,
>   Undir pretence and shewe of plaine simplicitie.[1]

A more genial note is struck in the *Mirror of Fools*, or *Brunellus*, of the Canterbury monk, Nigel Wireker, where the hero is an ass, Chaucer's 'Daun Burnell,' who visits Salerno to lengthen his tail and Paris to acquire learning, but, as he still keeps his bray after seven years among the English students by the Seine, decides to leave academic life and enter a monastery.

Many of these themes lent themselves to dialogue or debate, a genre inherited from the classical eclogue and reënforced by the disputatious habits of a scholastic age,

---

[1] *Latin Poems commonly Attributed to Walter Mapes*, ed. by Thomas Wright (London, 1841), pp. 273–274.

and also having its counterpart in the vernacular. Besides well known examples such as the debates between Soul and Body, Sheep and Wool, Rose and Violet, Ganymede and Helen, the Goliardic milieu appears more clearly in the contentions between Wine and Water, the poor clerk and the rich, the well fed priest and the begging barefoot student of logic, whose *ergo's* gain him no prebend. To the chancellor Philip de Grève is attributed the excellent *Debate between the Heart and the Eye*, later set to music by Henry of Pisa and sung by Friar Salimbene. One of the most popular themes was the relative merits of knights and clerks as lovers, subject of a contest between Phyllis and Flora and of the famous nuns' council at Remiremont, and passing before the end of the century into the vernacular poems of courtly love in *Le jugement d'Amour* and its many successors.

Here we reach a point from which we cannot advance on the Latin side alone without creating an indefensible salient, a point where Latin poetry merges in the broader poetical current of the time irrespective of the language in which it may find expression. Sooner or later, the student of the Latin poetry of the twelfth century must face the problem of its relations to the new poetry in French and Provençal, in German and Italian. For some generations all these run parallel, with much mutual influence. For a time French and, to a less degree, Provençal enjoy something of the international vogue of Latin, in language and, still more widely, in subject matter, until the final triumph of the national tongues in the later Middle Ages. All these national literatures have their roots in the Latin literature of the earlier period, all are dependent upon the Latin for many centuries in ways which for the most part still remain to be traced or more clearly defined. The twelfth century is the great period of divergence between Latin and vernacular, the culmination of the international poetry of the Middle Ages with its burst of activity in all fields of expression, its new forms of versification which make their fortune later in the vernacular. If we keep our eyes too close to the Latin and especially to the more classical types of Latin, we are in danger of viewing the age as one of a mere revival of learning and not a renaissance. A revival of learning it most certainly was, of the Latin classics, of the Roman law, of the science and philosophy of the Greeks and Arabs; but it was also an age of new creation in literature and art beyond the mere imitation of ancient models. The necessary limitation of this volume to the Latin phase of the movement must not prevent our recognizing that this was only a part of something much larger. The analogy of the Italian Renaissance is again suggestive, a revival of ancient learning and also of ancient art, but still more an age of new life and new knowledge which carry us well beyond the ancients. Not Constantinople but the West produced the Quattrocento. In the twelfth century as in the fifteenth the student of poetry must go far beyond the ancient texts.

BIBLIOGRAPHICAL NOTE

There is no *corpus* of the Latin poetry of the twelfth century. Much will be found in Migne, *Patrologia* (poorly edited), and in the general collections of Flacius Illyricus, *Varia . . poemata* (Basel, 1556), and P. Leyser, *Historia poetarum et poematum medii aevi* (Halle, 1721). Pending the publication of the third volume of Manitius, one may use the outline in Gröber, *Grundriss*, ii, 1, pp. 323–432. For a brief survey, see Taylor, *Mediaeval Mind*, ch. 33.

For rhythmics, see especially W. Meyer, *Gesammelte Abhandlungen zur mittellateinischen Rythmik* (Berlin, 1905). Good monographs on individual poets are B. Hauréau, *Les mélanges poétiques d'Hildebert de Lavardin* (Paris, 1882); cf. C. Pascal, *Poesia latina medievale* (Catania, 1907), pp. 1–68; Hauréau, *Des poèmes latins attribués à Saint Bernard* (Paris, 1890); W. Meyer, "Die Oxforder Gedichte des Primas," in Göttingen *Nachrichten*, 1907, pp. 75 ff. *The Complaint of Nature* of Alain de Lille is translated by D. M. Moffat (New York, 1908). The Medici Antiphonary is analyzed by Delisle, in *Annuaire-Bulletin de la Société de l'Histoire de France*, 1885, pp. 100–139; and by Dreves, *Analecta hymnica*, xx, xxi, where many of the pieces are printed. The poems of Baudri de Bourgueil have now been edited by Phyllis Abrahams (Paris, 1926).

The principal collection of mediaeval hymns is *Analecta hymnica medii aevi*, edited by G. M. Dreves and Clemens Blume, of which fifty-five volumes have appeared (Leipzig, 1886–). From this collection Dreves has made a selection in his *Ein Jahrtausend lateinischer Hymnendichtung* (Leipzig, 1909). The bibliographical guides are U. Chevalier, *Repertorium hymnologicum* (Louvain, 1897–1920); and C. Blume, *Repertorium Repertorii* (Leipzig, 1901). See also J. Julian, *Dictionary of Hymnology* (revised edition, London, 1915). Brief selections have been published by R. C. Trench (1849), F. A. March (1874), and W. A. Merrill (1904). Abaelard's hymns and *planctus* will be found in *Analecta hymnica*, xlviii. 141–232. Adam of St. Victor is edited and translated in three volumes by D. S. Wrangham (London, 1881); certain of the hymns ascribed to him are included among the many metrical translations of J. M. Neale.

On the drama, see E. K. Chambers, *The Mediaeval Stage* (Oxford, 1903), ii; W. Creizenach, *Geschichte des neueren Dramas*, i (second edition, Halle, 1911); and the many special studies of Karl Young (with full bibliographies), who has in preparation a comprehensive study of the liturgical drama. On the early miracle play, see G. R.

Coffman, *A New Theory concerning the Origin of the Miracle Play* (Menasha, 1914), with Young's correction in the *Manly Anniversary Studies* (Chicago, 1923), pp. 254–268; and Coffman's "A New Approach to Medieval Latin Drama," in *Modern Philology*, xxii. 239–271 (1925). The *Ludus de Antichristo*, most fully studied in W. Meyer's *Gesammelte Abhandlungen*, i. 136–339, is conveniently edited in *Münchener Texte*, i (1912); and translated by W. H. Hulme, in *Western Reserve University Bulletin*, xxviii, no. 8 (August, 1925).

The best single volume of Goliardic verse is J. A. Schmeller, *Carmina Burana* (third edition, Breslau, 1894). There is much in the early publications of Du Méril and Thomas Wright. A guide to the rhymes published to 1872 is given by W. Wattenbach in *Zeitschrift für deutsches Alterthum*, iii. 469–506. Much has since been published, important examples being K. Breul, *The Cambridge Songs* (Cambridge, 1915); J. Werner, *Beiträge zur Kunde der lateinischen Literatur des Mittelalters* (Aarau, 1905); M. Manitius, *Die Gedichte des Archipoeta* (Munich, 1913). The best translations are those of J. A. Symonds, *Wine, Women, and Song* (various editions). Out of the enormous number of modern essays, particular mention may be made of Ch. V. Langlois, "La littérature goliardique," in *Revue bleue*, l. 807–813, li. 174–180 (1892–93); H. Süssmilch, *Die lateinische Vagantenpoesie* (Leipzig, 1917); J. H. Hanford, "The Progenitors of Golias," in *Speculum*, i. 38–58 (1926); P. S. Allen, "Mediaeval Latin Lyrics," in *Modern Philology*, v, vi (1908–09), forerunner of a volume with the same title now in press.

On mediaeval parody, see F. Novati, *Studi critici e letterari* (Turin, 1889), pp. 175–310; P. Lehmann, *Die Parodie im Mittelalter* (Munich, 1922); and his *Parodistische Texte* (Munich, 1923). The dialogue is treated by H. Walther, *Das Streitgedicht in der lateinischen Litteratur des Mittelalters* (Munich, 1920); see also various studies of J. H. Hanford, particularly "The Mediaeval Debate between Wine and Water," in *Publications of the Modern Language Association of America*, xxviii. 315–367 (1913).

The vast field of the relations between Latin and vernacular literature has been very inadequately explored. Good examples of significant studies are J. Bédier, *Les légendes épiques* (second edition, Paris, 1914–21); E. Faral, *Recherches sur les sources latines des contes et romans courtois du moyen âge* (Paris, 1913), and "Le fabliau latin au moyen âge," in *Romania*, l. 321–385 (1924); J. R. Reinhard, "The Literary Background of the *Chantefable*," in *Speculum*, i. 157–169 (1926).

CHAPTER VII

THE REVIVAL OF JURISPRUDENCE

THE influence of Rome upon the mind of the twelfth century was not confined to the fields of language and literature. The Romans were a nation of rulers and lawyers more than a nation of philosophers and men of letters, as Virgil said in his eloquent lines on Rome's imperial mission:

Others shall beat out the breathing bronze to softer lines, I believe it well; shall draw living lineaments from the marble; the cause shall be more eloquent on their lips; their pencil shall portray the pathways of heaven, and tell the stars in their arising: be thy charge, O Roman, to rule the nations in thine empire; this shall be thine art, to lay down the law of peace, to be merciful to the conquered and beat the haughty down.[1]

Thrice, says Ihering, did Rome conquer the world: by her arms, by her church, and by her law; and, we may add, the ultimate conquest of her law was a spiritual conquest, after her empire was dead and her armies turned to dust. Nothing was more characteristic of the genius of the Romans than their law, and nothing has been more persistent and pervasive. The revival of Roman law was an essential part of any Roman renaissance. Such a revival belongs to intellectual quite as much as to institutional history, indeed at this point the two are indistinguishable. Roman law not only survived among the

---

[1] *Aeneid*, vi. 847–853 (Mackail's translation).

Roman population, it was revived and extended to peoples of Northern Europe, and it was then spread by modern colonization to lands beyond the seas of which the Romans had never even dreamed, to Quebec and Louisiana, to Spanish America and the Cape of Good Hope. Not so many years ago an appeal from South Africa to the British Privy Council turned upon the interpretation of a passage in the *Digest* of Justinian. In this long historical perspective the twelfth century occupies a central and a decisive position. Of all centuries the most legal, says Maitland, "in no other age, since the classical days of Roman law, has so large a part of the sum total of intellectual endeavour been devoted to jurisprudence." [1]

The revival of the Roman law was not merely a bringing out of neglected texts but a revival of jurisprudence as well. The early centuries of the Middle Ages in the West had plenty of law, but it was customary law, written down in part in the barbarian codes, supplemented at important points by the Frankish legislation, but ultimately broken up into the local custom of each particular district. Law in the Germanic and feudal periods rested not upon legislative enactment but upon the immemorial custom of the tribe or the fief. Even when some of these customs were put into written form, the change was merely one of convenience, not of the basis of authority; the old men knew the law as it had been in their fathers'

[1] Pollock and Maitland, *History of English Law*, i. 111.

time, and for them it did not change. Tradition, not reflection, determined everything. Scientific jurisprudence disappeared with the Roman empire, and while there are some traces of its reappearance among the Lombards of Northern Italy in the eleventh century, for most purposes it is true to say that it reëmerges only in conjunction with the full recovery of the *corpus* of Roman law in the late eleventh and twelfth centuries. Only in the Roman texts, and particularly in the *Digest*, could models of juristic method be found. Still, when once this method had been recovered, it could be applied to other bodies of law as well, in the first instance to the law of the church by Gratian and his successors, then, much more slowly, to the feudal customs and to the new law of the English royal court. Even in the twelfth century the new movement is something more than a revival of Roman rules of law, it is also a revival and extension of Roman system and Roman methods of thought.

In the early Middle Ages the Roman law had survived in two forms, as the customary law of the Roman population, and in the *Corpus Juris Civilis* as codified in the sixth century by Justinian. In the first form it rested chiefly on the Theodosian Code of 438, particularly as excerpted in the Germanic kingdoms of the West and gathered into such compilations as the *Lex Romana Visigothorum* or *Breviary of Alaric*, the *Ostrogothic Edict*, the *Lex Romana Burgundionum*, and the *Lex Romana Curiensis* of the Eastern Alps. The principle of the personality of law permitted individual Romans and the Roman church to retain their own law in most of the Germanic kingdoms, and where the Roman element was dense, as in parts of Italy and in Southern France, Roman law was thus practically the law of the region. While occasionally men of learning might there turn to these written law books, for most people the Roman law came to rest upon local custom, a popularized and in some respects degenerate form of law, which bore somewhat the same relation to the classical jurisprudence as the Vulgar Latin of these provinces bore to the classical speech. Such a law could and did keep alive the Roman tradition, but it could not produce a jurisprudence.

For this the ancient materials were preserved in the *Corpus Juris Civilis*, consisting of the *Code*, or codification of imperial legislation; the *Digest*, or summary of the writings of the Roman jurists; the *Institutes*, a textbook for the use of schools of law; and the *Novels*, or later legislation of Justinian. Of these the greatest permanent importance attached to the *Digest*, for the imperial legislation had departed in style and even in content from the simplicity and clarity of the best period of Roman jurisprudence, whereas the *Digest* preserved in the form of extracts the words and methods of the great jurisconsults Paul, Ulpian, and the others, at whose hands Roman law had become 'written reason,' an unsurpassed model of juristic analysis and technique. The maintenance of legal science in Western Europe depended upon access to the *Digest*, and the *Digest*, in Maitland's phrase, barely escaped with its life in the Dark Ages. In the West, indeed, the whole of Justinian's *Corpus* suffered from the fact that it had been drawn up and issued at Constantinople after several of the Western provinces had fallen away permanently from Rome; it had no validity in Gaul and Spain, and its influence in Italy was seriously affected by the Lombard conquest shortly after its promulgation there in 554. The *Corpus Juris Civilis* also suffered from its bulk, for while, as compared with the immense mass of legal literature which preceded, it might appear brief and succinct, well suited to transmission through a troublous time, yet to the Dark Ages it was a big book, filling several volumes at a time when parchment was scarce and when only the simplest compends remained in circulation in any field of knowledge.

Of course the Roman law did not disappear from the West, nor did it lie asleep, to use Schupfer's figure, like the enchanted princess, until the coming of the fairy prince in the twelfth century. Historians no longer accept the ancient legend which represents its revival as due to the discovery of a copy of the *Digest* at Amalfi in 1135, whence the Pisans carried it off and kept it until 1406, when it was taken to its permanent home in Florence. This story quite misrepresents the facts in its assumption of a hibernation of Roman law throughout the long preceding centuries, but it points to the truth in one respect, in its emphasis upon the *Digest* as the nucleus of the new development. Roman law was kept alive as custom and in the practice of notaries, and some instruction was given in the drafting of legal instruments, while modern research has unearthed certain collections of summaries, excerpts, and glosses, designed for the student and the practitioner; but in none of these can we properly speak of legal science. The *Digest* drops out of sight between 603 and 1076, when it is cited in a court in Tuscany, and from the whole intervening period only two manuscripts are known. Its life hung by a slender thread, and until it came forth into the light once more there could be no rebirth of jurisprudence. In these days of compends and extracts law had lost its independent status and had become subordinate to the liberal arts and chiefly to rhetoric, and men who had occasion to cite or discuss legal terms were satisfied with the brief extracts in that universal cyclopaedia, the *Etymologies* of Isidore.

By general agreement the renaissance of Roman law at the beginning of the twelfth century is connected with Bologna and the jurist Irnerius, to whom later writers went so far as to ascribe the foundation of Bologna's law school and the renewal of legal science. He was, says Odofredus in the next century, "a man of the greatest renown," "the lamp of the law and the first to throw light on our science." When, however, we seek to put concrete meaning into such phrases, we meet with difficulty. There were other centres of legal study before Bologna, such as Rome, Pavia, and Ravenna; and there were Bolognese jurists before Irnerius, notably Pepo, "bright and shining light of Bologna," who is found perhaps in 1065 and certainly in 1076 in the decision of the very case where the *Digest* first reappears. The real Irnerius must be sought in contemporary documents and in such of his writings as can now be recovered. Born not far from 1060, he comes into view toward the turn of the century, and can be traced until 1125 and perhaps some years later. He is no closet lawyer, for he belongs first to the party of the Great Countess, Matilda of Tuscany, and after her death in 1115 passes to the service of the Emperor Henry V, in whose train he often acts as judge and in 1118 as one of the jurisconsults who support the election of the anti-pope. Bologna, however, was the chief seat of his activity as teacher and writer. His writings, some of which are lost and some of which still await publication, consist of a great body of glosses on the text of the *Corpus Juris*, especially the *Digest*, and probably of a series of *Questions on the Subtleties of the Law*, with perhaps some minor fragments. As a teacher Irnerius drew large bodies of students by his remarkable skill in the classroom. He separated law finally from rhetoric and gave it full status as an independent subject of study, based no longer upon extracts and outlines but upon the text of the *Corpus Juris*, the whole of which could now be used to explain every part. His methods of instruction are doubtless reflected in his *Glosses*, where he sets himself to explain each difficult passage clearly and concisely, examining the verbal sense but also analyzing its meaning in the light of the relevant portions of the *Corpus*. At the same time, if we may judge from the *Questions*, he encouraged question and discussion and sought to solve apparent contradictions in the authorities. "A most subtle doctor," he remained clear and practical throughout. He appears at his best in his glosses on the *Digest*, which he rightly made the centre of his exposition. Though he was not the first of the glossators, he did more than any one else to fix their method and determine its course for generations to come. Thus much is clear, though we cannot often test his originality, and though much of his specific work disappeared, absorbed into the general body of professional doctrine.

The successors of Irnerius for something more than a hundred years are known collectively as the Glossators; indeed, his own glosses have to be picked out laboriously from the early manuscripts of the *Corpus Juris*, where they are usually to be identified by the initial I or Y with which he holds his own among many successors. He was not the only teacher of law in his own day, and by the middle of the century there were at least four of eminence, the so-called Four Doctors whom tradition makes his pupils. The story runs that his students came to Irnerius on his deathbed asking him to designate a successor, and that he replied, "Bulgarus has the golden tongue, Martinus fulness of legal knowledge, Hugo understanding of the law, Jacobus is myself":

Bulgarus os aureum, Martinus copia legum,
Mens legum est Ugo, Jacobus id quod ego.

So Jacobus succeeded his master, and each of the other
three had his characterization for posterity. All four
meet us in the legal literature as well as in the documents
of the age and were famous as counsellors of Emperor
Frederick Barbarossa. Martinus and Bulgarus represented divergent tendencies of thought, if hardly distinct
schools; while Martinus generally leaned toward equity,
it was also said that at times he "stuck to the letter like
a Jew." Already we see the beginning of those *Dissen-
siones Dominorum* which were to fill a volume with their
dissenting *dicta*. In the next generation, when Placentinus writes his *Summa* on the *Code* in order to drive the
work of Rogerius into desuetude, he takes pains to assure
the reader that the work is all his own, and we later hear
of the pilfering of others' glosses, in which process men
laid under contribution the great names of the later
twelfth century: Johannes Bassianus, Pilleus, Otto,
Hugolinus, and the others.

Whatever their other literary undertakings, the glossators always produced glosses. Originally these were
largely verbal, corresponding to the current interlinear
gloss on the Bible, but, as the explanations and parallel
citations grew in length, they ran over into the margins,
until many a codex would show more notes than text.
When the comment became too extended for the space
thus available, it took the form of an independent work,

long or short. Our period already shows a considerable variety of such treatises: the *summa*, or general analysis of a book, title by title; the discussion of cases relevant to each passage; the *brocarda*, or general maxims deduced from the text; and treatises concerned with particular topics, notably procedure. Nevertheless, the heart of the school lay in the systematic running commentary of the gloss, which was codified, *ca.* 1250, in the *Glossa ordinaria* of Accursius. By this time men had begun to compare the multitude of glosses to a plague of locusts which covered up the text, and when jurists began to gloss the gloss the method had outlived its usefulness. The text was now regularly accompanied by the gloss, indeed the maxim came to run that only the glossed portions would be recognized in court (*quidquid non agnoscit glossa non agnoscit curia*).

The glossators of Bologna were regularly teachers, and their books must be studied with this fact in mind. For one thing, while the course of study was based upon the whole *Corpus Juris*, the order and division were quite different from those of ancient or of modern times. Instead of starting with the elementary textbook of the *Institutes*, the Middle Ages began with the *Digest*, which, probably because of its piecemeal reception in the earlier period, was divided into three volumes: the *Old Digest* (books i–xxiv, 2), the *Digestum Infortiatum* (xxiv, 3–xxxviii), and the *New Digest* (xxxix–l). The first nine books of the *Code* formed a fourth volume, while the remaining three books, dealing with the public law of the later Empire and thus less important, were grouped with the *Novels* and *Institutes* in a fifth volume called the *Volumen parvum*. Exposition followed this order, the *Old Digest* and *Code* being reserved for the 'ordinary' or morning lectures, while the remaining portions were taken up in the 'extraordinary' lectures of the afternoon. We have no specific description of Bolognese lectures before that of Hugolinus at the beginning of the thirteenth century, but the method was traditional, though accompanied with question and discussion and some good humor, and we can safely trust as typical the somewhat fuller account of Odofredus, *ca.* 1250:

Concerning the method of teaching the following order was kept by ancient and modern doctors and especially by my own master, which method I shall observe: First, I shall give you summaries of each title before I proceed to the text; second, I shall give you as clear and explicit a statement as I can of the purport of each law [included in the title]; third, I shall read the text with a view to correcting it; fourth, I shall briefly repeat the contents of the law; fifth, I shall solve apparent contradictions, adding any general principles of law [to be extracted from the passage], commonly called 'Brocardica,' and any distinctions or subtle and useful problems (*quaestiones*) arising out of the law with their solutions, as far as the Divine Providence shall enable me. And if any law shall seem deserving, by reason of its celebrity or difficulty, of a repetition, I shall reserve it for an evening repetition, for I shall dispute at least twice a year, once before Christmas and once before Easter, if you like.

I shall always begin the *Old Digest* on or about the octave of Michaelmas [6 October] and finish it entirely, by God's help, with everything ordinary and extraordinary, about the middle of August. The *Code* I shall always begin about a fortnight after Michaelmas and by God's help complete it, with everything ordinary and extraordinary, about the first of August. Formerly the doctors did not lecture on the extraordinary portions; but with me all students can have profit, even the ignorant and the newcomers, for they will hear the whole book, nor will anything be omitted as was once the common practice here. For the ignorant can profit by the statement of the case and the exposition of the text, the more advanced can become more adept in the subtleties of questions and opposing opinions. And I shall read all the glosses, which was not the practice before my time.

Then comes certain general advice as to the choice of teachers and the methods of study, followed by some general account of the *Digest*. This course closed as follows:

Now, gentlemen, we have begun and finished and gone through this book, as you know who have been in the class, for which we thank God and His Virgin Mother and all His Saints. It is an ancient custom in this city that when a book is finished mass should be sung to the Holy Ghost, and it is a good custom and hence should be observed. But since it is the practice that doctors on finishing a book should say something of their plans, I will tell you something, but not much. Next year I expect to give ordinary lectures well and lawfully as I always have, but no extraordinary lectures, for students are not good payers, wishing to learn but not to pay, as the saying is: All desire to know but none to pay the price. I have nothing more to say to you, beyond dismissing you with God's blessing and begging you to attend the mass.[1]

The work of the Bolognese glossators constitutes a large and highly important part of the mental activity of the twelfth century, and at the same time has its place in the general history of the European intellect. It not only cleared the ground for future generations by purifying the text and establishing its literal meaning in the light of a mastery of the whole *Corpus*, but it performed a pioneer

[1] Paris, Bibliothèque Nationale, MS. Lat. 4489, f. 102; Savigny, *Geschichte des römischen Rechts im Mittelalter*, iii. 264, 541, 553; cf. Rashdall, *Universities*, i. 219.

task of dialectical analysis peculiarly suited to a logical age working on a rigidly limited body of material. If the glossators lacked the historical and philological equipment of the modern scholar, this was not their fault. What could be done in their time they did; and as there is always in law a large element of scholasticism, there was plenty of work for a scholastic age which could be handed on for the use of others. Even at its worst their method resulted in exegesis, not in allegory. The danger of such a method is over-refinement and tenuity, those cobwebs of learning which Lord Bacon described as "admirable for the fineness of thread and work, but of no substance or profit." This danger is less in a concrete subject like law than it is in metaphysics, and less in the earlier than in the later periods of any discipline, and there was less of it in the twelfth century than in the days of the Postglossators. If, on the other hand, there was then also less of the later adjustment and adaptation of Roman law to contemporary conditions, practical tact and understanding were not absent, even as early as Irnerius, for Roman law was a matter of life as well as of logic. Still it is the legal technique and sheer skill of mind of the glossators which have been most admired by modern jurists. Rashdall has summed up the matter as follows: [1]

In many respects the work of the School of Bologna represents the most brilliant achievement of the intellect of medieval Europe.

[1] *The Universities of Europe in the Middle Ages*, i. 254–255.

The medieval mind had, indeed, a certain natural affinity for the study and development of an already existing body of Law. The limitations of its knowledge of the past and of the material Universe, were not, to any appreciable extent, a bar to the mastery of a Science which concerns itself simply with the business and the relations of every-day life. The Jurist received his Justinian on authority as the Theologian received the Canonical and Patristic writings, or the Philosopher his Aristotle, while he had the advantage of receiving it in the original language. It had only to be understood, to be interpreted, developed, and applied. The very tendencies which led men of immense natural powers so far astray in the spheres of Theology, of Philosophy, and still more of Natural Science, gave a right direction to the interpretation of authoritatively prescribed codes of law. An almost superstitious reverence for the *littera scripta*; a disposition to push a principle to its extreme logical consequences, and an equally strong disposition to harmonize it at all costs with a seemingly contradictory principle; a passion for classification, for definition and minute distinction, a genius for subtlety — these, when associated with good sense and ordinary knowledge of affairs, are at least some of the characteristics of a great legal intellect. Moreover, the exercises which were of such doubtful utility in other branches of knowledge formed an excellent course of legal education. The practice of incessant disputation produced a dexterity in devising or meeting arguments and a readiness in applying acquired knowledge, of comparatively little value to the student of History or Physical Science, but indispensable to the Advocate and even to the Judge. While it fostered an indifference to the truth of things fatal to progress in Theology or Philosophy, it gave the pleader the indispensable faculty of supporting a bad case with good, and a good case with the best possible, arguments.

In estimating the place of the Civil Law in the history of medieval culture, we must carefully distinguish between its cultivation as a science and its pursuit as a profession. During the most brilliant period of its cultivation as a science its Professors were almost all congregated in Bologna itself. That period embraces the century and a half after its revival by Irnerius. It was in the hands of the 'Glossators' — of Irnerius, of the famous 'Four Doctors' . . . , of Rogerius, Placentinus, Azo, and Hugolinus — that the most real progress was made. The works of these men are, perhaps, the only productions of medieval learning to which the modern Professor of any science whatever may turn, not merely for the sake of their historical interest, not merely in the hope of finding ideas of a suggestive value, but with some possibility of finding a solution of the doubts, difficulties, and problems which still beset the modern student.

It is well to remember that this revival of Roman law did not take place in a vacuum, but was closely related to the larger currents of the age. It was a time of economic awakening in the Mediterranean and especially in Northern Italy, and the new trade and commerce demanded a law more flexible and more urban than the archaic and essentially rural custom of the Lombards. The towns came to prefer Roman law. It was an age of political consolidation, creating a demand for some 'common law' wider in its application than mere local custom and based on principles of more general validity. It was also an age of political movement and discussion, and all parties hastened to seek support in the new jurisprudence. Then, too, something may perhaps be set down to the general strengthening of the Roman tradition and the Roman appeal in literature and in thought. Thus Frederick Barbarossa, that 'imperial Hildebrand,' was quick to use the arguments of 'our Roman laws,' speaking of his imperial predecessors, Constantine, Valentinian, and Justinian, summoning (it is said) Saladin to give up the lands conquered by Crassus and Antony, securing in 1158, according to tradition, the support of the Four Doctors for his assertion of regalian rights over the Lombard towns, and ordering the insertion of his Roncaglian decrees in the *Corpus Juris* by virtue of his imperial position. Roman law was to prove a strong bulwark of absolutism, and we are not surprised to find the glossators mostly on the Emperor's side, although there is a tradition that Bulgarus had the courage to oppose Martinus on the limits of imperial authority in the very presence of Barbarossa, and we know that one of the glosses of Irnerius supports the same view of the limitations of imperial rights over the property of subjects. On the other hand the Roman senate, under the leadership of Arnold of Brescia, declared that Constantine and Justinian had ruled by authority of the Roman people. Their emissaries, if we may trust Otto of Freising, who was present, called on the Emperor to give security for the observance of the "good customs and ancient laws" which had been duly assured to Rome in the instruments of his imperial predecessors; whereas Frederick's answer emphasizes the fact that he is in lawful possession (*legitimus possessor*).[1] More than one could play at the game of Roman law, now as well as later.

This game could also be played at many places besides Bologna. If Bologna remained the home of the glossatorial school, the universities which arose in the following period were in large measure schools of law, and, as the university-trained jurists attained position and authority, they used their influence to depreciate local custom and statute in favor of the universal and underlying law of Rome. Then Italy, from the twelfth century to the six-

[1] Cf. *ante*, p. 119.

teenth century, became a centre for the diffusion of
Roman law throughout Europe. If its formal reception
in Germany and Scotland waited till the sixteenth century, there were other lands like France and Spain where
it spread much earlier. Everywhere this result came
about mainly through the study of law in universities,
at first by Transmontane students in Italy and then in the
newer institutions beyond the Alps, and through the influence of lawyers and judges thus trained. It was from
the universities that the Roman law passed into practice
and the civilian habit of mind permeated the European
intellect.

From one university to another Roman law was ordinarily carried by some travelling professor who lit the
torch of learning in a new place. In the South of France,
for example, Roman law had survived from early days
among the predominant Roman element in the population and was reënforced by the *Breviary* of Alaric, pro-
mulgated in Gascony in 506: while in our period the
South claims the *Exceptiones Petri*, a manual based on
excerpts from the *Corpus Juris*, dedicated apparently in
the later eleventh century to a judge Odilo of Valence on
the Rhone; perhaps the similar and somewhat later
Brachylogus; and certainly a Provençal summary of
Justinian's *Code* entitled *Lo Codi*, which was drawn up
for judges in the neighborhood of Arles in 1149 or there-
abouts. Yet the first school of law in the Midi, that of
Montpellier, traces its origin to a Bolognese glossator

named Placentinus who arrived some time after 1160. A native of Piacenza, as his name indicates, Placentinus taught there and at Mantua as well as at Bologna; after his first sojourn at Montpellier he spent two years again at Bologna, "provoking the other masters to envy by emptying their classrooms, and opening up the hidden secrets of the law," if we may believe his own statement, but dying at Montpellier in 1192. In spite of his wanderings he was everywhere a fruitful author, leaving *Summae* on the *Code* and *Institutes* as well as lesser *Summulae* and glosses and other works of the usual type. Not only was Roman law firmly anchored in the South, or *pays de droit écrit*, but by the thirteenth century it began to make headway in the North, or *pays de droit coutumier*, where local custom prevailed. The channels by which it flowed northward were partly the new university of Orleans, the chief northern university of law, and partly the royal court, where as early as *ca.* 1202 we find jurists, or legists as they are more commonly called, giving a decision respecting regalian rights which specifically invokes the *ius scriptum*. In France, too, the legists are found on the side of the king.

In England, on the other hand, the king had pronounced against the Roman law and had forbidden its teaching a full half-century before. To the modern reader the surprising thing is that here Roman law should have been considered important enough to forbid, for English law was local and Germanic, even to the Germanic speech which appears in no other of the barbarian laws, and there was no Roman inheritance to fall back upon. Nevertheless, at least on the literary side, England was affected by the Roman revival of the twelfth century. Many English ecclesiastics studied law at Bologna, and if this law was mainly canon law, they were quick enough to cite Roman authorities in their arguments, indeed the two systems "entered England hand in hand." John of Salisbury knew a good deal of Roman law with the rest of his classical learning; the abbot of Peterborough possessed the whole of the *Corpus Juris Civilis*, besides various parts of it and the *Summa* of Placentinus. England even had its Bolognese glossator, in the person of the Lombard Master Vacarius, who taught law in the household of Archbishop Theobald of Canterbury, and perhaps elsewhere, before 1154, and can be traced in England for nearly half a century thereafter. Though he also wrote on Lombard and canon law, his chief book was entitled *Liber Pauperum*, "The Poor Man's Book," "a compilation of the Codex and of the Digest arranged for students who had not the means to acquire costly books, nor the time to make a prolonged study of Roman sources." [1] In his gloss he takes the position that "the emperor is the sole author and interpreter of law," a doctrine whose application to England it would be interesting to see followed out. It was apparently from this book that the

---

[1] P. Vinogradoff, *Roman Law in Mediaeval Europe*, p. 53, where some illustrations are given from the Worcester MS. of the *Liber*.

name of *pauperistae* was applied to the students of law at
Oxford, where the academic study of Roman law persists
throughout the Middle Ages. Roman law, however, was
never 'received' by the king's judges, so that its study
led to no career. "The civilian, if he was not a canonist,
had no wide field open to him." Except as a diplomatist,
a chancery clerk, or a teacher, he "would find little to do
in England." [1] Roman law in England had no independent existence apart from the canon law, indeed their
close association seems to have been the cause of its
original disfavor with the English king.

Throughout Europe the canon law was in conflict,
actual or potential, with the secular state, as the struggle
of Henry II and Becket indicates. For the canon law was
the law of the universal church, which claimed authority
everywhere, not only in religious matters but in many
spheres now reserved to civil authority alone. The
church indeed was itself a state, an international state
reaching across national boundaries into the life of every
local community. Says Maitland: [2]

> The medieval church was a state. Convenience may forbid us to
> call it a state very often, but we ought to do so from time to time,
> for we could frame no acceptable definition of a state which would
> not comprehend the church. What has it not that a state should
> have? It has laws, lawgivers, law courts, lawyers. It uses physical
> force to compel men to obey its laws. It keeps prisons. In the thir-
> teenth century, though with squeamish phrases, it pronounces sen-

---

[1] Pollock and Maitland, *History of English Law*, i. 123-124.
[2] F. W. Maitland, *Roman Canon Law in the Church of England*, p. 100.

tence of death. It is no voluntary society. If people are not born into it, they are baptized into it when they cannot help themselves. If they attempt to leave it, they are guilty of the *crimen laesae maiestatis*, and are likely to be burnt. It is supported by involuntary contributions, by tithe and tax.

We must divest ourselves of modern prepossessions which lead us to think of the canon law as occupied merely with the clergy and ecclesiastical discipline — it is so easy to imagine a church composed only of priests! The mediaeval church, it is true, claimed jurisdiction over the clergy, but this meant all cases in which a tonsured clerk was concerned, whether as plaintiff or defendant, whether the issue was civil or criminal; and clerk was an inclusive term, as those found who ran afoul of the benefit of clergy. So much *ratione personae*, by virtue of the person involved. *Ratione materiae*, by virtue of the subject matter, it claimed jurisdiction over all questions of ecclesiastical organization and administration, questions touching the property and property rights of the church, questions growing out of the sacraments, such as marriage and family relations, also wills, vows, pledges, and contracts resting on good faith. On the criminal side it was concerned with sin as such, often likewise with crime or the public aspect of sin, particularly all false doctrine, heresy, and schism, perjury and usury, and various sexual offences. In all these matters the laity was affected quite as much as the clergy. Not all of these claims were admitted by secular rulers, but many of them were, so that there existed beside the lay tribunals a whole system of courts Christian held by the bishop and his subordinates, with an ultimate appeal to Rome.

The twelfth century was a period of great importance in the growth of those centralizing tendencies in the church which are often summed up in the phrase, the papal monarchy. Monasteries were placed under the immediate protection of the Holy See, episcopal independence was discouraged, and appeals to Rome were favored. An ever increasing mass of legislation and decision poured forth from the papal curia respecting cases from every part of Latin Christendom. As litigation expanded, more lawyers and judges were required, and the need for specialized professional training made itself felt. The conditions of the time demanded a systematization of the canon law for use in the classroom and the courts.

Unlike its elder sister the Roman law, the canon law had a continuous history as the law of the continuous institution of the Roman church. And if this history begins in the days of the Roman empire, the greater part of it lies within the Middle Ages. The sources of the canon law — the Bible, the Fathers, the canons of councils, and the decretals of the Popes—had been from time to time arranged, by Dionysius the Little, by the Pseudo-Isidore, by Burchard of Worms, at the very threshold of the twelfth century in the collections ascribed to Ivo of Chartres. There was, however, confusion and contradiction in the authorities, and *ca.* 1140 Gratian, a monk of San Felice of Bologna, set himself to produce a *Concord*

of Discordant Canons which should make matters clear
and straight. Usually called the *Decretum*, this consists
of three parts: one hundred and one *distinctiones* dealing
with the sources of law and the law of ecclesiastical persons and officials; thirty-six *causae* or selected cases discussed in the light of the canons; and five *distinctiones* on
worship and the sacraments. Gratian not only collects,
he seeks to explain and reconcile, using the antithetical
method of Abaelard's *Sic et non*, but stressing the contradictions less and seeking to reconcile and harmonize at
any cost. Falling in with the current habit of thought,
this book had an immediate success both as a textbook
and as a work of reference. Though never formally
adopted by the church, it became generally recognized
as an authority and formed the first part of the *Corpus
Juris Canonici*. Down to Gratian's time canon law had
been closely associated with theology in a somewhat
subordinate position; with an authoritative textbook of
its own, it now acquired full independence, and Dante
places Gratian in Paradise side by side with Peter Lombard, the Paris theologian whose *Sentences* had followed
Gratian's method.

Again unlike the Roman law, the canon law did not
constitute a closed *corpus*, but continued to grow both by
legislation and by judicial decision. The most active
legislator of the twelfth century, Alexander III, Pope
from 1159 to 1181, was himself a canonist, having been
professor at Bologna where he composed the so-called

Summa Magistri Rolandi, one of the earliest in the long series of commentaries on Gratian. Decretals in his name and the name of his immediate successors piled up so rapidly that Stephen of Tournai, between 1192 and 1203, likens them to a pathless forest. Pathless the forest was until men began to group the decretals by subjects in the so-called *Five Compilations*, an arrangement which began *ca.* 1190 and was made permanent in the great book of *Decretals* issued by Gregory IX in 1234 and forming the second part of the *Corpus Juris Canonici*. Meanwhile the canon law had become a subject of university study side by side with the Roman, so that many students found it advisable to take degrees in both subjects as a J.U.D. or LL.D., and the same professor might lecture on the two laws. Within the universities and without, the canon law developed a parallel literature in the glosses, *summae*, and special treatises which begin to find their place on the shelves of libraries. Here again the glosses grew, until Dante complains that for them "the Gospel and the great doctors are deserted." Canon law also led to a career as the administrative and judicial sides of the church developed in the thirteenth century; indeed, the canon law was stigmatized as a lucrative profession for which men deserted the higher but less remunerative subject of theology.

In the development of canon law, as in its origins, Roman law had its considerable part; Gratian implies Irnerius as well as Abaelard. The church was originally a Roman institution, it 'lived by Roman law' in the days of the personality of law, and thus carried with it much Roman jurisprudence. From the ninth century we have even a manual of Roman law arranged for canonical use, the *Lex Romana canonice compta*. There was plenty of Roman law in the writings of the younger canonists like Ivo and Gratian, and it is no accident that Gratian's work was done at Bologna. Beginning with Alexander III a change is perceptible. The church continues to borrow Roman law, but it does not cite it as having authority as such, for the Roman law knows no Pope and emphasizes the Emperor everywhere, and the church was now strong enough to stand alone without lending its authority to law which it might find cited against it. In 1219 the Pope even forbade the study of Roman law by priests and altogether prohibited its teaching at the University of Paris.

As the law of the universal church, the canon law reached many places where the Roman law did not penetrate, as England, or penetrate in this period, as Germany, and it thus served as a vehicle for the transmission of the Roman law which it had absorbed and of the new method of jurisprudence. Moreover, the canon law developed a special procedure of its own, the inquisitorial procedure of the thirteenth century which had a profound influence on criminal justice on the Continent, while in England it shaped certain branches of law, like wills, which were finally taken over by the civil courts. This, however, is a later chapter of legal history which would carry us far beyond the twelfth century.

The revival of jurisprudence in the twelfth century also manifested itself outside the sphere of civil and canon law, in the countries still ruled by feudal or local custom. Some of this influence was direct, like the use of Roman maxims and Roman system where the substance of Roman law was excluded; some of it was indirect, the example of written law and systematic treatment working upon custom which was still unwritten but needed now to be written down in order to hold its own against the *lex scripta*. At the same time something must be set down to the growth of bureaucracy and royal power and to the spread of the literary habit; the revival of jurisprudence was a phase of the revival of the state. The earliest monuments of feudal law date from the later eleventh century, the *Usages* of Barcelona (1068 and following), and perhaps the beginnings of the Lombard *Leges feudorum*. After 1199 we have the *Très ancien coutumier* of Normandy, and from the thirteenth century various compilations of French feudal custom. Legislation, dormant since the ninth century, reappears in the assizes of Roger of Sicily, Henry II, and the kings of Jerusalem, in the ordinances of Philip Augustus, and in the earliest mentions of the Spanish Cortes. Along with the new administrative procedure of the Anglo-Norman Exchequer a new law is making in the decisions of the English royal court. This law is being recorded in regular rolls from the time of Richard I, while the administrative procedure is evident in the Exchequer rolls as early as 1130. From the reign of Henry II we have the first systematic description of the workings of this system in the *Dialogue on the Exchequer* of Richard Fitz Neal and the *Treatise on the Laws and Customs of the Kingdom of England* ascribed to Ranulf de Glanvill (1187–89), monuments of the new law as well as of the new statecraft.

Glanvill writes in Latin, as the writs and decisions of the king's court are in Latin. He starts off with an imitation of the opening words of Justinian's *Institutes*, and soon cites the famous maxim of absolutism, "The will of the prince has the force of law," without the qualifying clause respecting the popular source of princely authority which follows in the original passage of the *Digest*. Yet he takes pains to justify the laws of England from the reproach that, unlike the *leges scriptae*, they have not been written down. All this is preface, and when he comes to the body of his work there is, as Maitland has shown, little that is Roman beyond a few definitions and the method of the dilemma. The work itself begins:

Of pleas some are civil, some are criminal. Again, of criminal pleas some pertain to the crown of our lord the king, others to the sheriffs of the counties. To the king's crown belong these: the crime which in the *leges* [i. e., the Roman laws] is called *crimen laesae maiestatis*, — as by slaying the king or by a betrayal of his person or realm or army, — the concealment of treasure trove, breach of his peace, homicide, arson, robbery, rape, forgery, and the like.[1]

---

[1] Maitland's translation (*History of English Law*, i. 165).

The substance of Glanvill's treatment is thoroughly English, consisting essentially of a classification and discussion of the writs of the king's court, and shows us the law actually growing under the hands of the king's judges, as the common law was to continue to grow in the future. English law, too, never became a closed *corpus*. Already many of its distinctive features are evident, such as the system of original writs and the institution of trial by jury, the jury of England and of "kingless commonwealths beyond the seas." The age of Henry II is an epoch of the first importance in the history of the common law.

In one respect, the English common law was at a disadvantage in the twelfth century. Like the customary law of other countries, it was not taught in universities, university instruction throughout the Middle Ages being reserved for Roman and canon law. Even the law of the king's court could not be studied in an English university. Driven from the universities of Oxford and Cambridge, the common law took refuge in those curious and characteristic establishments, the Inns of Court at London, and it was in some measure owing to these that it escaped destruction or injury in the great renaissance of the sixteenth century when Roman law triumphed in Germany and in Scotland.

In still another sphere the twelfth century was a fertile age of jurisprudence, namely in the written law of the Italian cities and in the growth of commercial and maritime law to which these so largely contributed. In the town laws Roman law and Germanic custom were curiously intermingled, and here again the practical needs of a growing administration had their share in the movement of reducing law to written form. The Pisan *Constitutum usus* dates from 1160, the customs of Alessandria from 1179, and there are some others before the end of the century. New legislation also makes its appearance in the municipal *statuti*, the beginning of a rich and varied body of local law for which the Italian towns are later distinguished. On the threshold of the thirteenth century Boncompagno of Bologna tells us that "every city in Italy makes its statutes or constitutions under which the *podestà* or consuls carry on business and punish violators irrespective of any law which may seem to contravene the statute." Moreover, numerous commercial treaties between cities laid a solid foundation for international relations, and if we cannot with certainty assign to our period the earliest codes of maritime law, we can at least discern the existence of a consular system for residents in foreign cities, and of a special jurisdiction for the dusty-footed merchants who frequented fairs and markets and claimed the rapid processes of the piepowder courts. The trading and manufacturing population is developing its own law as well as its own institutions of government.

From the twelfth century on, law once more becomes, what it had been in Roman days, a major interest of the European mind, a subject worthy of the highest intellectual effort. Henceforth theology has a rival, and it is a secular rival. Even canon law is now independent. Beside the Scriptures and the Fathers now stand other works of authority, secular works for the most part, pagan works even, without religious sanction. The acceptance of the 'human, heathen *Digest*' forecasts the acceptance of books still less Christian, of Aristotle, Hippocrates, even Averroës "who made the great comment." The ecclesiastic, too, has a rival. So long as the clergy had a monopoly of learning, it had a monopoly of those public employments in which book-learning was required: when no one else could draft a document or look up a precedent, chancellors and secretaries were perforce ecclesiastics, indeed chancery and chapel are often indistinguishable. Faithful servants the clergy usually were, but they bore a divided allegiance, and the strain of serving two masters increased greatly in our period with the consolidation of the church and its sharper definition. Witness again the history of Henry II and Becket! It was a great advantage to European royalty that, just when the clergy began to fail it, a class of educated laymen should appear, trained in law as well as in letters, from whom the expert administrators and agents of the future could be taken. With the growth of bureaucracy even the church leaned more heavily on its lawyers, and it was natural that kings should turn to the lay jurist or legist. For good and ill, the lawyer had come as an active element in the world's government, and he had come to stay.

BIBLIOGRAPHICAL NOTE

The great work on Roman law in the Middle Ages is still that of F. C. von Savigny, *Geschichte des römischen Rechts im Mittelalter* (second edition, Berlin, 1834–51, 7 vols.), with a partial French translation (Paris, 1839, 4 vols.). Subsequent investigation has added much on points of detail, especially the many monographs of H. Fitting. The best book on Irnerius is E. Besta, *L'opera d'Irnerio* (Turin, 1896), who edits the glosses on the *Old Digest*. On Placentinus see the book of P. de Tourtolon (Paris, 1896); on Vacarius, F. Liebermann, in *English Historical Review*, xi. 305–314, 514–515 (1896). P. Vinogradoff, *Roman Law in Mediaeval Europe* (London and New York, 1909), is an excellent sketch, with bibliography; the substantial chapter by H. D. Hazeltine in the *Cambridge Medieval History* (v, ch. 21) covers canon law as well, with an elaborate bibliography. For Roman and canon law in the universities, see H. Rashdall, *The Universities of Europe in the Middle Ages* (Oxford, 1895).

For the sources of canon law since Gratian the standard work is J. F. von Schulte, *Geschichte der Quellen und Literatur des canonischen Rechts von Gratian bis auf die Gegenwart* (Stuttgart, 1875–80), supplemented for the later twelfth century by E. Seckel, in *Neues Archiv*, xxv. 521–537 (1900), and by H. Singer in Vienna *Sitzungsberichte*, phil.-hist. Klasse, clxxi (1912). For the three preceding centuries a comprehensive treatment has long been in preparation by Paul Fournier, who has published many preliminary studies. On the relations of canon law to theology, see J. de Ghellinck, *Le mouvement théologique du XIIᵉ siècle* (Paris, 1914). The standard edition of the *Corpus Juris Canonici* is that of E. Friedberg (Leipzig, 1879–81), who has also studied the *Quinque Compilationes* (Leipzig, 1882).

The relation of Roman and canon law to the common law is admirably treated in F. Pollock and F. W. Maitland, *History of English Law* (second edition, Cambridge, 1898), i, bk. i, chs. 1, 5, 6. See also Maitland, *Roman Canon Law in the Church of England* (London, 1898); and for a suggestive parallel, his Rede lecture on *English Law and the Renaissance* (Cambridge, 1901). Note also W. S. Holdsworth, *History of English Law* (London, 1922–26, 9 vols.). There are standard histories of law for most Continental countries in our period: for Germany by R. Schröder; for France by P. Viollet; for Italy by F. Schupfer, C. Calisse, E. Besta, etc. See also the introductory *General Survey* in the *Continental Legal History Series*, edited by J. H. Wigmore (Boston, 1912). *Select Cases concerning the Law Merchant*, edited and translated by C. Gross for the Selden Society (London, 1908), begin only with 1270.

CHAPTER VIII

HISTORICAL WRITING

ONE of the best expressions of the intellectual revival of the twelfth century is to be seen in the writing of history; indeed, from many points of view this is one of the great periods of mediaeval historiography. Old forms take on greater breadth and fulness, new forms develop, and the amount of historical writing greatly increases as it reflects more fully the growing activity of the age. Curiously enough, classical influence, so marked in other phases of twelfth-century literature, scarcely shows itself in history; it is not a period of the revival of classical models, but of new life which seeks spontaneous expression in a more abundant and more varied historiography, both in Latin and, later in the century, in the vernacular.

Of the two principal Roman historians, Tacitus was practically unknown to the Middle Ages. His *Annals*, or rather those books which alone have survived the wreck of time, thanks to a single copy, were now so completely hidden that it was once maintained that they were really a forgery of Poggio Bracciolini in the fifteenth century. The first four and one-half books of the *Histories* owe their preservation to a copy made at Monte Cassino in the eleventh century.[1] Of the minor works the *Germania* alone meets us, in a citation from a manuscript kept at the monastery of Fulda in the ninth century, thereafter to disappear until brought to light with its fellows in 1455, when Enoch of Ascoli carried to Italy the copy from which all modern manuscripts of the *Germania* and the *Dialogue on Oratory* are commonly supposed to be derived. Only with the beginnings of modern politics in the sixteenth century does Tacitus come to his own as an influence on historical writing and political thinking. He was quite beyond the comprehension of a feudal age.

For Livy the number of manuscripts is somewhat greater, but the evidence of actual use is almost as small. In the eleventh century Lambert of Hersfeld seems to use him, but in the twelfth John of Salisbury, the best classical scholar of the age, knows him only at second hand. 'The lost decades' which saddened the humanists had been lost before this time — and still remain lost, in spite of the efforts of Martino Fusco and of the daily press. Livy appears regularly in the mediaeval lists of ancient authors, but only as a name, and he is not much more when Dante speaks of *Livio che non erra*, 'the impeccable Livy.' Dante, it is true, seems to get from Livy something of the feeling for the Roman past which appears in the *De monarchia*, but enthusiasm for Livy first

[1] This is the accepted view respecting the MS. tradition of both *Annals* and *Histories*, though recent researches also claim authority for the Vatican codex 1958.

appears with Rienzi and Poggio; and two centuries of humanism lie between the inerrant Livy of Dante and Machiavelli's *Discourses on the First Ten Books*.

Caesar, Sallust, and Suetonius were not unknown to the twelfth century, but their influence was slight. Manuscripts of Caesar are rare and few historians know him. Sallust, "the favorite model of style for the historians of the ninth and tenth centuries," can be traced in Adam of Bremen and later in Rahewin, but he had small influence in the twelfth century, unless it be in such extracts from the *Catiline* and *Jugurtha* as are incorporated into the *Gesta* of the Angevin counts. Suetonius was copied in the twelfth century and was much cited by John of Salisbury, but he can show no subsequent imitator equal to Einhard in his *Life of Charlemagne*; indeed, the mediaeval biography rarely affects classical models. The Latin historians who really delighted the mediaeval, as they did the later Roman, world were the epitomators, Florus, Justin, and Eutropius, whose popularity was paralleled by that of the summarizers and excerptors in other fields, like Solinus. This is only another way of saying that the Middle Ages cared little for the form of things Roman, and lacked the outlook on the world which was reflected in ancient historical writing; and when, as in the twelfth century, there was some revival of the sense of form, men preferred to clip phrases from the Roman poets. Thus Suger, in his prose biographies of French kings, imitates Lucan, not Suetonius. Moreover, classical historiography was powerfully influenced by classical rhetoric, particularly public oratory, and the basis for this had disappeared from mediaeval life. And, if mediaeval historians still justify themselves in the ancient way as purveyors of moral instruction, the purpose is no longer to exalt patriotism and civic morality, as in Livy's glowing preface, but to point the way to another and better world. "We have written these things, both good and bad," says the Anglo-Saxon Chronicler in concluding his sketch of William the Conqueror, "that virtuous men might follow after the good, and wholly avoid the evil, and might go in the way that leadeth to the kingdom of heaven."

It is, accordingly, in Christian, not in pagan, Rome that we must seek the antecedents of mediaeval historiography, both in its general view of life and in its specific forms and types. Christian Europe, far down into modern times, took its philosophy of history from Augustine and its chronological system from Eusebius, and the two were combined in the mediaeval chronicle or general history. Indeed, a universal history in the full sense had not been possible before the triumph of Christianity; for, while the worldwide supremacy of Rome might suggest general history in an external fashion, a sense of the fundamental unity of mankind was necessary to a really vital conception of universal history. As heirs to both the classical and the Jewish tradition, the early Christian historians faced the task of combining and coordinating two histories which had grown up in entire independence of each other. The effort to reduce to a common denominator the materials found in the Roman historians and in the Old Testament was in the first instance a question of chronology, which the *Canons* of Eusebius of Caesarea solved for the subsequent Christian ages. His system formed and joined two parallel chronologies by synchronizing certain outstanding figures and events like Abraham and Ninus, Moses and Cecrops, Samson and the Trojan War; and the chronicle or epitome of history which in this way he carried to 325 A.D. became, as translated by St. Jerome, the foundation of the general histories of the Middle Ages. St. Augustine added to this the theory of the six ages of the world, corresponding to the six days of Creation — for in the sight of the Creator a thousand years are "as one day"— with the seventh as the unending Sabbath of eternity. In this system, which was further developed and popularized by Isidore, the first age extended from Adam to Noah, the second from Noah to Abraham, and so on, with the sixth from the birth of Christ to the end of the world, an event which the Middle Ages, like the early Christians, expected quickly. In the pages of Orosius, who wrote his *Seven Books against the Pagans* in 417, this sixth age coincided with the Roman empire, the last of the four great monarchies in the vision of the prophet Daniel, so that the persistence of Rome was assured until the end of all things earthly. The complement of all this was Augustine's distinction between the earthly city of Rome which would pass away and the eternal city of all the faithful, the city not made with hands, invisible in the heavens, whose builder and maker is God. Thenceforth Christendom had its philosophy of history, turned away from the world that now is and fixed on the world to come, and this dualism of thought dominates the Middle Ages.

Out of these materials, Roman and Christian, the Roman subordinated to the Christian, the general histories of the Middle Ages were made, in their chronology, their division into periods, and their historical philosophy. Beginning commonly with the Creation, they copied Eusebius, Jerome, and the continuators of these until they reached their own times, when they added that account of contemporary events which is the only portion possessing special interest for us. In course of time some of the more economical, and more merciful, writers began with the Christian era, but this method of reckoning spread but slowly as a substitute for the Roman era, after its first introduction in the sixth century, and Constantinople continued to count from the beginning of the world, there placed in 5509 B.C. — not in 4004, the twenty-second of October at six in the afternoon, as the good Archbishop Usher fixed it in the chronology which still meets us in the margin of the King James version. Even the date of the Christian era was in dispute at the close of the eleventh century, a certain school maintaining on astronomical grounds that the current reckoning was twenty-two years too late, so that the year 1100 ought really to be 1122. Meanwhile the basis for the general histories of the twelfth century had been fixed in the chronicles of Marianus Scotus, who died at Mainz in 1082, and his successor Sigebert of Gembloux, whose rather bald chronological outline comes to 1112.

A second type of mediaeval record, the annals, might well have claimed a classical origin, for the ancient historians used the annalistic form so regularly, from the summers and winters of Thucydides to the *annus terribilis* of Tacitus's *Histories*, that *annales* became the standard term for history as contrasted with contemporary memoirs (*historiae*). It would, however, be hard to patent the idea of writing history year by year, and, as a matter of fact, the annals of the Middle Ages, in spite of some survivals of the Roman consuls' lists, had an independent origin in the Easter tables of the eighth century. In an unlettered age such as that, few dared trust their own reckoning of a date so fundamental as Easter for the whole ecclesiastical year, and authoritative Easter tables for a series of years, such as those of Bede, were copied and passed about from church to church and monastery to monastery. Containing usually nineteen years to a page, their wide margins offered convenient space for entries under each year, and later, when the table had served its purpose, those marginal or interlinear entries were drawn off as separate annals. Very rude and brief these were at first, with many gaps and many items of purely local interest, as we may see from the following example, written at St. Gall:

709. Hard winter. Duke Gottfried died.
710. Hard year and deficient in crops.
712. Great flood.
714. Pippin, mayor of the palace, died.
718. Charles Martel devastated Saxony with great destruction.
720. Charles fought against the Saxons.
721. Theudo drove the Saracens out of Aquitaine.
722. Great crops.
725. The Saracens came for the first time.
731. The blessed Bede the presbiter died.
732. Charles fought against the Saracens at Poitiers on Saturday.[1]

This is all that our annalist had to record for these years, even of that so-called battle of Tours in 732 which certain of his modern successors were to make one of the decisive battles of history, without which victory, an American student declared, "we should all be polygamous Mohammedan Turks instead of Christians worshipping the one true God"!

In course of time such local annals grew by passing from monastery to monastery, or they might be grafted on a general history, going back to the Creation or the year 1, and a really informed writer might thus turn them into a general chronicle, which would still keep the arrangement by years. In the main, however, the annals, whether of monasteries or cathedrals, retained their local character, which corresponded to the extremely localized life of the age.

[1] *Monumenta Germaniae Historica, Scriptores,* i. 73. The intervening years are left blank.

Still another type of historical writing was fixed in the early Middle Ages, the lives of the saints. Written at first according to the rules of the Roman rhetoric, which prescribed that a biography should regularly be a panegyric, these biographies also perpetuated the memory of ancient shrines where saints and martyrs now wrought the miracles once performed by pagan divinities. They soon, however, developed a character of their own, till they became the most distinctive form of biographical writing which the Middle Ages produced. Unfortunately, they tend to a striking uniformity of type, in which each saint acquires the conventional virtues of other saints and goes to Heaven after performing a host of miracles copied from the Bible or the exploits of his holy predecessors. Such works, written primarily for edification, and often rewritten from age to age in the current forms of language and thought, are likely to contain more of subjective than of objective truth; if they often preserve personal and local details, they are chiefly valuable as a reflection of the mediaeval mind and the kind of religious life then chiefly admired.

These three general types of Christian historiography, chronicles, annals, and lives of saints, the twelfth century inherited and continued, but in its own way and with a fulness and variety which reflect a new and more active age. Of hagiography, to take them in the reverse order, there was a plenty, whether in the formal lives, the special collections of miracles, or the records of the finding and translation of relics. The lives of earlier saints were re-written, particularly for special occasions, like the trans-lation of King Edward the Confessor at Westminster in 1163, and such an occasion might even start a new series of legends like the *chanson* of Duke Richard which Bédier has connected with the solemn opening of the tombs of the Norman dukes at Fécamp in 1162. So the miracles of St. Nicholas, growing as his relics and cult passed north-ward from Bari, might play a decisive part in the making of the liturgical drama.

Then the twelfth century had its own saints, though in less abundance than the more credulous Merovingian age, like the holy men of the orders of Cluni and Cîteaux, notably St. Bernard, and that most famous and most characteristic of twelfth-century martyrs, St. Thomas Becket. Killed in 1170 and canonized in 1172, Becket to the minds of contemporaries at once represented the church in its conflict with the state; and before the end of the century we have a whole body of Becket literature, in French and Icelandic as well as in Latin, including many miracles wrought at the tomb in Canterbury which had already begun to draw the stream of pilgrims that became immortal in the pages of Chaucer. The acquisition of holy relics was a matter of business as well as of religion, for the miracles performed at a shrine drew pilgrims and gifts in their train, especially when they were further ad-vertised through being taken up in the popular epics. Of

all centres Constantinople was reputed to possess the
greatest store of ancient relics, and those who passed that
way in ever increasing numbers sought to beg or steal
what of these treasures they could. A Canterbury monk
tells us of his experiences in securing a fragment of St.
Andrew there *ca.* 1090, while a monk of Pairis, in Alsace,
has left a rather unedifying account of the exploits of his
abbot in the great looting of 1204:

While the victors were eagerly plundering the conquered city,
which was theirs by right of conquest, the abbot Martin began to
cogitate about his own share of the booty, and lest he alone should
remain empty-handed, while all the others became rich, he resolved
to seize upon plunder with his own consecrated hands. But, since he
thought it not meet to handle any booty of worldly things with those
hands, he began to plan how he might secure some portion of the
relics of the saints, of which he knew there was a great quantity in
the city. . . . [Having found a suitable church with a chest of relics]
the abbot hastily and eagerly thrust in both hands, and, being stoutly
girded, filled with the fruits of the holy sacrilege both his own and his
chaplain's bosom. He wisely concealed what seemed the most valuable and departed forthwith. Moreover what and how worthy of
veneration those relics which the holy robber appropriated were, is
told more fully at the end of this work [a trace of Christ's blood, a
piece of the Cross, "a not inconsiderable piece of St. John" the Baptist, the arm of St. James, and relics of many saints and holy places].
When he was hastening to the ships, so stuffed full, if I may use the
expression, those who knew and loved him saw him as they were
themselves hastening to the booty from the ships, and inquired
joyfully whether he had stolen anything, or with what he was so
loaded down as he walked. With a joyful countenance, as always,
and with pleasant words he said: "We have done well." To which
they replied: "Thanks be to God." [1]

---

[1] P. Riant, *Exuviae sacrae Constantinopolitanae* (Geneva, 1877–78), i.
104–122. Cf. D. C. Munro, *The Fourth Crusade* (Philadelphia, 1901), pp.
16–18.

Such a flood of relics tended in time to depreciate their value and even throw doubt on their genuineness, particularly when they became articles of commerce, until Chaucer can speak of the "pigges bones" of his Pardoner, and Erasmus write his satire on the Virgin's milk of Walsingham. Another occasion for doubt was the many duplicates of the same relic, each claiming to be the real original. By the close of the Middle Ages at least five churches in France claimed to have the authentic relic of Christ's circumcision, nor was Pope Innocent III able to settle the question of the real original when it came to him early in the thirteenth century.[1] A century earlier Guibert, abbot of Nogent, wrote, shortly before his death in 1119, a curious treatise *De pignoribus sanctorum* in which he showed striking scepticism on such points. Either St. John the Baptist, he argues, had two heads, or one of those preserved at Constantinople and Saint-Jean d'Angely is false. The body of St. Firmin at Amiens bears no mark of identification, whereas both head and members are at Saint-Denis with an attesting parchment. If the neighboring monastery of Saint-Médard of Soissons has a tooth of our Lord, then is he not fully risen, and the doctrine of the Resurrection is thereby invalidated. Such arguments were later used by another Picard critic, one John Calvin. Guibert inveighs against raising money by carrying about miracle-working relics of doubtful genu-

[1] H. Denifle, *La désolation des églises en France* (Paris, 1897–99), i. 167.

ineness, as in the recent processions for the rebuilding of Laon cathedral.

Our chief interest in Guibert's work is as an expression of the spirit of historical criticism. This was never so completely absent from the Middle Ages as is often supposed, for textual and chronological problems were sure to arise, and historians had to face in some fashion the problem of conflicting statements. In such matters the twelfth century shows some progress, as illustrated in a writer like Otto of Freising and in more specific ways. Toward the beginning of the century Marianus Scotus and others attack the current chronology; in 1198 Innocent III lays down sound criteria for examining doubtful papal documents; while Guibert shows much good sense in the criticism of what may be called archaeological materials — evidence of a critical attitude which foreshadows Petrarch's examination of the Austrian privileges and Lorenzo Valla's attack on the Donation of Constantine.

The annals of the twelfth century show no sudden change from their predecessors. Drought and flood, plague, pestilence, and famine, eclipses and comets, the death and accession of abbots and bishops, still constitute the greater part of their subject matter. At the same time the annals become fuller and more varied as there is more to record and as the growth of travel brings more news of the outside world, so that a group of such records in England, edited as the *Annales monastici* in the 'Rolls Series,' foreshadows their place in the thirteenth century as a record of the first importance in insular affairs. So, out of the local records of St. Albans, the thirteenth century will make the great history of Matthew Paris. Growing interest attaches, especially in Italy, to the annals of the several cities, reflecting the more intense life of the commercial and industrial republics, and often developing into the city chronicles of the succeeding age. In these respects the South is still in advance in the twelfth century; the *Chroniken der deutschen Städte* and similar records in England and the Low Countries belong to the later Middle Ages. On the whole, as the twelfth century wears on, history grows less local, partly with the growth of communication, partly with the increasing importance of courts and centralized monarchies. A striking example is furnished by the abbey of Saint-Denis, that ancient mausoleum of French kings, which by the thirteenth century has become a sort of official centre of French historiography, whether in the form of royal biography or national annals.

The universal chronicle is a conspicuous feature of historical writing in the twelfth century. In France it had entirely disappeared in the local records of the preceding period, and in Germany, while preserving its general character, it had become rather bald and dry in the pages of Marianus and Sigebert. With such works as a starting-point, we witness a revival in France at the hands of Robert of Torigni and Ordericus, and in Italy in Romualdus of Salerno, while in Otto of Freising the German historiography of the Middle Ages reaches its highest point.

The persistence of the older general history is clearly apparent in one of the best works of the twelfth century, that of Robert of Torigni, abbot of Mont-Saint-Michel, which indeed he entitles an *Appendix to Sigebert* "in preference to all modern chronographers." Begun at Bec, where Robert first became monk, this chronicle was continued at the Mount from his coming as abbot in 1154 to his death in 1186. Few spots are by nature so set apart for monastic seclusion and religious meditation as this remote rock, cut off from the mainland by tide and shifting sands, and looking out past stormy Breton headlands to the pathless ocean where the sun of mortal life goes down in death. Nowhere, we might suppose, would a chronicle be more local and more turned toward the unseen world, away from the little lives of men. As a matter of fact, while Abbot Robert was devoted to the affairs of the monastery, its church, its library, the relics and reliquaries of its saints, all this took him perforce into the outer world where lay the abbey's possessions, in Normandy, England, Maine, Brittany, and the Channel Islands, and to the courts of kings and prelates. Kings also visited the Mount in his time, as did pilgrims from beyond the seas, and all brought grist to the abbot's historical mill. So his chronicle, year by year, records doings in far-off Spain, Sicily, and Syria, as well as in the Anglo-

Norman realm, even bits of distant intellectual history like the new version of Aristotle made by James of Venice in 1128, the coming of Master Vacarius and the Roman law to England twenty years later, and the translations from the Greek by the Pisan judge Burgundio. Nor is there much of the unseen world here. A hard-headed man of affairs without much imagination, Robert has an eye for chronology, especially the succession of bishops and abbots, and the building and dedication of churches, all of which he sets down briefly and soberly, after the fashion of an annalist, in the midst of the portents of nature and the campaigns of princes. Robert, however, maintains a sharp distinction between his chronicle and the brief annals which continued to be kept at the Mount. Thus, under 1165, the annals record merely the accession of the archbishop of Rouen, Rotrou, while the chronicle recounts also the itinerary of Henry II and his queen, his interview with Louis VII and his negotiations with Frederick Barbarossa, the birth of Philip Augustus and the future queen of Sicily, the journey of Pope Alexander III to Sicily, changes of bishops at Bayeux and Chartres and of abbots at Saint-Wandrille and Marmoutier, the death of the king of the Scots, a stroke of lightning at the Mount, and — longest entry of all — the gold and silver reliquary which the abbot has made for the bones of St. Lawrence, brought from Italy by a predecessor more than a century before. And the continuity with Sigebert appears in the notation of this year as the thirteenth of

Frederick of the Romans, the twenty-eighth of Louis of the French, and the eleventh of Henry of the English.

Likewise local appears at first sight the *Ecclesiastical History* of another Norman monk of the twelfth century, Ordericus Vitalis of Saint-Évroul. Ordericus never became abbot, but spent his whole life in this one establishment, with rare excursions into the outer world. Much there is, certainly, concerning the monastery and its neighborhood, especially the wars of neighboring barons, but many other sources, oral and written, came to the author in his long life, so that he could write on an ample scale from the beginning of the Christian era, with much on Sicily and the East as well as on Normandy and his native England. Working year after year, save when the cold of winter forced him to lay aside his pen, he produced the chief historical work which the century saw in France. Unable to study personally "the affairs of Alexandria, Greece, and Rome," he relies upon the older chroniclers for the earlier Christian centuries, but for more recent times he uses the recent Norman and English historians and the lives of saints. He also draws freely upon the documents in the archives of his monastery and upon collections of contemporary Latin verse, to which he himself contributed. Of Marianus and Sigebert he had once a glimpse, but a glimpse only, and his work follows his own rather discursive plan, from the birth of Christ to 1141. Its five printed volumes are not only a mine of information for the life of the age; they show a sure touch and a ripe knowledge of men, such as is not always associated with the cloister. "The best French historian of the century," he was a monk to the end, when he reviews his religious career with the lively hope of the eternal rewards promised him in his youth.

An excellent example of the bishop-historian is Otto of Freising (d. 1159), with whom general history takes on a philosophic cast; he was both historian and philosopher, both monk and bishop. Uncle of the Emperor Frederick Barbarossa, his connections with the imperial family brought him into the leading events of his time and carried him as far as Rome and Jerusalem on expeditions which he describes with the sure touch of the eyewitness. Then, too, he had studied at Paris in his youth, and was the first to bring into Germany the *New Logic* of Aristotle, by which his own thinking was profoundly affected, so that he takes a keen interest in the scholastic conflicts of the age and introduces into his historical writings a certain amount of the logic of the syllogism and the discussion of substance and attribute. Master of the deeper learning of the Latin world, he was profoundly influenced by Augustine's *City of God*, to the point of entitling his *Chronicle* a treatise on the two cities, the earthly and the heavenly. The whole of the eighth or final book is devoted to the coming of Antichrist and the establishment of the heavenly Jerusalem, whose glory is dimly prefigured in the apocalyptic description of pearly gates and golden streets. "Placed as it were at the end of time," his eager heart expects the approaching climax, while the earlier part of his history is one long tragedy of change and decay, each book of which "ends in misery." One is reminded of Santayana's phrase concerning the church's large disillusion as to this world and minute illusions as to the world to come! When, however, Otto comes to the actual division of his confused material by books and periods, he shows a very reasonable historical perspective. What would have been the first four, or pre-Roman, ages of Augustine are combined in the first book, while the second extends from the founding of Rome to the birth of Christ. The terminal points of the succeeding three books, Constantine, Odoacer, the treaty of Verdun, remind us of the heavy-typed dates of the modern manual, while the sixth ends with the death of Hildebrand in 1085, and the seventh, the most detailed, extends from the First Crusade to 1146. This perspective is distinctly Roman, for Otto finds the unity of the Christian centuries in the Roman empire, the fourth and iron kingdom of Orosius. Transferred from Rome to the Greeks, then successively to Franks, Lombards, and Germans, the empire moves westward in its course, just as the learning of the East has passed to the Greeks, the Romans, and finally to the Gauls and Spaniards of the author's day. Like his imperial nephew, Otto has a high theory of the Emperor's authority, placed above the law in phrases which recall the *Corpus Juris*, and responsible to God alone.

The more prosperous reign of Frederick I, that high light of the mediaeval empire, gave Otto occasion to write history in a less pessimistic vein, and the two books of Frederick's biography, or *Gesta*, down to 1156, give us a very favorable specimen of Otto's many-sided powers as an historian, even if we hesitate to rank him, as does one enthusiastic German writer, with Tacitus and Thucydides. No better account than his has reached us of one of the great journeys to Rome for the imperial crown, the *Römerzug* of 1154–55, and no one has written in the same compass a better description of those Lombard communes with which the Emperor had to contend:[1]

In the government of the cities and in the management of civil affairs they also imitate the skill of the ancient Romans. Furthermore they love liberty so well that, to guard against the abuse of power, they choose to be ruled by the authority of consuls rather than by princes. They are divided into three classes, namely, 'captains,' vavassors, and the people. To prevent the growth of class pride, the consuls are chosen from each class, not from one only, and, for fear that they may yield to the lust of power, they are changed nearly every year. Hence it has come to pass that, since almost the whole country belongs to the cities, each of them forces the inhabitants of its diocese to join it, and one can hardly find, within so wide a circuit, a man of rank or importance who does not recognize the authority of his city. . . . In order that there shall be no lack of forces for coercing their neighbors, the cities stoop to bestow the sword belt and honorable rank upon youths of inferior station, or even upon laborers in despised and mechanical trades whom other peoples exclude like the pest from the more honorable and liberal pursuits. To this practice it is due that they surpass the other cities of the world in riches and power; and, besides their industry, the long continued absence of their rulers beyond the Alps has further contributed to this end. In one respect they are unmindful of their ancient nobility

---

[1] *Gesta Friderici*, ii. 13, substantially as translated in J. H. Robinson, *Readings in European History*, i. 303–304.

and betray their barbarian origin; for, although they boast of living under law, they do not obey the law. They rarely or never receive their ruler with respect, although it is their duty to show him willing and respectful obedience. They do not obey the decrees that he issues by virtue of his legal powers, unless they are made to feel his authority by the presence of his great army.

In biography the twelfth century is particularly rich. This was not a specialty of the earlier Middle Ages, when few strongly marked personalities stand out, and a picture such as Einhard draws of Charlemagne is a striking exception which owes as much to Suetonius as to Einhard. Much of mediaeval biography, like mediaeval portraiture, deals with types, and the edge of personal characterization is usually blunt. As Schmeidler has pointed out, literary portraiture as we understand it is rare in the Middle Ages, when it does not often occur to a writer to stop his narrative in order to depict a man or group of men. The exception proves the rule when Acerbus Morena of Lodi, in breaking off his account of Barbarossa's Italian campaigns in 1163 with a striking characterization of the Emperor, Empress, and chief personages of his following, expresses the hope that his readers will not find this superfluous or out of place. A favorite form of biography was the catalogues and series of local biographies, or *Gesta*, of the bishops, abbots, or counts of a particular place. More detailed and more interesting than the bald annals, they are still essentially local records. Even those of the widest interest for Christendom, the lives of the Popes known as the *Liber pontificalis*, are for

many centuries chronicles of purely local happenings —
the annals of the Roman bishopric.

If this was true at the centre of Roman Christendom,
small wonder that the earliest *Gesta abbatum vel pontificum* lacked the personal touch and the European outlook.
In the twelfth century such records become ampler and
often more biographical; indeed, many new series of this
sort owe their origin to this age. At Rome Cardinal Boso
revives the fading tradition of the *Liber pontificalis* by a
revision of the earlier lives and by fuller biographies of the
pontiffs of his own time, especially after his appearance
at the curia in 1149. Boso's chief merit is fulness: he
draws freely upon the papal archives, and his life of
Alexander III, incomplete as it is, is much the longest of
the whole papal series; but the result is still annals rather
than biography. For the most part, too, they are the
annals of a city. Thus the life of Adrian IV (1154–59), the
only English Pope, fits into the conventional local scheme,
with none of the amplitude of that remarkable fragment
which another Englishman, John of Salisbury, had devoted to four preceding years in his *Historia pontificalis*
(1148–52); for the relations with Frederick Barbarossa
and William of Sicily we find more facts in Otto of Freising and Romualdus, though Boso lays more weight on the
incident of holding the Pope's stirrup. In the following
extracts from the life of Adrian IV even the eulogy is
copied from the biographies of the seventh and eighth
centuries, where all the Popes are most kind, most eloquent, etc.:

He sat four years, eight months, six days, . . . a man most kind, mild, and patient, skilled in the English and Latin tongues, a master of polished eloquence, eminent both in song and sermon, slow to anger and quick to forgive, a cheerful and generous giver, and distinguished for the whole disposition of his character. . . . He had a very necessary and commodious cistern dug in the Lateran, where he also renewed many things wasted by age; in Mid-Lent he dedicated with his own hands the greater altar of the church of SS. Cosmas and Damian over the stone which the blessed Pope Gregory had consecrated. [He enlarged the patrimony of St. Peter with many lands and buildings, and, having recovered possession of Orvieto, was the first Pope to sojourn therein.] He died at Anagni 1 September [1159] and was taken to Rome and buried honorably near Pope Eugene at St. Peter's. Written by Boso, cardinal priest of S. Pudenziana, who, chamberlain of the aforesaid Pope throughout his pontificate and deacon of SS. Cosmas and Damian, remained with him in continuous and familiar association until his death.[1]

Even in biography, the papal tradition proved too strong for the twelfth century, as it has for every succeeding century.

The *Liber pontificalis* found many imitators among the historians of bishoprics, as at Ravenna, Le Mans, Auxerre, and Toul; but by the twelfth century these begin to reflect their age somewhat more freely. Thus the ancient series of the *Acts of the Bishops of Le Mans* is now taken in hand by a writer of classical tastes and training with the weakness for rhymed prose which is a symptom of the time. Instead of charters inserted in the text, we have bits of verse; and of the poet Hildebert we read that the subtlety of his song was famed far and wide, so that even the eloquence of a Cicero could scarcely set forth his praises worthily. So the chronicle of the bishops of Cam-

---

[1] Ed. Duchesne, ii. 388–397.

brai, one of the best of such works in the eleventh century, is now continued in verse, though the verse is not classical. In the twelfth century the widely used *Gesta* of the archbishops of Trier shows much interest in antiquity, not only using freely Caesar's *Gallic War*, but giving this illustrious city a pre-Roman origin in the person of one Trebetas, son of Ninus, *ca.* 2000 B.C., whose descendants are celebrated in Latin epitaphs and made the authors of the city's Roman monuments, like the still surviving *Porta Nigra*. Such fables of remote urban origins are characteristic not only of the Middle Ages but also of the Italian Renaissance.

A broader theme, likewise worthy of a later age, is the survey of English episcopal and monastic history by William of Malmesbury in his *Gesta pontificum Anglorum* down to his own time (1125). The model as well as the foundation is, of course, Bede, no unworthy model at that, but there is much of the author's own research, as we can see more at length in his special history of Glastonbury Abbey. The *Gesta pontificum* is paralleled by the *Gesta regum*, which likewise branches off from Bede but becomes with its continuation a precious source for the author's own time. Indeed William has an honorable place in English historiography as

the first writer after Bede who attempted to give to his details of dates and events such a systematic connexion, in the way of cause and consequence, as entitles them to the name of History. He certainly aspires to the art of the historian; and to some extent he succeeds in tracing the development of institutions, the results of political measures, the tendency of significant events. He prides himself, and with some reason, on his skill in the delineation of character. He tries, as indeed the instinct of self-preservation not less than the sense of historical justice recommends to him, to be fair and equitable in the view of dynastic parties; and he avails himself of the privilege of his mixed blood to take a somewhat neutral position in the rivalry of Norman and Englishman. He is a man of great reading, unbounded industry, very forward scholarship, and of thoughtful research in many regions of learning. If the result is not altogether adequate, it is at least nearer to the historic ideal than anything that comes before.[1]

The line between ecclesiastical and feudal biography is hard to draw, for the great ecclesiastics were also feudal princes, while the biographies of lay lords were largely written by clerks or chaplains. A noteworthy exception is the fragment concerning the counts of Anjou which bears the name of one of these counts, Fulk Rechin, in 1096. Dealing with one of the great feudal families of France, it breathes the spirit of the feudal age, nowhere better expressed than in the following succinct life of Count Geoffrey Martel: [2]

My uncle Geoffrey became a knight in his father's lifetime and began his knighthood by two wars against his neighbors, one against the Poitevins, whose count he captured at Mont Couër, and another against the people of Maine, whose count, named Herbert Bacon, he likewise took. He also carried on war against his own father, in the course of which he committed many evil deeds of which he afterward bitterly repented. After his father died on his return from Jerusalem, Geoffrey possessed his lands and the city of Angers, and fought Count Thibaud of Blois, son of Count Odo, and by gift of King Henry received the city of Tours, which embittered the war with

---

[1] W. Stubbs, preface to his edition of the *Gesta Regum* (1887) i, p. x.

[2] *Chroniques des Comtes d'Anjou,* ed. L. Halphen and R. Poupardin (Paris, 1913), pp. 235–237.

Count Thibaud, in the course of which, at a battle between Tours and Amboise, Thibaud was captured with a thousand of his knights. And so, besides the part of Touraine inherited from his father, he acquired Tours and the castles round about — Chinon, L'Ile-Bouchard, Châteaurenault, and Saint-Aignan. After this he had a war with William, count of the Normans, who later acquired the kingdom of England and was a magnificent king, and with the people of France and of Bourges, and with William count of Poitou and Aimeri viscount of Thouars and Hoël count of Nantes and the Breton counts who held Rennes and with Hugh count of Maine, who had thrown off his fealty. Because of all these wars and the prowess he showed therein he was rightly called the Hammer, as one who hammered down his enemies.

In the last year of his life he made me his nephew a knight at the age of seventeen in the city of Angers, at the feast of Pentecost, in the year of the Incarnation 1060, and granted me Saintonge and the city of Saintes because of a quarrel he had with Peter of Didonne. In this same year King Henry died on the nativity of St. John, and my uncle Geoffrey on the third day after Martinmas came to a good end. For in the night which preceded his death, laying aside all care of knighthood and secular things, he became a monk in the monastery of St. Nicholas, which his father and he had built with much devotion and endowed with their goods.

A good end, and just in the nick of time! Knighthood and secular things as long as possible, and the quiet of the monastery well prepared for the last moments! So in 1159 Robert de Neufbourg, seneschal and justiciar of Normandy, entered the abbey of Bec, where he spent a whole month of fruitful penance before his death, and was buried in the chapter house "which he himself had wonderfully built at his own expense."

Of the feudal biographies from the hands of clerks, one of the best comes from the end of the century in the history of the counts of Guines and lords of Ardres written by the priest Lambert of Ardres, near Calais. Though he

puts part of his narrative into the mouth of the lord's
nephew, the whole is of a piece; and the turgid Latin style,
with its quotations from Scripture and the Roman poets,
the Latin verse, and the elaborate ancient examples of the
preface show plainly the clerk. These lords were of the
lesser feudalism, dependants of the counts of Flanders,
whose court they imitated by establishing twelve peers
of their own, but, while they play only a subordinate part
in the general history of their age, they bring us all the
closer to the realities of local life. The best portrait is
that of Count Baldwin II (1169–1206), just and generous,
a great builder, a drainer of marshes like the doughty
Hercules of old, a mighty hunter who listened more gladly
to the bark of the greyhound than to the chant of the
chaplain; a mighty drinker, who smashed all the water
vessels in the castle and served the archbishop of Rheims
only strong Burgundy when he begged for water; deeply
stricken by the death of his countess yet renewing his
youth like the eagle; a very Solomon or Jupiter with the
fair sex, father of uncounted sons and daughters begotten
at home and at large, of whom thirty-three came to his
funeral; unable to read but eager to hear, exchanging
jongleurs' tales for the heavier learning of the clergy, and
collecting a library of the various translations which he
had ordered from Latin into the Romance vernacular —
altogether we may well agree that there were few like
him. Then there are glimpses of feudal society scattered
through the work — the huge bear brought from England

and baited almost to death for the delectation of the
people of Ardres, who, however, found themselves bur-
dened for the upkeep with a loaf from every oven, an
obligation which persisted long after there was no bear to
bait; the peasant forced to give her daughter in default
of a lamb to the lady of the castle; the wild largesse of the
newly knighted Arnold to the minstrels, mimes, jongleurs,
mountebanks, and followers of every sort who had come
to the festivity, and his journeyings in many lands; the
amiable, God-fearing Lady Petronilla, who danced and
played with dolls and swam and dived in the fish pond to
the joy of all spectators. Most valuable, perhaps, is
Lambert's account of the castles: the three-story wooden
keep and mound, built early in the twelfth century but
still in use, ampler than most such dwellings, since it contained on the first floor not only the great hall but the
master's bedchamber and two other bedrooms, a heated
dressing-room, the buttery and pantry, though the
kitchen for greater safety formed a separate building
with the quarters of pigs and poultry; and then toward
the close of the century the round stone castle which
Baldwin built at Guines, with a flat leaden roof and
many rooms, including a labyrinth; and the tower which
he reconstructed at Tournehem and equipped with its
infernal dungeons; the great fosse at Ardres, dug in
hunger and misery under the lash of stern taskmasters;
his sky-scraping fortress (*celo contiguam*) at Sangatte
among the dunes of the coast, so defended that if Trojan

Ilium had been manned and equipped in proportion it would still be standing in all its glory!

Of the less rugged feudalism of the close of our century we have a remarkable picture in the *Histoire de Guillaume le Maréchal*, a French poem of more than 19,000 lines discovered and edited in masterly fashion by the late Paul Meyer. Soldier of fortune in his youth, companion at arms of that pattern of knightly *largesse*, the Young King, pilgrim to Jerusalem and Cologne, the Marshal rose to be earl of Striguil and Pembroke and, from 1216 until his death in 1219, regent for Henry III, so that his life is intermingled with the history of four reigns in England and with many events of moment in Ireland and France. His biographer tells us much of the life of the time, especially its tournaments, French sports introduced into England by Richard Lion-Heart and often differing little from actual warfare, and of the large profits made therefrom by a skilful combatant like the Marshal, who, with one companion, captured in less than a year one hundred and three knights, besides horses and armor not entered on the clerk's accounts. Withal the Marshal was a model of feudal virtue, whom Philip Augustus declared the most loyal man he had ever known. Rich in contemporary details, fresh and original in its materials, this unique biography belongs to the new age of vernacular history, being written for the earl's family in language they could understand:

Quant [li] lignages, frére & suers
Orront ce, molt lor iert as cuers,
Que li buens Mar. lor frére
Willemes a fèt de lor pére
Feire tele uevre cum cestui.
& Dex lor dount joie de lui,
Car bien sai que molt s'esjorront
De cest [livre], quant il l'orront,
Por les granz biens & por l'enor
Qu'il orront de lor anseisor!

Ci fine del conte l'estorie,
E Dex en perdurable glorie
Dont que la sue ame soit mise
Et entre ses angles assise!
Amen.

Of autobiography the twelfth century gives us comparatively little, in the modern sense perhaps nothing. We are still in the naïve Middle Ages, and far from the self-consciousness of Petrarch's *Letter to Posterity*. Introspective biography is still strongly religious and monastic, reminding us of those who had earlier striven for 'the gift of tears' or that Richalm whose visions have been set forth by Coulton.[1] For such inner records St. Augustine had left another model, his *Confessions*, and their influence is clear in such a work as the *De vita sua* of Guibert, abbot of Nogent in Picardy from 1104 to *ca.* 1124. Though this confused and scattering work contains much local history, monastic, feudal, and municipal, it has little on Guibert's own work as abbot. So far as it is a personal record it is rather internal — remorse for the sins of youth and the lapses of later years, sincere affec-

[1] *Five Centuries of Religion*, i. 35 ff.

tion for a pious mother who led a semi-monastic life, the temptations of profane learning and the sure refuge of scriptural study and comment, narratives of miracles of saints and visions of demons and divination by texts of Scripture — the whole reflecting many curious aspects of monastic and popular belief, though most readers will hardly find in him, with his latest editor, "the ancestor of memoir writers."

A very different type of monastic autobiography, wholly external and of this world, is seen in Suger's account of his career as head of the great monastery of Saint-Denis, *De rebus in administratione sua gestis*. Abbot from 1122 to his death in 1151, Suger gave much of his time to the administration of the kingdom as well, acting as regent during the absence of Louis VII in the East, while at Saint-Denis he showed himself a capable administrator, increasing the revenues, arranging the archives, and rebuilding the church. Accordingly, we are not surprised that his tale is of lands and rents and buildings and relics and precious stones, not of the internal life of the monastery, still less of his own inner life. This last, it is true, was not his theme, but neither does it appear to have been his special interest. So his other writings comprise no sermons or theological treatises, but tell of his royal masters and their doings. Urged by the brethren to record for posterity the fruits of his prosperous rule, he has undertaken to set this down, "for no hope of vainglory or temporal reward," but as a precaution lest by neglect his church might lose any of its newly acquired or recovered rights or possessions. In and about Saint-Denis he has augmented the income from the weekly *tonlieu*, the *cens*, the *péage*, the mills, and the great fair of the *Lendit*; increased the rents and the amount of land under cultivation, planting vineyards to insure a supply of wine, for which it had before been necessary to pawn the chalices and vestments of the abbey; and bought a town house half a dozen miles away, near the gate of Saint-Merry, "for the more honorable lodging of ourselves, our horses, and our successors, since the business of the kingdom frequently requires our presence." Respecting the remoter possessions of the monastery, as far as the English Channel, a score of chapters tell us of their enlargement and recovery and increased yield from the efforts of one who had busied himself with the ancient title deeds and grants of immunity preserved in the abbey's archives. Greatest detail, however, is given to the rebuilding and decoration of the abbey church, in the style of transition from Romanesque to Gothic, in accordance with an ambition cherished since Suger was a boy in the monastery school. Old and cramped, this was greatly enlarged and replanned, choir, nave, and transepts, with new altars and chapels, doors, and towers, and wonderful windows "rich in sapphires." The great dedication of 11 June 1144, at which twenty archbishops and bishops dedicated as many altars, as more fully narrated in an accompanying treatise, was the crowning point in Suger's ecclesiastical career, a monument to his prudence, his energy, his worldly pomp and glory, and his enlightened patronage of the arts. Suger's light was not to be hidden under a bushel, for his name appears more than once in the sonorous inscriptions over the portals. "Who am I," he asks, "and what my father's house, that I should have presumed to begin and hoped to complete so beautiful a structure, had I not by the mercy of God and his holy martyrs devoted myself mind and body to this work?" We read throughout of earthly riches which he compares to the treasures of Jerusalem and Constantinople, of gold and jewels and mosaics and enamels and costly vestments, of the gems with their mystical meanings, discernible only by the learned, of the scriptural allegories set forth in Latin verse beneath the "splendid variety of the new windows which the hands of many masters of many nations had executed." Of all the precious stones "only the carbuncle was lacking." The cost of item after item is proudly set down — the great golden chalice weighing one hundred and forty ounces and set with jacinth and topaz, the doors gilded "at great expense," seven hundred livres and more for the windows, forty-two gold marks for the high altar, four hundred livres spent for gems for the crucifix "which were worth considerably more."

"Tax not the royal saint with vain expense," said Wordsworth. Vain it had certainly seemed to the austere St. Bernard, some years earlier, as he thundered against the luxury of the new abbey churches. Grant, he says, that the honor of God is served by their immense height, their unnecessary length and breadth, their costly finishings, their strange decorations which distract the attention of the worshippers. As a monk I ask you, why the gold — unless it be to draw more gold from the faithful? Why the spreading candelabra, the golden reliquaries, the gorgeous images of the saints, which serve only to delight the curious while the poor go in want? What have cloistered brethren in common with the grotesque figures which look down on them — unclean monkeys, fierce lions, spotted tigers, centaurs and half-men, knights in battle, hunters sounding their horns, and monsters conpounded of various animals? So great and so marvellous is the variety of these that one is tempted to read the marble rather than the written page and to spend the entire day in admiration of them rather than in meditation on the law of God. "Alas, if there be no shame for this foolishness, why at least is there no sorrow for the cost?" [1]

"Vanity of vanities, saith the preacher," and St. Bernard was first and foremost a preacher, and a fundamentalist preacher at that. Vain above all to him were pride of intellect and absorption in the learning of this world, and his harshest invectives were hurled at the most brilliant intellect of his age, Abaelard, that "scrutinizer of

[1] Migne, *Patrologia Latina*, clxxxii. 916.

majesty and fabricator of heresies" who "deems himself able by human reason to comprehend God altogether." Between a mystic like Bernard and a rationalist like Abaelard there was no common ground, and for the time being the mystic had the church behind him. With Abaelard we have another type of autobiography, the intellectual, in that long tale of misfortune which he addressed to an unknown friend under the title of *Historia suarum calamitatum*.

Abaelard, it is true, was a monk and an abbot, but he became such by force of circumstances and not from choice. Even when he retires into the forests of Champagne or the depths of Brittany, he has always one eye on Paris and his return thither; indeed, his *Historia calamitatum* seems to have been written to prepare the way for his coming back, to serve an immediate purpose rather than for posterity. It shows nothing of monastic humility or religious vocation, but, on the contrary, is full of arrogance of intellect and joy of combat, even of the lust of the flesh and the lust of the eyes and the pride of life. Its author was a vain man, vain of his penetrating mind and skill in debate, vain of his power to draw away others' students, vain even of his success with the fair sex — so that he "feared no repulse from whatever woman he might deign to honor with his love" — always sure of his own opinions and unsparing of his adversaries. He relies on talent rather than on formal preparation, venturing into the closed field of theology and even improvising lectures on those pitfalls of the unwary, the obscurest parts of the prophet Ezekiel. He was by nature always in opposition, a thorn in the side of intellectual and social conformity. In the classroom he was the bright boy who always knew more than his teachers and delighted to confute them, ridiculing old Anselm of Laon, whose reputation he declared to rest upon mere tradition, unsupported by talent or learning, notable chiefly for a wonderful flow of words without meaning or reason, "a fire which gave forth smoke instead of light," like the barren fig tree of the Gospel or the old oak of Lucan, mere shadow of a great name. In the monastery of Saint-Denis he antagonized the monks by attacking the traditions respecting their founder and patron saint. Always it is he who is right and his many enemies who are wrong. And, as becomes a history of his misfortunes, he pities himself much. Objectively, the facts of Abaelard's autobiography can in the main be verified from his other writings and the statements of contemporaries. Subjectively, the *Historia calamitatum* confirms itself throughout, if we discern between the bursts of self-confidence the intervals of irresolution and despondency in what he tries to present as a consistently planned career. The prolixity and the citations of ancient authority are of the Middle Ages, as are the particular problems with which his mind was occupied, but the personality might turn up in any subsequent epoch — 'portrait of a radical by himself'! Yet, just as Heloise's joy in loving belongs to the ages, Abaelard's joy in learning is more specifically of the new renaissance, of which he is the bright particular star.

If the autobiography of Abaelard reveals the new intellectual life of the twelfth century, the advances in political organization are reflected in the writings which now deal in detail with royal courts and their doings. From one point of view these may be regarded as merely a phase of the movement which produced the *chansons de gestes*: if feudal lords listened eagerly to the deeds of their ancestors in the vernacular, the more learned forms of history might well be fostered, or even supervised, by more cultivated rulers such as Henry Plantagenet or the Latin princes of Jerusalem. Henry Plantagenet did much for history in the Anglo-Norman vernacular, as will appear below, and he has even been accused of encouraging Arthurian romance as a literary basis for a new British imperialism. There is, however, a new note in the court histories of the later twelfth century, the bureaucratic, and it is no accident that the best of these centre about the most fully developed administrations of the epoch, the Norman kingdom of Sicily and the Anglo-Norman kingdom of the North. In France historiography is not fully focussed upon the king before the reign of Philip Augustus; in the Empire we have accounts of rulers rather than courts in the historical literature which gathers about Frederick I or the *Carmen* which Petrus de Ebulo dedicates to Henry VI; indeed, this last is Sicilian rather than German, even to its accompanying illustrations of palace life at Palermo. In the Norman kingdoms, on the contrary, bureaucracy is so well established by the twelfth century that we can already discern a court in the administrative sense, with archives, finance, and a professional clerical staff for which a record of the court and its doings is the most natural thing in the world. Even a literature of administration makes its appearance, as we have seen, in the *Tractatus de legibus et consuetudinibus regni Anglie* ascribed to the justiciar Glanvill, and in the *Dialogue* of Richard FitzNeal which describes in detail the workings of the English Exchequer; and we are not surprised to learn that the author of the *Dialogue* has written a heavily documented history in three columns, the first dealing with the English church, the second recounting the great deeds of Henry II, the third treating of many matters both public and relating to the court. This precious *Tricolumnis* has long since been lost, but many of its contents must have passed into the court histories of the reign. Two of these survive from the pens of royal clerks, the anonymous *Gesta Regis Henrici* which long went under the name of Benedict of Peterborough, and its continuation to 1201 by Roger of Hoveden. Both show minute acquaintance with the itinerary of the king and the doings of the royal family, describe embassies and elaborate court ceremonies like the coronation of Richard I, give long lists of barons and castles, and insert complete texts of many official documents, all with a fulness and care for detail which give them a high place among the sources for English constitutional history. Indeed, their simple, matter-of-fact style has been compared to the sobriety and terseness of the documents of the royal chancery, both reflecting the frugal, methodical habits of a household where even the daily allowances of bread and wine and candle ends were fixed by royal ordinance.

The more opulent court of Sicily, though in frequent relations, by marriage and otherwise, with that of the Angevins, possessed a Greek and a Saracen element foreign to the North. Three languages were necessary for the documents of its chancery and the voluminous registers of its lands and revenues, so that the bureaucracy was larger and stronger. Moreover, while the household of Henry II was still ambulatory, the restless king ever on the march, that of his son-in-law William II had its headquarters at Palermo, where the court establishment and the mass of the officials permanently remained, so that its life suggests in many ways that of the Byzantine and Mohammedan East, and the chronicle of its doings would remind us more of a palace history of Bagdad or Constantinople. Time has not dealt kindly with the records of Sicilian royalty, but for the years 1154–69 we have an intimate record of its doings in the *Liber de regno Sicilie* which commonly bears the name of Hugo Falcandus, the work of a member of the curia, probably a notary. "Occupying himself," as he says, "chiefly with the things done about the court," he shows familiar acquaintance with its factions and its procedure, with the life of the palace and the rich capital in which it is set, its port and shops and covered streets. He is a pronounced partisan, holding up the good to admiration and the bad to execration, even as the ancient Romans kept the *imagines* of their ancestors that examples of virtue and evil might ever be before their eyes. He has a marvellous Latin style, vivid, pointed, flexible, and free, with something of the ancient manner and a gift for characterization quite rare in the Middle Ages. There is in him a distinct suggestion of the great writers of Roman antiquity and the Italian Renaissance; whatever his origin, he is at least by adoption a fellow-countryman of Tacitus and Guicciardini.

The growing activity and diversity of European life in the twelfth century is reflected in a large increase in the narratives of brief episodes or particular events, some of which are among the best historical productions of the age. Examples of such writings concern the murder of Charles the Good, count of Flanders, in 1127; the English Battle of the Standard in 1138; the revolt of the Young King of England in 1173; the exploits of Dermot McMurrough in Ireland; the campaigns of Frederick I in Italy; the capture of Lisbon in 1147; and of course the various crusading expeditions, as we shall see more fully below.

Another distinctive mark of the historiography of the twelfth century is its reflection of the expansion of Latin

Christendom to the North and East and in the Mediterranean. Already *ca.* 1075 Adam of Bremen had dedicated to the archbishop of Hamburg that remarkable account of the beginnings of Christianity in the Scandinavian lands which is one of the most informing documents offered by the Middle Ages to the history of exploration. Besides recording the missionary labors which brought the Scandinavian countries within the sphere of Christian civilization, Adam has also something to say of those newer lands to the West, Iceland, Greenland, and Vineland the Good, discovered beyond the dark seas to the westward by intrepid Norse voyagers. The Eastern Baltic and the lands beyond, however, are still a region of myth and fable, peopled by Amazons and Cyclopes, men colored blue and red and green, and Cynocephali who barked and wore their heads on their chests, figures to be found in Pliny and Solinus as well as in the seamen's tales of Adam's own age. This darkness was soon to be dispelled as colonization turned eastward, and already in the twelfth century we can trace with some fulness that eastward expansion of the Germans at the expense of the Slavs which constitutes one of the most fundamental chapters in the history of Central and Eastern Europe. This expansion, in part a religious and missionary movement, is reflected not only in the annals of the newly established bishoprics and monasteries, but in historians like Helmold and Saxo Grammaticus. Helmold's *Chronica Slavorum* recounts the Germanization of the territories between Elbe

and Saale in a long story of border warfare against Sorbs
and Wends and Rugians, of the foundation of new cloisters and new bishoprics like Lübeck and Schwerin, and
of the deeds of holy prelates against the idolaters, all to
the glory of those who rendered this land illustrious by
the sword, the tongue, and the shedding of their own
blood in the righteous cause — in short, German and
Christian *Kultur* imposed by force, as the Teutonic
Knights in the next century were to impose it on the still
heathen Prussians farther east. Meanwhile the Slavic
peoples who retained their independence were producing
their own histories, as seen most notably in Cosmas of
Prague, the father of Bohemian national history. So
Hungary in the twelfth century produces the first life of
its royal saint, Stephen, while the so-called Nestor in-
augurates Russian historiography.

In the South we have already noted the interest taken
by Ordericus in the expansion of the Normans in Spain,
Sicily, and Syria, an expansion in each instance at the
expense of the Saracen. The conquest of Sicily by the
Normans, however, was rather an adjunct to their conquest of Southern Italy from Lombards and Greeks than
a primary object of the early leaders; the expedition
lacked the character of a religious war, and the Saracen
population persisted in the island, which became a fruitful centre of interchange between the peoples of the two
faiths. And if King Roger led expeditions against the
Saracens in Africa, he fought Greek and Latin Christians

with equal impartiality. By the twelfth century Sicilian historiography has lost the note of expansion and become, as we have seen, the record of a court.

In Spain the Christian reconquest has by this time recovered a large part of the Peninsula, and the historical record, hitherto uncertain and fragmentary, begins to take on amplitude and coherence. There is still, however, a strong tincture of legend, and it is significant that the two principal collections of the period group romantic stories about the hard nucleus of fact contained, respectively, in the pilgrimages to Compostela and the adventures of the Cid. And it is even more significant that these collections in their turn go on to make history by holding before men's eyes for many generations the figures of Roland and the Cid, and thus moulding the ideals of Europe as late as Cervantes and Corneille. The *Codex Calixtinus* of Santiago de Compostela has been described and its influence has been traced in the admirable study of Bédier in the third volume of that *Légendes épiques* which must be read by every student of the subject. Put together about the middle of the twelfth century, this codex contains a remarkable collection of miracles wrought at the shrine of St. James; a guide for pilgrims journeying thither by the great roads which led past other noble shrines in France; and the famous Latin chronicle of the Pseudo-Turpin which is intimately connected with the whole cycle of romance strung along these same routes of pilgrimage. French in origin, this material is a monument to the active intercourse between France and Spain in the twelfth century, and before the end of the century these Galician collections are copied and accepted north of the Pyrenees, where they give Latin support to the popular epics in a strange interplay of history and romance. Naturally the struggle with the infidel is stressed in this age as the French pour into the Peninsula in the new holy war. Charlemagne's single expedition to Spain is multiplied by three and spread over fourteen years, conquering the whole land and avenging Roland, who in the *Chanson de Roland* dies with his face toward Spain and his indestructible sword beneath him:

> Turns his face toward the pagan army.
> For this he does it, that he wishes greatly
> That Charles should say and all his men,
> The gentle count has died a conqueror.

More definitely of the *Reconquista* is the Cid "of the splendid beard," the historic Cid of the border wars of the late eleventh century, "the rough and turbulent free-booter, the destroyer of churches, whose lance was equally at the service of Moor or Christian — provided the pay were good" [1] — already on his way to become the pattern of religious zeal and knightly virtue, symbol of the triumph of the Cross over the Crescent, whom Philip II wished canonized as a saint. The Cid Campeador died in 1099, and the next century produced the *Poema de mio Cid* and the Latin *History* of the Leon manuscript, in

---

[1] H. B. Clarke, *The Cid Campeador* (New York, 1897), p. iv.

which he already appears as one who "while he lived in this world always obtained a noble triumph over his adversaries and was never overcome by any one."

Of the Crusades it is not easy to speak briefly. At once wars of religion and of feudal conquest, a commercial and a colonizing movement as well as a phase of the long struggle between East and West, they occupy much of the European stage from 1096 to 1204 and even later, and they give the period much of its movement and color. Their chronicles, Latin, French, Greek, Arabic, Armenian, have been collected in a great folio series by the Académie des Inscriptions et Belles-Lettres, and there further remain the many Western historians of the age who have much to say incidentally of the crusading expeditions. A summary account of the Western sources alone would fill a volume and tell us much of European historiography. Three examples must suffice. First of all, there is the fervent fighting Crusader, who cries *God wills it* on all occasions, to whom the Crusaders are the knights of Christ, the Greeks treacherous, the Turks barbarians and enemies of God. Such a one is the unknown author of the *Gesta Francorum*, which is our most valuable narrative of the First Crusade and the source of most later accounts. Written by an eyewitness in the intervals of events, and completed before 1101, this is a plain and unadorned account by a knight who had all the Crusader's ignorance of the Orient. Knowing no book but the Bible, his simple narrative is vivid and impressive, as he recounts the terrible hardships of the road, the fierce fighting about Antioch, the incredible slaughter in the Holy City. The author admires the Turks as fighters; indeed, if they were only firm in the faith of Christ and the triune God, "none could be found more mighty and brave and skilful in war; yet by God's grace we conquered them" — a grace which he sees manifest in such wonders as the Holy Lance and the miraculous army with the white standards of St. George and other saintly leaders. No 'armchair fighter' in some distant cloister this, but a real Crusader, with the undimmed enthusiasm and the naïve piety of one who might have shouted at Clermont and who, in any case, never turned aside till the Crusader's work was done.

If we read only such accounts as the *Gesta*, we should get the impression of the Crusades as a series of holy wars in which the 'joyful spectacle' of Turks' heads on pikes finds its counterpart in the 'hogs' and 'sows' and 'may Allah curse them!' of the Mohammedan writers. Such impressions must be corrected by calling to mind the colonizing side of the movement, the factories of the Italian cities, the steady immigration from the West, the feudal lordships and the military-religious orders, the peaceful relations with the Moslem population, the gradual adoption of Oriental modes of life, and the tolerant outlook of the resident Christian population. Listen to the following complaint of the consequences of a religious war with Mohammedan Egypt:

Boundless greed has forced us violently out of the most calm tranquillity into a troubled and anxious position! The treasures of Egypt and all its boundless wealth were at our service; our kingdom was secure on that side; we had no one to fear from the South. No danger threatened those who wished to come to us by sea; our men could without fear and under good conditions enter Egypt for trade and commerce. The Egyptians, in turn, brought us foreign riches and wares wholly unknown to our people. Their coming always yielded us advantage and honor. In addition, the immeasurable tribute which they paid yearly was a source of strength and increase both to the royal and to private treasuries. But now all has turned out to our loss; the most fine gold is changed, my harp also is turned to mourning. Wherever I turn, danger threatens us on all sides. We can no longer cross the sea in safety, every neighboring land about us belongs to the enemy, and the kingdoms which surround ours are preparing for our destruction.[1]

The author of this passage was an ecclesiastic, nay an archbishop, the famous William of Tyre, whose *Historia Hierosolymitana*, in twenty-three books, written between 1169 and 1184, is the most voluminous of all the crusading histories and one of the chief works of the age. Though untrustworthy for the early period, it is full of information concerning the Latin Kingdom in the author's own time, and presents steadily the point of view of the resident Christians in contrast with the more fanatical newcomers. William is an excellent illustration of the culture of the Latin East. Born in Syria, he was educated in the West and quotes his classics freely, yet he also knows Greek and Arabic. Chancellor of the Latin Kingdom, he displays its organization and its vicissitudes and the discords which hastened its end a few years later; but he

[1] William of Tyre, xx. 10. Cf. D. C. Munro, in *Essays on the Crusades* (Burlington, 1903), p. 28.

has a native's fondness for the country and its milk and honey. If he goes round about Zion and tells the towers thereof, he also describes the other cities of Syria and Egypt, especially his own metropolis of Tyre, with its hoary antiquity, its walls and harbor, its Tyrian purple, its manufactures of fine glass, and its well watered gardens and fields of sugar cane. The good archbishop writes more like a Syrian than a Crusader; indeed, we might almost be listening to the Moslem traveller, ibn Jubair, who visited Tyre in 1184 and describes the tolerance of its Christian inhabitants and the quiet and peaceful life of the 'true believers' who live under them and worship in their own mosques.

By the time of the Fourth Crusade (1201–04) the long struggle between the religious and the secular motives turns definitely in favor of the secular. Begun as a well planned expedition against the centre of Mohammedan power in Egypt, this Crusade was diverted by commercial and political influences, until it ended in the conquest of Constantinople and the establishment there of a short-lived Latin empire — a 'crime against civilization' by its wanton destruction of the material remains of Byzantine culture, and against Christendom by breaking down the great military buffer against invasion from Asia. The classic narrative of the expedition comes from the pen of Geoffrey de Villehardouin, a knight of Champagne who was one of the leaders and became marshal of the new kingdom in the East, and a very engaging account it is, in the vivid and vigorous vernacular which has gained him an honorable place in the history of French literature. Its literary charm, however, long gave it undue historical weight, for Villehardouin makes the diversion to Zara and Constantinople appear merely as a series of accidents rather than a well directed plan, and the suppressions in his more or less official narrative need to be corrected from others. Even then, between the lines of the marshal, we can see the lower civilization of the Latins as compared with the Greeks whom they overthrew. He says, indeed, that when the Crusaders reached Constantinople and saw "the high walls and the rich towers round about it and the rich palaces and lofty churches, so many that no one could believe if he did not see with his own eyes, and the length and the breadth of the city which of all others was sovereign, there was none so bold whose flesh did not tremble"; but he recounts complacently the plunder and destruction of all this splendor. To him it is all a great military exploit, as indeed it was, just as when he later rode about the land taking lesser cities, and he is blind to the higher side of Byzantine civilization. Like the other great lords of the expedition, he has the soul of a freebooter. Villehardouin was a layman and wrote in French, and we have now entered the thirteenth century. Before its close another lay historian, Joinville, will wonder whether crusading is worth while as compared with life in his castle in Champagne, and Rutebeuf's *Descroizié*

will argue frankly for staying at home as a safer invest-
ment:

> Hom puet mult bien en cest payx
> Gaaignier Dieu cens grant damage.

As regards external form, the historical works of the
twelfth century reflect the humanism of the age in a fondness for Latin verse. Often, as in Ordericus, this is manifested by incorporating epitaphs, extracts from the rolls
of the dead, and other occasional poems; but in several
instances the chronicle itself is written in verse, whether
Latin hexameter of the classical type or mediaeval
rhymed couplets. Such compositions were especially
popular in Italy. Thus Moses of Bergamo, whom we
shall later meet at Constantinople, celebrated the glories
and early history of his commune in a poem of three
hundred and seventy-two rhyming hexameters, while an
unknown Pisan has left us a versified account of the expedition of his countrymen against Majorca in 1114.
Much historical poetry centred about the deeds of the
Hohenstaufen emperors in Italy, such as the *Ligurinus*
of Gunther (1187), the *Pantheon* and *Gesta Friderici* of
Geoffrey of Viterbo, and the fulsome eulogies of Petrus
de Ebulo. Such works were, however, not limited to
Italians: Geoffrey was educated at Bamberg, while Gunther, who wrote so skilfully that his poem was long considered a production of some later humanist, was a monk
of Pairis in Alsace. France is represented, though in more
halting fashion, by the *Philippis*, in which William the

Breton, early in the thirteenth century, celebrated the deeds of Philip Augustus.

Of greater permanent significance than these far-off imitations of the ancients is the use of the vernacular as the language of history. This movement appears about the same time in France and Germany, in the Regensburg *Kaiserchronik* of *ca.* 1150 and at the Anglo-Norman court, but France soon takes the lead. True, the vernacular is to be found much earlier, in that *Anglo-Saxon Chronicle* whose splendid prose constitutes one of our most faithful and most vivid narratives of English history, but this comes to an end in 1154, with the accession of the first Plantagenet king, the French of whose court soon became a language of history. The new movement was Norman in its origin, and continued throughout the century. Appearing first in verse, the new style found its best representative in that Master Wace of Jersey whose *Roman de Brut* and *Roman de Rou* traced the origins of the British and Norman lines of rulers from Brutus and Rollo respectively. Often disdained as a mere rhymester, Wace is now known to have based his work on the older Norman historians and on specific local sources of information which entitle him to be regarded as an historian and not merely as a poet. Indeed, his terse and sober style was too plain for the courtiers of his age, and he had to give way to more diffuse compositions in the style of the feudal romances. Before the end of the century Normandy has also begun to produce an historical literature in prose, which soon spreads to other parts of France in Villehardouin, Joinville, and other less famous writers in the vernacular.

By 1200 vernacular history had come to stay, and this fact is one of more than linguistic or literary significance, since it involved ultimately the secularization and popularization of history. So long as history was confined to Latin, it perforce remained primarily an affair of the clergy and reflected their preoccupations and view of the world. When it came to be written for laymen, it must make its appeal to them, first at the courts which gave its writers their support, later in the towns whose chronicles meet us in the later period of the Middle Ages. History for laymen and history for the people necessarily meant history in the language of the lay world, that world of courts and towns which had grown so fast in the course of the twelfth century.

BIBLIOGRAPHICAL NOTE

No survey of mediaeval historiography exists such as the modern period owes to E. Fueter or the classical to H. Ulrici, J. B. Bury, and J. T. Shotwell. There is, however, a general bibliographical guide to collections and editions in A. Potthast, *Bibliotheca historica medii aevi* (second edition, Leipzig, 1896); and there are useful general accounts by countries. Of these the most comprehensive and the most valuable for detailed information and suggestion is A. Molinier, *Les sources de l'histoire de France* (Paris, 1901–06), of which the second volume covers the twelfth century. Likewise excellent is W. Wattenbach, *Deutschlands Geschichtsquellen im Mittelalter* (sixth edition, Berlin, 1893–94). There is nothing parallel for England, though individual writers are summarily treated in C. Gross, *Sources and Literature of English History to about 1485* (second edition, London, 1915). U. Balzani, *Italy*, is the best volume in the popular series *Early Chroniclers of Europe* (London, 1883; third Italian edition, Milan, 1909). R. Ballester y Castell, *Las fuentes narrativas de la historia de España durante la edad media* (Palma, 1908), is slight.

Good small volumes on special aspects of our subject are: C. Jenkins, *The Monastic Chronicler* (London, 1922); R. L. Poole, *Chronicles and Annals* (Oxford, 1926); H. Delehaye, *The Legends of the Saints* (New York, 1907); B. Schmeidler, *Italienische Geschicht-schreiber des XII. und XIII. Jahrhunderts* (Leipzig, 1909); B. Lasch, *Das Erwachen und die Entwickelung der historischen Kritik im Mittelalter* (Breslau, 1887); Marie Schulz, *Die Lehre von der historischen Methode bei den Geschichtschreibern des Mittelalters* (Berlin, 1909).

The best introduction to the historians of our period will be found in the prefaces to the critical editions prepared by great modern scholars such as Stubbs, Waitz, Liebermann, and Delisle, whether in the great collections of the *Rolls Series* and the *Monumenta Germaniae Historica,* or elsewhere like Delisle's Ordericus and Robert of Torigni. See also Paul Meyer's edition of Guillaume le Maréchal (Paris, 1891–1901); B. Schmeidler's Adam of Bremen (Hanover, 1917); and R. L. Poole's *Historia pontificalis* (Oxford, 1927).

Certain chroniclers of our period (Ordericus, William of Malmesbury, etc.) are translated into English in the *Bohn Antiquarian Library*; and (Robert of Torigni, Gervase of Canterbury, etc.) in J. Stevenson, *The Church Historians of England* (London, 1853–58). Others may be found in separate versions, e. g., *The Autobiography* of *Guibert, Abbot of Nogent-sous-Coucy,* translated by C. C. S. Bland (London, 1925); Jocelin of Brakelonde, translated by Ernest Clarke (London, 1903); Villehardouin, in *Everyman's Library.* Still others (Otto of Freising, William of Tyre, etc.) are announced in the *Records of Civilization* published by Columbia University, in which series the early part of the *Liber pontificalis* has already been issued. French translations of Ordericus, Suger, various historians of the Crusades, etc., are in F. P. G. Guizot, *Collection des mémoires relatifs à l'histoire de France* (Paris, 1823–35); others, accompanying the Latin text, in the new series, *Les classiques de l'histoire de France au moyen âge,* edited by L. Halphen. Many German chronicles of the period (Otto of Freising, Adam of Bremen, Helmold, Cosmas of Prague, annals, etc.) are translated in *Die Geschichtschreiber der deutschen Vorzeit* (Berlin and Leipzig, since 1849).

Recent critical studies of writers discussed in this chapter are: B. Schmeidler, "Der Briefwechsel zwischen Abälard und Heloise eine Fälschung?," in *Archiv für Kulturgeschichte,* xi. 1–30 (1913); A. Hofmeister, "Studien über Otto von Freising," in *Neues Archiv,* xxxvii. 99–161, 635–768 (1911–12); E. Besta, *Il "Liber de regno Siciliae,"* in *Miscellanea A. Salinas* (Palermo, 1907), pp. 283–306; F. L. Ganshof, "A propos de la Chronique de Lambert d'Ardres," in *Mélanges Ferdinand Lot* (Paris, 1925), pp. 205–234, an answer to the attempt of W. Erben (*Neues Archiv,* xliv. 314–340) to place this chronicle in the fifteenth century. For Wace, cf. my *Norman Institutions,* pp. 268–272.

CHAPTER IX

THE TRANSLATORS FROM GREEK AND ARABIC

THE Renaissance of the twelfth century, like its Italian successor three hundred years later, drew its life from two principal sources. Each was based in part upon the knowledge and ideas already present in the Latin West, in part upon an influx of new learning and literature from the East. But whereas the Renaissance of the fifteenth century was concerned primarily with literature, that of the twelfth century was concerned even more with philosophy and science. And while in the Quattrocento the foreign soui :e was wholly Greek, in the twelfth century it was also Arabic, derived from Spain and Sicily and Syria and Africa as well as from Constantinople. To these new springs of intellectual life we must now direct our attention.

That the literature and science of Europe had their immediate origin in Greece and passed thence to Rome is one of the commonplaces of history. In spite, however, of the Greek derivation of Roman literature and art there was little direct translation of Greek classics after the Scipionic age. Adaptation of course there was, very direct in the case of Terence and Cicero and the so-called Latin *Iliad*, but the great works of the Greeks remained for the most part untranslated in classical antiquity. And, of course, men continued to write in Greek long after the political triumph of Rome. Not only Hippocrates in the time of Herodotus, but Galen in the second century of the Christian era, wrote their medical works in Greek. Euclid was followed by the Alexandrine mathematicians and by the geography and astronomy of Ptolemy (*ca.* 160 A.D.). To Aristotle and Plato succeeded the Greek Neoplatonists. Accordingly, when the encyclopedists of the fifth to the eighth centuries gathered up ancient learning for their own and later times, it was Latin learning alone on which they drew. Boethius, it is true, that last of the ancients, had a plan for translating the whole of Aristotle and Plato, but he completed only the logical works of Aristotle and adaptations of Greek mathematics, and even the logic largely disappeared in the confused period which followed. Those indefatigable compilers, Isidore and Bede, knowing no Greek, were perforce limited to Latin sources, and their science, thin and barren and often fantastic, carried on a bare modicum of ancient learning to the mediaeval world. Based upon the briefer manuals of the later Empire, this knowledge was by them further condensed into small packages as a viaticum for the long journey through the Dark Ages, and it was desiccated and often predigested in the process.

To these meagre manuals the early Middle Ages made no significant additions from the Greek. Some direct acquaintance with Greek medicine lingered on in Southern Italy, but it was relatively small. In the ninth century Hilduin and John the Scot translated the Pseudo-Dionysius. In the eleventh century some hagiology passed to Amalfi and Naples. As a whole, however, the period before the twelfth century was distinguished by its ignorance of Greek. Here and there a phrase, an alphabet, a list of numerals, and the traces of Greek in the West in the early Middle Ages are soon exhausted. Even the alphabet was lost: at the hands of the mediaeval scribe a Greek word becomes gibberish or is omitted with *grecum* inserted in its place — it was 'all Greek' to him. Even in the twelfth century the leading humanist, John of Salisbury, "never quotes a Greek author unless he is available in a Latin translation."

Meanwhile throughout the Eastern Empire, and especially at Constantinople, the Greek tradition lived on. There Greek was the official language of law and government, the language of the Orthodox church, of learning, and of literature. Additions to knowledge and letters were relatively small, but the ancients were reverently copied and studied. Commentaries and encyclopaedias, grammars and dictionaries, books of quotations and elegant extracts, kept alive acquaintance with classical Greek. Copied and recopied, the ancient classics were preserved. The words of the immortals, as Frederic Harrison says,[1] were here servilely repeated, but without

[1] *Byzantine History in the Early Middle Ages* (London, 1900), pp. 36–37.

this "the immortals would have died long ago," as they had already died in the West.

Moreover, if Greek literature had no expansion to the West in this period, the learning of the Greeks spread widely to the eastward by translation into Syriac, Hebrew, and Arabic, not to mention the ecclesiastical writings which were turned into Armenian, Georgian, and Coptic, these versions sometimes preserving works of which the Greek originals have been lost, but exerting no influence on Latin Europe. The Semitic versions, on the other hand, are of the greatest importance for the West, constituting as they did the chief vehicle for the transmission of Greek science and philosophy to Latin Europe, together with the additions which had been made en route. The route was at times long and devious, from Greek into Syriac or Hebrew, thence into Arabic and thence into Latin, often with Spanish as an intermediary, but it was much travelled and led at last to the Latin West.

The story begins in Syria, where the rich Aramaic literature was fed in part by translations of Aristotle and Greek theologians. Some of these remained in Syria to await the Arab conqueror of the seventh century, others were carried by Nestorian refugees to the Persian court and thus again to the Arabs. The Saracens, with no native philosophy and science of their own, but with a marvellous power of assimilating the culture of others, quickly absorbed whatever they found in Western Asia, while in course of time they added much from their own observation and from the peoples farther to the East. Arabic translations were made directly from the Greek, as in the case of Ptolemy's *Almagest* (A.D. 827), as well as from Syriac and Hebrew. Certain of the caliphs especially favored learning, while the universal diffusion of the Arabic language made communication easy and spread a common culture throughout Islam, regardless of political divisions. The most vigorous scientific and philosophical activity of the early Middle Ages lay in the lands of the Prophet, whether in the fields of medicine and mathematics or in those of astronomy, astrology, and alchemy. To their Greek inheritance the Arabs added something of their own: observation of disease sufficiently accurate to permit of identification; large advances in arithmetic, algebra, and trigonometry, where we must also take account of Hindu contributions; and the standard astronomical tables of the Middle Ages. The reception of this science in Western Europe marks a turning-point in the history of European intelligence.

Until the twelfth century the intellectual contacts between Christian Europe and the Arab world were few and unimportant. They belong almost entirely to the age of the Crusades, but they owe very little to the Crusades themselves. The Crusaders were men of action, not men of learning, and little can be traced in the way of translations in Palestine and Syria. The known translators in Syria, Stephen of Pisa, *ca.* 1127, and Philip of

Tripoli a century later, are little more than names to us, the former associated with the medicine of Ali-ben-Abbas, the latter with that widely popular work, *The Secret of Secrets*, which passed under the name of Aristotle. Adelard of Bath also visited Syria early in the twelfth century, but we do not know that he carried any texts away with him. North Africa had been Mohammedan since the seventh century, and although it boasted comparatively few schools of its own, it was the great highway between the East and Spain. Thither in course of time came certain adventurous Italians like Constantine the African — Italian at least by adoption, for he died a monk of Monte Cassino — and Leonard of Pisa. Constantine seems to have given a new impulse to medicine by his translations of Galen and Hippocrates and Isaac the Jew, while Leonard of Pisa, son of a Pisan customs official in North Africa, acquired there a familiarity with Arabic mathematics which made him the leading European mathematician of the thirteenth century. There was one Italian land which took more direct part in the movement, namely Sicily. Midway between Europe and Africa, Sicily had been under Arab rule from 902 to 1091, and under the Normans who followed it retained a large Mohammedan element in its population. Moreover, it had many commercial relations with Mohammedan countries, while King Roger conducted campaigns in Northern Africa and Frederick II made an expedition to Palestine. Arabian physicians and astrologers were employed at the Sicilian court, and one of the great works of Arabic learning, the *Geography* of Edrisi, was composed at King Roger's command. A contemporary scholar, Eugene the Emir, translated the *Optics* of Ptolemy, while under Frederick II Michael Scot and Theodore of Antioch made versions of Arabic works on zoölogy for the Emperor's use. Frederick also maintained a correspondence on scientific topics with many sovereigns and scholars of Mohammedan lands, and the work of translation went on under his son and successor Manfred, while we should probably refer to this Sicilian centre some of the versions by unknown authors.

Nevertheless the most important channel by which the new learning reached Western Europe ran through the Spanish peninsula. "Spain," says W. P. Ker,[1] "from the Rock in the South, which is a pillar of Hercules, to the Pass in the North, which is Roncesvalles, is full of the visions of stories." It has its romance of commerce, from the 'corded bales' of the Tyrian trader to the silver fleets of the Indies; of discovery and conquest, as personified in Columbus and the conquistadores; of crusading and knight errantry in the Cid and Don Quixote. It has also its romance of scholarship, of adventure in new paths of learning and even in forbidden bypaths. In consequence of the Saracen conquest, the Peninsula became for the greater portion of the Middle Ages a part of the Mohammedan East, heir to its learning and its science, to its

[1] *Two Essays* (Glasgow, 1918), p. 23.

magic and astrology, and the principal means of their introduction into Western Europe. When, in the twelfth century, the Latin world began to absorb this Oriental lore, the pioneers of the new learning turned chiefly to Spain, where one after another sought the key to knowledge in the mathematics and astronomy, the astrology and medicine and philosophy which were there stored up; and throughout the twelfth and thirteenth centuries Spain remained the land of mystery, of the unknown yet knowable, for inquiring minds beyond the Pyrenees. The great adventure of the European scholar lay in the Peninsula.

In general, the lure of Spain began to act only in the twelfth century, and the active impulse toward the spread of Arabic learning came from beyond the Pyrenees and from men of diverse origins. The chief names are Adelard of Bath, Plato of Tivoli, Robert of Chester, Hermann of Carinthia, with his pupil Rudolf of Bruges, and Gerard of Cremona, while in Spain itself we have Dominicus Gondisalvi, Hugh of Santalla, and a group of Jewish scholars, Petrus Alphonsi, John of Seville, Savasorda, and Abraham ben Ezra. Much in their biography and relations with one another is still obscure. Their work was at first confined to no single place, but translation was carried on at Barcelona, Tarazona, Segovia, Leon, Pamplona, as well as beyond the Pyrenees at Toulouse, Béziers, Narbonne, and Marseilles. Later, however, the chief centre became Toledo. An exact date for this new movement cannot be fixed, now that criticism has removed the year 1116 from an early title of Plato of Tivoli, but the astronomical tables of Adelard are dated 1126, and this whole group of translators, save Gerard of Cremona, can be placed within the second quarter of the twelfth century. They owed much to ecclesiastical patronage, especially to Raymond, archbishop of Toledo, and his contemporary Michael, bishop of Tarazona. Besides a large amount of astrology, inevitable in an age which regarded astrology as merely applied astronomy and a study of great practical utility, their attention was given mainly to astronomy and mathematics.

The latter half of the twelfth century saw the most industrious and prolific of all these translators from the Arabic, Gerard of Cremona. Fortunately we have a brief biographical note and list of his works, drawn up by his pupils in imitation of the catalogue of Galen's writings and affixed to Gerard's version of Galen's *Tegni*, lest the translator's light be hidden under a bushel and others receive credit for work which he left anonymous. From this we learn that, a scholar from his youth and master of the content of Latin learning, he was drawn to Toledo by love of Ptolemy's *Almagest*, which he could not find among the Latins. There he discovered a multitude of Arabic books in every field, and, pitying the poverty of the Latins, learned Arabic in order to translate them. His version of the *Almagest* bears the date of 1175. Before his death, which came at Toledo in

1187 at the age of seventy-three, he had turned into Latin the seventy-one Arabic works of this catalogue, besides perhaps a score of others. Three of these are logical, the *Posterior Analytics* of Aristotle with the commentaries of Themistius and al-Farabi; several are mathematical, including Euclid's *Elements*, the *Spherics* of Theodosius, a tract of Archimedes, and various treatises on geometry, algebra, and optics. The catalogue of works on astronomy and astrology is considerable, as is also the list of the scientific writings of Aristotle, but the longest list of all is medical, Galen and Hippocrates and the rest, who were chiefly known in these versions throughout the later Middle Ages. Indeed, more of Arabic science in general passed into Western Europe at the hands of Gerard of Cremona than in any other way.

After Gerard of Cremona, Roger Bacon lists Alfred the Englishman, Michael Scot, and Hermann the German as the principal translators from the Arabic, all of whom worked in Spain in the earlier thirteenth century. Alfred was a philosopher, concerned especially with expounding the natural philosophy of Aristotle, although he was also known for his version of two pseudo-Aristotelian treatises. Michael Scot first appears at Toledo in 1217 as the translator of al-Bitrogi *On the Sphere*, and by 1220 he had made the standard Latin version of Aristotle *On Animals*, not to mention his share in the transmission of the commentaries of Averroës on Aristotle and his own important works on astrology. Hermann the German, toward the middle of the century, was likewise concerned with Aristotle and Averroës, particularly the *Ethics*, *Poetics*, and *Rhetoric* and the commentaries thereon. Lesser writers of the same period concerned themselves with astrology and medicine.

None of these men from beyond the Pyrenees seems to have known Arabic when he came to Spain, some not when they left, and they worked perforce through interpreters, usually converted Jews. Thus while Gerard of Cremona used a Mozarab named Galippus, Michael Scot is said to have owed much to a Jew named Andrew, who is probably identical with Master Andrew, canon of Palencia, whom the Pope praises in 1225 for his knowledge of Arabic, Hebrew, Chaldee, and Latin, as well as the seven liberal arts. Sometimes Jews are themselves the authors or translators, as in the case of Petrus Alphonsi, John of Seville, Abraham ibn Ezra, and the astronomers of Alfonso X. Apparently their interpreting frequently took the form of translating from Arabic into the current Spanish idiom, which the Christian translator then turned into Latin. This fact helps to explain the inaccuracies of many of the versions, although in general they are slavishly literal, even to carrying over the Arabic article. We must also bear in mind that there was a large amount of translation from Arabic into Hebrew and then later into Latin, as any one can verify by turning to Steinschneider's great volume on Hebrew translations.

In this process of translation and transmission accident and convenience played a large part. No general survey of the material was made, and the early translators groped somewhat blindly in the mass of new matter suddenly disclosed to them. Brief works were often taken first because they were brief and the fundamental treatises were long and difficult; commentators were often preferred to the subject of the commentary. Moreover, the translators worked in different places, so that they might easily duplicate one another's work, and the earliest or most accurate version was not always the most popular. Much was translated to which the modern world is indifferent, something was lost which we should willingly recover, yet the sum total is highly significant. From Spain came the philosophy and natural science of Aristotle and his Arabic commentators in the form which was to transform European thought in the thirteenth century. The Spanish translators made most of the current versions of Galen and Hippocrates and of the Arab physicians like Avicenna. Out of Spain came the new Euclid, the new algebra, and treatises on perspective and optics. Spain was the home of astronomical tables and astronomical observation from the days of Maslama and al-Zarkali to those of Alfonso the Wise, and the meridian of Toledo was long the standard of computation for the West, while we must also note the current compends of astronomy, like al-Fargani, as well as the generally received version of Ptolemy's *Almagest*, for the love of which Gerard of Cremona made the long journey to Toledo. The great body of Eastern astrology came through Spain, as did something of Eastern alchemy.

This Spanish tide flowed over the Pyrenees into Southern France, to centres like Narbonne, Béziers, Toulouse, Montpellier, and Marseilles, where the new astronomy appears as early as 1139 and traces can also be found of the astrology, philosophy, and medicine of the Arabs on into the fourteenth century. Here the share of Jewish translators was large, perhaps even larger relatively than in Spain; and many of the versions came by way of the Hebrew.

Besides these known works in the several Mediterranean lands, a place must also be kept for the numerous translations from the Arabic of which both author and land are unknown. Here we must group, not only much scattered material of minor importance, especially in astrology, but also certain fundamental works like the *Physics*, *Metaphysics*, and several lesser works of Aristotle on natural science, as these appear in the West about 1200. There is also at least one anonymous version from the Arabic of the *Almagest* and the *Quadripartitum* of Ptolemy. With minor exceptions no names of translators are attached to the Latin literature of alchemy which purports to come from the Arabic, like the writings of the so-called Geber.

The indebtedness of the Western world to the Arabs is well illustrated in the scientific and commercial terms which its various languages have borrowed untranslated from the Arabic. Words like algebra, zero, cipher tell their own tale, as do 'Arabic' numerals and the word algorism which long distinguished their use as taught by al-Khwarizmi. In astronomy the same process is exemplified in almanac, zenith, nadir, and azimuth. From the Arabic we get alchemy, and perhaps chemistry, as well as alcohol, alkali, elixir, alembic, not to mention pharmaceutical terms like syrup and gum arabic. In the field of trade and navigation we have bazar and tariff, admiral and arsenal, and products of Mohammedan lands such as sugar and cotton, the muslin of Mosul and the damask of Damascus, the leather of Cordova and Morocco. Such fossils of our vocabulary reveal whole chapters of human intercourse in the Mediterranean.

If Arabic learning reached Latin Christendom at many points, direct translation from the Greek was in the twelfth century almost wholly confined to Italy, where the most important meeting-point of Greek and Latin culture was the Norman kingdom of Southern Italy and Sicily. Long a part of the Byzantine Empire, this region still retained Greek traditions and a numerous Greek-speaking population, and it had not lost contact with the East. In the eleventh century the merchants of Amalfi maintained an active commerce with Constantinople and Syria; Byzantine craftsmen wrought great bronze doors for the churches and palaces of the South; and travelling monks brought back fragments of Greek legend and theology to be turned into Latin. Libraries of Greek origin, chiefly of biblical and theological writings, were gathered into the Basilian monasteries, and more comprehensive collections were formed at the Norman capital. King Roger and his successors directly encouraged translation into Latin, indeed the two principal translators of the age were members of the royal administration, Henricus Aristippus and Eugene the Emir, both of whom have left eulogies of King William I which celebrate his philosophic mind and wide-ranging tastes and the attractions of his court for scholars.

Archdeacon of Catania in 1156, when he worked at his Plato in the army before Benevento, Aristippus was the principal officer of the Sicilian curia from 1160 to 1162, when his dismissal was soon followed by his death. Besides versions of Gregory Nazianzen and Diogenes, which, if completed, have not reached us, Aristippus was the first translator of the *Meno* and *Phaedo* of Plato and of the fourth book of Aristotle's *Meteorology*, and his Latin rendering remained in current use during the Middle Ages and the early Renaissance. An observer of natural phenomena on his own account, he was also instrumental in bringing manuscripts to Sicily from the library of the Emperor Manuel at Constantinople. One of these possesses special importance, a beautiful codex of Ptolemy's *Almagest*, from which the first Latin version was made by a visiting scholar about 1160. The translator tells us that he was much aided by Eugene the Emir, "a man most learned in Greek and Arabic and not ignorant of Latin," who likewise translated Ptolemy's *Optics* from the Arabic. The scientific and mathematical bent of the Sicilian school is seen in still other works which were probably first turned into Latin here: the *Data*, *Optics*, and *Catoptrics* of Euclid, the *De motu* of Proclus, and the *Pneumatics* of Hero of Alexandria. A poet of some importance in his native Greek, Eugene is likewise associated with the transmission to the West of two curious bits of Oriental literature, the prophecy of the Erythraean Sibyl and the Sanskrit fable of *Kalila and Dimna*. If it be added that the new versions of Aristotle's *Logic* were in circulation at the court of William I, and that an important group of New Testament manuscripts can be traced to the scribes of King Roger's court, we get some further measure of the intellectual interests of twelfth-century Sicily, while the medical school of Salerno must not be forgotten as a centre of attraction and diffusion for scientific knowledge.

Italy had no other royal court to serve as a centre of the new learning, and no other region where East and West met in such constant and fruitful intercourse. In other parts of the peninsula we must look less for resident Greeks than for Latins who learned their Greek at Constantinople, as travellers, as diplomats, or as members of the not inconsiderable Latin colony made up chiefly from the great commercial republics of Venice and Pisa.

At a theological disputation held in Constantinople before the Emperor in 1136, we are told that "there were present not a few Latins, among them three wise men skilled in the two languages and most learned in letters, namely James a Venetian, Burgundio a Pisan, and the third, most famous among Greeks and Latins above all others for his knowledge of both literatures, Moses by name, an Italian from the city of Bergamo, and he was chosen by all to be a faithful interpreter for both sides." Each of these scholars is known to us from other sources, and they stand out as the principal Italian translators of the age, beyond the limits of the Sicilian kingdom. James of Venice was the translator of the *New Logic* of Aristotle; Moses of Bergamo, who found his eastern connections by way of Venice, has left us fragmentary remains of a many-sided activity, as grammarian, translator, poet, and collector of manuscripts, which justifies us in considering him a prototype of the men who 'settled *hoti*'s business' in the fifteenth century. Burgundio the Pisan is a well known figure in the public life of his native city who made several visits to Constantinople. Although translation from the Greek seems to have been the occupation of his leisure moments only, his output was more considerable than that of any of his Latin contemporaries. Much of it was theology, including works of Basil and Chrysostom and John of Damascus which exerted a distinct influence on Latin thought. Philosophy was represented by Nemesius, law by the Greek quotations in the *Digest*, agriculture by an extract from the *Geoponica*. He was perhaps best known as the author of the current translations of the *Aphorisms* of Hippocrates and ten works of that Galen whom another Pisan, Stephen of Antioch, helped bring in from the Arabic. His epitaph celebrates the universal learning of this *optimus interpres*:

Omne quod est natum terris sub sole locatum
Hic plene scivit scibile quicquid erat.

Less noteworthy than Burgundio, two other members of the Pisan colony at Constantinople should also be mentioned, Hugo Eterianus and his brother Leo, generally known as Leo Tuscus. Hugo, though master of both tongues, was not so much a translator as an active advocate of Latin doctrine in controversy with Greek theologians, a polemic career which was crowned with a cardinal's hat by Lucius III. Leo, an interpreter in the Emperor's household, translated the mass of St. Chrysostom and a dream-book (*Oneirocriticon*) of Ahmed ben Sirin. The interest in signs and wonders which prevailed at Manuel's court is further illustrated by one Paschal the Roman, also a translator of religious matter, who compiled another dream-book at Constantinople in 1165 and is probably the author of the version of Kiranides made there in 1169; as well as by other occult works which found their way westward about this time, perhaps in part from the imperial library. Indeed the relations, formal and informal, between the Greek empire on the one hand, and the Papacy and the Western empire on the other, offered many occasions for literary intercourse; and while we hear most of the resultant disputes between Greek and Latin theologians, it is altogether likely that other materials came west in ways which have so far escaped detection.

North of the Alps there is little to record in the way of translation, although it is probable that certain of the anonymous translators who worked in Italy came from other lands. In Germany we have the *Dialogi* with the Greeks written down by Anselm of Havelberg about 1150, and the *De diversitate persone et nature* which another emissary of the Western Empire brought back in 1179. Before the middle of the century a monk in Hungary, Cerbanus, translated the *Ekatontades* of Maximus the Confessor and perhaps also a treatise of John of Damascus. In 1167 a certain William the Physician, originally from Gap in Provence, brought back Greek codices from Constantinople to the monastery of Saint-Denis at Paris, where he later became abbot (1172–86), while the works of the Pseudo-Dionysius were translated by John Sarrazin, who also visited the Greek East in search of manuscripts.

Finally there remain to be mentioned the anonymous translations, made for the most part doubtless in Italy. Where we are fortunate enough to have the prefaces, these works can be dated approximately and some facts can be determined with respect to their authors, as in the case of the first Latin version of the *Almagest*, made in

Sicily about 1160, and a version of Aristotle's *Posterior Analytics* (1128–59) preserved in a manuscript of the cathedral of Toledo. In the majority of cases no such evidence has been handed down, and we have no guide beyond the dates of codices and the citations of texts in a form directly derived from the Greek. Until investigation has proceeded considerably further than at present, the work of the twelfth century in many instances cannot clearly be separated from that of the earlier Middle Ages on the one hand, and on the other from that of the translators of the thirteenth and fourteenth centuries who follow in direct succession. Often we know only that a particular work had been translated from the Greek before the time of the Italian humanists. The most important body of Greek material with which the twelfth century may have occupied itself anonymously is the writings of Aristotle. The *Physics*, *Metaphysics*, and briefer works on natural history reach Western Europe about 1200; the *Politics*, *Ethics*, *Rhetoric*, and *Economics* only in the course of the next two generations. In nearly every instance translations are found both from the Greek and from the Arabic, and nearly all are undated. At present about all that can be said is that by the turn of the century traces are found of versions from the Greek in the case of the *Physics*, *De caelo*, *De anima*, and the *Parva naturalia*, and perhaps of the *Metaphysics*.

On the personal side these Hellenists of the twelfth century have left little of themselves. James of Venice is only a name; the translator of the *Almagest* is not even that. Moses of Bergamo we know slightly through the accident which has preserved one of his letters; others survive almost wholly through their prefaces. Characteristic traits or incidents are few — Moses lamenting the loss of his Greek library, and the three pounds of gold it had cost him; the Pisan secretary of Manuel Comnenus trailing after the emperor on the tortuous marches of his Turkish campaigns; Burgundio redeeming his son's soul from purgatory by translating Chrysostom in the leisure moments of his diplomatic journeys; a Salerno student of medicine braving the terrors of Scylla and Charybdis in order to see an astronomical manuscript just arrived from Constantinople, and remaining in Sicily until he had mastered its contents and made them available to the Latin world; Aristippus working over Plato in camp and investigating the phenomena of Etna's eruptions in the spirit of the elder Pliny; Eugene the Emir, in prison at the close of his public career, writing Greek verse in praise of solitude and books. Little enough all this, but sufficient to show the kinship of these men with "the ancient and universal company of scholars."

Apart from much unacknowledged use during the Renaissance, these translators from the Greek made a solid contribution to the culture of the later Middle Ages. Where they came into competition with translations from the Arabic, it was soon recognized that they were more faithful and trustworthy. At their best the Arabic versions were one remove further from the original and had passed through the refracting medium of a wholly different kind of language, while at their worst they were made in haste and with the aid of ignorant interpreters working through the Spanish vernacular. In large measure the two sets of translators utilized the same material. Both were interested in philosophy, mathematics, medicine, and natural science; and, as most of the Greek works in these fields had been turned into Arabic, any one of these might reach the West by either route. If Plato could be found only in the Greek, Aristotle was available also in Arabic, and for most of his works there exist two or more parallel Latin versions. Theology, liturgy, and hagiography, as well as grammar, naturally came from the Greek alone, while astrology was chiefly Arabic. Nevertheless in the realm of the occult and legendary we have from the Greek Kiranides and the dream-books, *Kalila and Dimna* and the Sibyl, some alchemy perhaps, and the *Quadripartitum* of Ptolemy and other bits of astrology. In many instances it was more or less a matter of accident whether the version from the Greek or that from the Arabic should pass into general circulation; thus the Sicilian translation of the *Almagest*, though earlier, is known in but four copies, while that made in Spain is found everywhere. The list of works known only through the Greek of the twelfth century is, however, considerable. It comprises the *Meno* and *Phaedo* of Plato, the only other dialogue known to the Middle Ages being the *Timaeus*, in an older version; the advanced works of Euclid; Proclus and Hero; numerous treatises of Galen; Chrysostom, Basil, Nemesius, John of Damascus, and the Pseudo-Dionysius; and a certain amount of scattered material, theological, legendary, liturgical, and occult.

The absence of the classical works of literature and history from this list of translations from the Greek is as significant as it is from the curriculum of the mediaeval universities. We are in the twelfth century, not the fifteenth, and the interest in medicine, mathematics, philosophy, and theology reflects the practical and ecclesiastical preoccupations of the age rather than the wider interests of the humanists. The mediaeval translations "were not regarded as *belles lettres*. They were a means to an end." It is well, however, to remember that these same authors continue to be read in the Quattrocento, in translations new or old; they are merely crowded into the background by the newer learning. In this sense there is continuity between the two periods. There is also a certain amount of continuity in the materials of scholarship — individual manuscripts of the earlier period gathered into libraries at Venice or Paris, the library of the Sicilian kings probably forming the nucleus of the Greek collections of the Vatican. To what extent there was a continuous influence of Hellenism is a more difficult problem, in view of our fragmentary knowledge of conditions in the South. The Sicilian translators of the twelfth

century are followed directly by those at the courts of
Frederick II and Manfred, while in the fourteenth century we have to remember the sojourn of Petrarch at the
court of Robert of Naples, and the Calabrian Greek who
taught Boccaccio. The gap is short, but it cannot yet be
bridged.

On the scientific side the renaissance of the twelfth
century was thus a Greek as well as an Arabic renaissance; and the unique significance of Arabic science in
that period now finds itself diminished by the translations made directly from the Greek. The Latin world
could have got its Aristotle and its Galen, its Ptolemy
and Euclid, largely through these Graeco-Latin versions.
It *could* have got much Greek science in this way, but
for the most part it *did* not. The current language of
science was by this time Arabic. The whole scientific
movement from Spain and Provence was Arabic in its
origin, and so in part was that from Southern Italy. The
versions from the Arabic often antedated those from the
Greek, or at least in most cases took their place in current
use. These brought the added prestige of the accompanying Arabic commentaries and manuals, some of which
profoundly colored European thought. The Arabic translations had 'a better press.' To the translations must
be added the science of the Arabs themselves, assimilating and often going beyond the Greek, in medicine
and mathematics, in astronomy and astrology, probably
also in alchemy. This is not all: with the Arabs and

Jews of the Middle Ages scientific knowledge was a thing of supreme importance, and this spirit of devotion to science passed to the Latins who came in contact with their learning. With interest came method: a rationalistic habit of mind and an experimental temper. These, of course, could have been found among the ancient Greeks and were inherent in their writings, but they had been fostered and kept alive in the Mohammedan countries, and it was chiefly from these that they passed to Western Christendom.

BIBLIOGRAPHICAL NOTE

This chapter has been taken for the most part from my *Studies in the History of Mediaeval Science* (second edition, Cambridge, Mass., 1927), especially chs. 1 and 8, where full references will be found to the contemporary and modern authorities. See also my sketch entitled "Arabic Science in Western Europe," in *Isis*, vii. 478–485 (1925). In this article and in the present chapter the terms 'Arabic' and 'Arab' are used in a linguistic and cultural and not in an ethnographic sense.

CHAPTER X

THE REVIVAL OF SCIENCE

AT no point is the intellectual revival of the twelfth century more marked than in the domain of science. In 1100, Western Europe was limited to the compends of Isidore and Bede and scattered fragments of Roman learning; by 1200, or shortly thereafter, it had received the natural science and philosophy of the Arabs and thus the larger part of Greek learning. The intervening hundred years, or, let us say, the century from *ca.* 1125 on, made available Euclid and Ptolemy and the mathematics and astronomy of the Arabs, the medicine of Galen and Hippocrates and Avicenna, and the rich cyclopaedia of Aristotelian wisdom. Something now came to be known of Greek and Arabic alchemy, and much of Arabic astrology, and the experimental spirit was clearly manifested. We can speak with entire propriety of a scientific renaissance, though we cannot limit ourselves quite so sharply as in the case of literature to the twelfth century itself, and shall at times be obliged to reach forward into the thirteenth century for clearer illustrations of what the preceding century had begun.

The general scientific culture of the early Middle Ages is best reflected in its most popular cyclopaedia, the *Etymologies* of Isidore of Seville. Compiled in Spain shortly before the author's death in 636, it quickly spread beyond the Pyrenees, and some hundreds of copies must soon have passed into circulation. As we have seen, this was one of those books which no respectable library could be without, and its celebrity is further attested by its constant use for references and excerpts. It was popular because it was compendious and succinct in an age which wanted all its learning in tabloid form, because it was bookish, because it was credulous, because it made use of allegorical and mystical interpretation. No one criticised it for dealing with words rather than things and for caring supremely for etymologies and definitions. Like most of its successors in every age, it was based chiefly upon previous cyclopaedias; preserving extracts from works now lost, it gives us a "conglomerate of ten centuries" which is at the same time a "cross section of the mind of the Dark Ages." The very fact that Isidore was only a compiler gives him a representative quality which a more original work would have lacked. As Brehaut puts it: [1]

The view held in the dark ages of the natural and the supernatural and of their relative proportions in the outlook on life, was precisely the reverse of that held by intelligent men in modern times. For us the material universe has taken on the aspect of order; within its limits phenomena seem to follow definite modes of behavior, upon the evidence of which a body of scientific knowledge has been built up. Indeed at times in certain branches of science there has been danger of a dogmatism akin to, if the reverse of, that which prevailed in medieval times with reference to the supernatural. On the other hand, the certainty that once existed in regard to the supernatural world has faded away; no means of investigating it that commands

---

[1] *An Encyclopedist of the Dark Ages*, pp. 67–68.

confidence has been devised, and any idea held in regard to it is believed to be void of truth if inconsistent with the conclusions reached
by science. In all these respects the attitude of Isidore and his time
is exactly opposite to ours. To him the supernatural world was the
demonstrable and ordered one. Its phenomena, or what were supposed to be such, were accepted as valid, while no importance was
attached to evidence offered by the senses as to the material. It may
even be said that the supernatural universe bulked far larger in the
mind of the medieval thinker than does the natural in that of the
modern, and it was fortified by an immeasurably stronger and more
uncritical dogmatism.

The twenty books of the *Etymologies* which stood for
the sum of human knowledge during many centuries
covered the seven liberal arts, medicine and law, the
church and the alphabet, man and animals (the longest
book is on animals), the earth and the universe, political
as well as physical geography, architecture and surveying, agricultural and military sciences, ships and household utensils, and the practical arts in general. One is
tempted to quote at length from Brehaut's translation,[1]
but the following extracts give fair examples of the author's methods and habit of mind:

iv. 13. On the beginning of medicine.
1. Inquiry is made by certain why the art of medicine is not
included among the liberal disciplines. Because of this, that they
embrace separate subjects, but medicine embraces all. For the
physician is commanded to know grammar, in order to be able to
understand and set forth what he reads.
2. In like manner rhetoric, too, that he may be able to define by
true arguments the diseases which he treats. Moreover logic, to
scrutinize and cure the causes of infirmities by the aid of reason. So,
too, arithmetic, on account of the number of hours in paroxysms
and of the days in periods.
3. In the same manner geometry, on account of the qualities of
districts and the situations of places, in respect to which it teaches

---

[1] Cf. the text in W. M. Lindsay's edition (Oxford, 1911).

what one ought to observe. Moreover, music will not be unknown to him, for there are many things that are read of as accomplished by this discipline in the case of sick men, as it is read of David that he saved Saul from an unclean spirit by the art of melody. The physician Asclepiades, too, restored one who was subject to frenzy to his former health by music.

4. Lastly, he will know astronomy, by which to contemplate the system of the stars and the change of the seasons, for as a certain physician says, our bodies change too, along with the qualities of the heavens. Hence it is that medicine is called 'a second philosophy.' For both disciplines claim the whole man. For as by one the soul is cured, so is the body by the other.

XI, 1, 125. *Iecur* (liver) has its name because in it fire (*ignis*) has its seat, and from there it flies up into the head. Thence it spreads to the eyes and the other organs of sense and the limbs, and by its heat it changes into blood the liquid that it has appropriated from food, and this blood it furnishes to the several parts to feed and nourish them. In the liver pleasure resides and desire, according to those who dispute about natural philosophy.

XI, 3, 23. The race of the Sciopodes is said to live in Ethiopia. They have one leg apiece, and are of a marvellous swiftness, and the Greeks call them Sciopodes from this, that in summertime they lie on the ground on their backs and are shaded by the greatness of their feet.

XII, 7, 18. The swan (*cygnus*) is so called from singing (*canendo*), because it pours forth sweet song in modulated tones. And it sings sweetly for the reason that it has a long curving neck, and it must needs be that the voice, struggling out by a long and winding way, should utter various notes.

XII, 7, 44. The crow (*cornix*), a bird full of years, has a Greek name among the Latins, and augurs say it increases a man's anxieties by the tokens it gives, that it reveals ambushes, and foretells the future. It is great wickedness to believe this, that God intrusts his counsels to crows.

XIV, 6, 6. Scotia, the same as Hibernia, an island very near Britain, narrower in the extent of its lands but more fertile; this extends from Africa toward Boreas, and its fore parts are opposite to Hiberia and the Cantabrian Ocean. Whence it is also called Hibernia. But it is called Scotia because it is inhabited by tribes of the Scots. There are no snakes there, few birds, no bees; so that if any one scatters among beehives elsewhere dust or pebbles brought thence, the swarms desert the combs.

The common mind of the early twelfth century is well exemplified in the *Liber floridus* compiled by Lambert, canon of Saint-Omer, in 1120, of which we have the original illustrated copy, with the author's portrait, preserved at Ghent. Here Lambert noted down, as it came, whatever he read in science, history, theology, and miscellaneous matter of every sort, from the rivers of Paradise and the Greek alphabet to a cure for the toothache. His science, if it may so be called, comprises the movements of the heavenly bodies, the weather, the regions and peoples of the earth, the Roman numerals and fractions, the names and properties of gems, plants, and animals, including Leviathan, who typifies Antichrist. Except for certain marvels culled from the chroniclers, there is nothing here that carries us beyond the obvious sources, which are usually cited by name: Isidore and Bede, Pliny, Martianus Capella, Macrobius, and the Latin Fathers.

We must not suppose that the revival of the twelfth century began by discarding Isidore and his fellows and suddenly abandoning their unscientific habits of thought, which were to persist until the seventeenth century and even later. These habits were deep rooted, for the decline of science went back far into Roman days, as Pliny abundantly attests, and in passages such as we have quoted Isidore had largely followed his Roman guides. The hand of Pliny and Isidore is, for example, still heavy upon Bartholomew the Englishman, who wrote, *ca.* 1230, a highly popular encyclopaedia *On the Properties of Things*, in which, with many developments and much similar matter of fable, we recognize our old friends the snakes of Ireland, the fiery liver, the sweet-throated swans, and other hardy perennials of popular tradition. What the twelfth century could do was to put the West once more in possession of the scientific writings of the Greeks, to open up the knowledge of their Arabic commentators and expositors, and to stimulate scientific activity in every field. The mass of written material was enormously increased and greatly diversified, so that a certain amount of specialization begins. These were great steps forward, even if they do not bring us fully into the modern spirit.

These changes are illustrated in the principal cyclopaedia of this age of cyclopaedias, the *Speculum maius* of Vincent of Beauvais, written toward the middle of the thirteenth century, a mirror of the knowledge of the epoch which Mâle has taken as the best guide to the sculpture of its cathedrals. Finding the multitude of books too great for the ordinary reader, this Dominican friar tells us that he has collected certain extracts or flowers from the vast whole and classified them under the three headings of the *Speculum naturale*, *Speculum doctrinale*, and *Speculum historiale*, treating respectively of natural science, philosophy, and history. The result is an enormous work, filling three huge folio tomes in the printed edition of 1624, as over against the one octavo of Isidore's *Etymologies*. Perhaps one-half of the whole, say three thousand folio pages, deals with science in the more particular sense. The *Speculum* is a compilation, and a compilation made with scissors and paste, with none of the pithy condensation of which Isidore was master. The sources speak for themselves and at length, and they are very numerous, including, besides the ever present Isidore and Pliny, the new Aristotle, many Arabic writers, especially on medicine, and a fair sprinkling of more recent Latins such as Adelard of Bath and William of Conches. The arrangement of the *Speculum naturale* is also characteristic of the age, not only in the minutely scholastic classification and subdivision into thirty-two books and 3718 chapters, but in the subordination of this vast material to the order of the six days of Creation after the manner of the *Exameron* of St. Ambrose. So the *Speculum doctrinale* starts from the Fall of man and treats of the various forms of philosophy by which he may rise again. Nothing so comprehensive was attempted again until the *Encyclopédie* of the eighteenth century.

That the science of Vincent's time was superior in quality as well as in quantity to that current before 1100, is clearly evident in the writings of another man of encyclopedic learning, the Universal Doctor, Albertus Magnus. Commenting upon the whole of Aristotle, and other treatises then believed to be the work of Aristotle, he is at his best in the discussion of animals, plants, and minerals. "Original everywhere, even where he seems to copy," he is ready to differ from the Prince of Philosophers when the facts seem to require it, and he adds much from his own observation and experiment. He tells us that "natural science is not simply receiving what one is told, but the investigation of causes in natural phenomena." The griffin, who ranges at large in Bartholomew the Englishman, Albert considers a creature of story-tellers, unsupported by experiments of philosophers or the arguments of philosophy, and so with the story of the pelican restoring its young with its own blood. So elsewhere in the *De animalibus*—of which Albert's autograph copy is still preserved at Cologne — he tells us, after mentioning various remedies for diseases of falcons: "These are the medicines, tested by experts, which are mentioned for falcons, but the wise falconer will as the result of experience add to or subtract from them on occasion, as shall seem beneficial to the health of the birds; for experience is the best teacher in all such things."

We shall get a better measure of the progress made in the twelfth century by surveying rapidly the several fields of science. Let us begin with mathematics. In the scheme of mediaeval education comprised in the seven liberal arts, four of these, or the *quadrivium*, were considered mathematical, namely, arithmetic, geometry, astronomy, and music; but their mathematics was very elementary indeed. How elementary, appears not only from the textbooks of Boethius and Bede, with their very simple outlines of arithmetical and astronomical reckoning, but also from the extraordinary reputation which

Gerbert acquired when he went somewhat beyond these masters. Confined to the material contained in Boethius and in fragments of the Roman *agrimensores*, Gerbert seems to have revived the practical use of the abacus, or counting-table of the Romans, which had a great vogue in the eleventh and twelfth centuries. Though he gave certain mysterious names and symbols to its counters, he did not use the Arabic method of reckoning by position, and devotes tedious chapters to a description of the 'iron process' of long division with Roman numerals. In geometry he knew only the most elementary parts of Euclid; in astronomy, in spite of the wonder which his simple apparatus excited, he does not seem to have gone beyond Bede. The mathematical labors of the following century in Lorraine and at Chartres were devoted to keeping alive the Gerbertian tradition. Nevertheless, the number of manuscripts *ca.* 1100 which deal with the elements of arithmetical and astronomical computation is a clear indication of the intellectual revival.

Early in the twelfth century 'the whole of Euclid's *Elements* of geometry appeared in a Latin translation, apparently from the Arabic, and a generation later his *Data* and *Optics* were accessible to more advanced students. Geometry had reached substantially the position which it occupied until recent times. In 1126 Adelard of Bath brought the trigonometrical tables of al-Khwarizmi to the West. In 1145 Robert of Chester translated the *Algebra* of the same author into Latin, thus introducing the name as well as the processes of this science into Christian Europe. This book 'on the restoration and opposition of numbers' (*Liber algebre et almucabola*) "laid the foundations of modern analysis," as the curious reader may see from Professor Karpinski's English translation, where the equations are given in modern notation. Al-Khwarizmi's name, softened into 'algorismus' and finally in Chaucer into 'augrim,' became attached to the new Indian arithmetic, of which the first Latin version meets us about the same time. Arabic numerals came in the course of the century, very possibly transmitted through the operations of trade rather than in academic manuals; but by the end of the century the learned world is divided between the algorists, who upheld the new method of reckoning, and the older abacists, who secured legislation against the use of the new-fangled figures at Florence as late as 1299. In 1202 appeared the earliest book of Leonard of Pisa, the *Liber abaci*, followed by the epoch-making treatises in which this mathematical genius gave solutions of quadratic and cubic equations and otherwise showed his "sovereign possession of the mathematical knowledge of his own and every preceding generation." Mathematics had reached a point from which it was not to make notable advances until the time of Descartes. The decisive importance of the twelfth century is nowhere more evident.

The astronomical manuscripts of the beginning of the century consist mainly of copies or extracts from the manuals of Bede and the Carolingian computist Helperic, with some attention to ecclesiastical chronology as touching the date of the Christian era. The few references which are found to the Arabic astrolabe do not indicate any further acquaintance with Arabic astronomy, so that the Anglo-Norman *Cumpoz* of Philippe de Thaon in 1119 reflects only the older Latin tradition. In the following year, however, another Englishman, Walcher of Malvern, begins to reckon by degrees, minutes, and seconds, as he has learned them from a Spanish Jew named Petrus Alphonsi, and in 1126 Adelard of Bath translates the astronomical tables of al-Khwarizmi. These were soon followed by the tables of al-Battani and al-Zarkali and by the brief manual of al-Fargani. Ptolemy's famous *Almagest*, that comprehensive summary of ancient astronomy, was translated from the Greek about 1160 and from the Arabic in 1175. Henceforth the full reception of the astronomical knowledge of the ancient world depended upon the assimilation of this work.

Meanwhile the Aristotelian physics had begun to filter in through Arabic writers, and the conflict of this with Ptolemy, as well as with Plato's *Timaeus*, puzzled an age which desired at all costs to reconcile its standard authorities. Aristotle's *Physics* was translated not long before 1200, but his *Meteorology* had been accessible before 1162 and the *De caelo* perhaps as early, while fragments of Aristotle's physical doctrines came in through various channels in the course of the century. As we ap-

proach 1200, we find an increasing number of brief treatises which discuss the nature of the universe and its
elements and the phenomena of earthquakes and tides
and volcanoes. The meteorology of the age is definitely
Aristotelian.

Its geography, strangely enough, remains essentially
Roman, limited for the most part to Ptolemy and Isidore.
There was, we have seen, a widening of Europe's geographical horizon by the crusading expeditions and by
explorations to the North and Northeast, with a corresponding expansion of the sphere of European civilization, but there was no accompanying reception of Arabic
geography. "The works of the foremost Mohammedan
geographers, Al-Mas'udi, Ibn Hauqal, Al-Istakhri, were
unknown in Europe during the Middle Ages, and formal
Arabic geography certainly contributed next to nothing
to the knowledge of the earth possessed by the Occi-
dentals of the Crusading age." [1]

While our period did not avail itself of these important
sources of new knowledge, it is not true that its geography
was entirely traditional. The geography of observation
was never wholly absent even from the encyclopaedias,
whereas it is abundantly illustrated in letters, chronicles,
and descriptive writings of various sorts. Not only accounts of striking phenomena like earthquakes and volcanoes, but many more ordinary bits of observation
meet us throughout the period. Among works of travel

[1] J. K. Wright, *Geographical Lore of the Time of the Crusades*, p. 77.

a special place belongs to Giraldus Cambrensis, whose *Topography of Ireland, Description of Wales,* and *Itinerary through Wales* fall in 1188 and the years soon after. Giraldus is credulous and prejudiced, willing to write at length on the interior of Ireland, which he knows only from hearsay, nor does he disdain Solinus and the conventional interpretation of allegory; yet he gives us much first-hand description of lakes, rivers, mountains, and bits of climatology, as well as a group of most interesting facts respecting the tidal phenomena of the coasts of the Irish Sea, pieced together perhaps from the reports of sailors and fishermen, whose accurate information on such subjects the student of books is too prone to overlook. The geography of Giraldus is very human withal, too human for many modern Welsh and Irish critics, for Giraldus discusses language, manners and customs, and the influence of climate on temperament, listing the praiseworthy and blameworthy characteristics of his fellow-Welshmen, and even noting the resemblances between the language of the Welsh fairies and the Greek of Priscian.

The regional geography of the age shows gradations of knowledge depending upon the opportunity for observation. By the thirteenth century it may be summed up as follows from the point of view of Western Europe: [1]

First, there were the well known regions about which knowledge was derived and kept fresh through active commercial, diplomatic,

---

[1] Wright, p. 257.

ecclesiastical, military, and scholarly enterprise. These regions may be said to have included most of Europe west of the Elbe and Hungary. They also included the overland routes to Constantinople, the shores of the Mediterranean, and the Holy Land. From the point of view of the Scandinavian peoples, who were great travelers, they took in not only the foregoing regions but also the Baltic coasts, southern Norway and Sweden, and Iceland. Beyond the bounds of the well-known areas lay a second group of areas about which a fair amount of reasonably trustworthy information was at hand, derived from one of three sources: (1) reports of occasional travelers; (2) more or less reliable hearsay; (3) classical descriptions drawn from literary sources. Much of Western Asia and North Africa fell within this category, and, for the Scandinavians, Greenland. Beyond lay the third group of regions known only through the vaguest of rumors — the domains of fabulous monsters and legendary men. To some writers India was such a land, to others Russia and northern Scandinavia, to still others the legendary isles that lay concealed in the Western Ocean. Finally, beyond them came those regions lying without the known world, about which the men of the Middle Ages themselves would have acknowledged that they knew nothing.

Such divisions are also partly a matter of individual temperament. To the untravelled mind all unseen lands are alike, and in the Middle Ages the unknown and the marvellous lay very close by. The way is short from the Western Ireland of Giraldus's description to the voyages of St. Brandan and his crew past the 'spray-swept Hebrides,' with their strange combination of actual ice bergs and glowing images from Ezekiel and the Apocalypse, and that lonely figure of Judas let loose from his fiery crater to 'cool him on the floe' of the Western Ocean. Now and for long afterwards geography easily merges in romance.

Another phase of twelfth-century science was the revival of astrology. Professor Thorndike's researches have shown that astrological beliefs and practices did not disappear in the early Middle Ages so completely as is commonly supposed, but the examples are relatively few when compared with the enormous mass of later literature. As revived in the twelfth century, astrology was to last until finally destroyed by the cosmology of Copernicus. Let us not, however, turn too quickly away from this delusion of our ancestors, for astrology was to them merely applied astronomy, 'humanized astronomy,' if you like, a natural sequence to the phenomena of summer and winter, day and night and tides, which were directly occasioned by the movements of the heavenly bodies. Not only has astral religion been one of the most widely prevalent faiths in human history, but astrology could claim the support of Ptolemy and, it was thought, Aristotle, as well as the whole series of Arabic astrologers. "The stars in their courses fought against Sisera," sang the daughter of Israel, long before the time of Ptolemy. It must be said, however, that the Arabs went much beyond the classical doctrines of Ptolemy's *Tetrabiblos* and added to genethliac astrology, which was concerned with the conjunction of heavenly bodies at the moment of birth, a more popular science of interrogations and elections for every occasion in life. In the second quarter of the twelfth century this Arabic literature began to pour into Europe in a perfect flood. Indeed to many this seemed to offer the most practical proof of the utility of the new learning. The Latin world thus became acquainted, not only with the *Tetrabiblos* of Ptolemy and the *Centiloquium* of the Pseudo-Ptolemy, but also with the *Greater Introduction* of Albumasar, the *Judgments* of al-Kindi and Messahala, the *Revolutions* of Zael, the so-called *Astrology* of Aristotle 'compiled from the two hundred and fifty-five volumes of the Indians,' works of Hermes and Thoth, books of portents and of rains, as well as more special treatises of aeromancy, hydromancy, geomancy, spatulamancy, and other forms of divination. By 1228 Michael Scot has summed up this literature in the 'new astrology' of his *Liber introductorius*, *Liber particularis*, and *Physiognomy*. In Italy public astrologers had their regular offices and consultations, indeed one of them has left us a portion of his daily registers. Even universities had their professors of astrology, while kings and princes consulted these practitioners both in affairs of state and in minute personal matters like blood-letting and marital relations. Guido of Montefeltro kept in his employ one of the most distinguished and successful of mediaeval astrologers, Guido Bonatti, who is said to have directed his master's military expeditions from a campanile with the precision of a fire alarm: first bell, to arms; second, to horse; third, off to battle. Ezzelino da Romano also had Bonatti among his many astrologers, along with Master Salio, canon of Padua, Riprandino of Verona, and "a long-bearded Saracen named Paul, who came from Baldach on the confines of the Far East, and by his origin and appearance and actions deserved the name of a second Balaam." Frederick II is said to have profited by Bonatti's skill as well as by the constant advice of his official astrologers Michael Scot and Theodore of Antioch, but in his great defeat before Parma his enemies exulted over the destruction of the troop of astrologers and magicians who surrounded this devotee of Beelzebub and other demons.

Alchemy, originally "the holy and divine art of making gold and silver," is perhaps the most obscure phase in the history of mediaeval science. The difficulty is in part inherent in the subject itself, for alchemists were concerned with various kinds of secret processes which became public slowly and often anonymously, and they had a bad reputation as early as Dante. When a mediaeval investigator thought he had turned mercury into gold, he was in no hurry to publish the method under his name. Partly, however, the obscurity is merely the result of insufficient investigation of the Greek, Arabic, and Latin texts. The practice of imitating the precious metals goes back to classical and even Oriental antiquity, particularly in Egypt, and a rich alchemical literature has been preserved in the Greek writers of the time of the Roman empire. A literature of recipes and processes rather than of theories, much of it was carried over into mediaeval Europe, reaching the West by literary channels as well as by direct transmission in the arts. Just how much the Arabs added in the process of transmission, is still an open question. Gibbon indeed declared that the science of chemistry owes its origin and importance to the industry of the Saracens: "They first invented and named the alembic for the purpose of distillation, analysed the substances of the three kingdoms of nature, tried the distinction and affinities of alcalis and acids, and converted the poisonous minerals into soft and salutary medicines." Yet a century after Gibbon the originality of the Arabs in all these respects had been considerably diminished by fuller acquaintance with the literature of Greek alchemy, so that Berthelot denied to them any significant contribution in this field, ascribing rather to Western alchemists whatever advances were made in the Middle Ages. Quite recently the publication of Arabic texts tends to restore to the Arabs something of their earlier importance. Until further research has made clear the exact position of Arabic alchemy, it is impossible to say how much of the European alchemy of the later ages is of Arabic origin and how much is due to actual experimentation in Latin Christendom. This is one of the most promising subjects for investigation in the field of mediaeval science; it is being approached by a new catalogue of Greek alchemical manuscripts, in course of publication by the International Union of Academies, and by special monographs on the Arabs which need to be paralleled by similar studies on the Latin West.

In any case the intense European activity in the field of alchemy belongs to a later period than we are now considering. Most of the Latin treatises, anonymous, pseudonymous, or of mythical authorship, occur in manuscripts of the fourteenth to the sixteenth centuries and still await publication. Nevertheless, the twelfth century can show three alchemical translations from the Arabic by Gerard of Cremona, besides the questionable Morienus which bears the date of 1144, while various alchemical works are ascribed to writers of the early thirteenth century, such as Michael Scot and Friar Elias of Cortona. Without pronouncing an opinion on these questions of authorship, we may at least be certain that the fundamentals of alchemical doctrine were by this time familiar to the West, as is seen in the cyclopaedias of Vincent of Beauvais and Albertus Magnus. An authentic chapter of Michael Scot written before 1236 tells us that the seven metals are compounds made up of varying proportions of quicksilver, sulphur, and earth; that "metals may be sophisticated by the art of alchemy through the addition of powders and the mediation of the four spirits of quicksilver, sulphur, orpiment, and sal ammoniac"; that gold may be treated so as to make a food useful to the old who wish to be younger and more vigorous — evidently the so-called elixir of life of the Arab alchemists. With these principles recognized, the way was open for the experimental literature which meets us in the later thirteenth century. By the middle of the following century a monk of Bologna catalogues his library of seventy-two alchemical works; by 1376 such Latin treatises had been translated into Greek. The story of alchemy is continuous from the days of Hellenistic Egypt to the seventeenth century, indeed up to this point it is chemistry in the making. Not only was much permanent chemical knowledge acquired as a by-product of alchemical research, but the most recent chemical theories and experiments incline us to much greater tolerance toward these early attempts to transmute one metal into another.

In medicine, the twelfth century saw the full recovery of the medical literature of the Greeks, the translation of the more important works of the Arab physicians, and the flourishing period of the University of Salerno, the earliest medical school in modern Europe. Greek medicine, it is true, had never wholly disappeared from the South of Italy, where Cassiodorus had created his library in the sixth century and where certain Latin versions of Greek medical writers can be traced in Beneventan copies as early as the tenth century — a meagre tradition but apparently enough to start the medical school of Salerno. Just when or how this centre of study came into being no one knows. By the tenth century Salerno is a seat of the healing art, and by the eleventh century its school is well established. The versions of Constantine the African developed, though they did not start, the activity of the school, and by the twelfth century Salerno has a medical literature of its own. This is primarily a literature in Latin but not wholly so; for, says Stephen of Pisa in 1127, "in Sicily and at Salerno, where students of such matters are chiefly to be found, there are both

Greeks and men familiar with Arabic." These Salernitan masters, Gariopontus, 'Trotula,' Urso, Roger, Nicholas, and others, dealt with many matters of medicine and surgery, as can be seen in their recently published works. Although like the Arabs they avoided dissection of the human body, they have left a treatise on the anatomy of the pig. Their writings on pharmacology and diseases of the eye were widely used. In general they emphasized bathing and diet — the baths of Salerno and other warm springs of the region were famous even in verse — and simple, sensible remedies. Their therapy was later popularized in a poem of 362 lines, the *Regimen sanitatis Salernitanum*, some of whose maxims are still in circulation: "After breakfast walk a mile, after dinner rest a while," etc. A more adequate statement of the early teaching of Salerno appears in the various versified treatises of Gilles de Corbeil, who came from the schools of Salerno and Montpellier to Paris to be physician to Philip Augustus and possibly to exercise some influence on medical teaching in the university.

While the revival of medicine in the West and the reestablishment of the medical profession proceed in the first instance from early Salerno, further advance in medical science required the full assimilation of the medical knowledge of the ancient world, particularly the works of the father of medicine, Hippocrates, whose writings are still read with profit for their method and for their high standard of professional ethics, and those of his voluminous successor, Galen. Something of their teaching had come from the Arabic through Constantine of Africa, whose versions still make up the larger part of the twenty-six treatises composing the medical library of the bishop of Hildesheim in 1161; but the great majority of their writings were brought to the West in the later twelfth century, partly from the Greek by the Pisan Burgundio, but chiefly through the Arabic by Gerard of Cremona. These were supplemented by Arabic commentaries and abridgements like those of Ali-ben-Abbas and the Jew Isaac, some of which were translated into German before 1200, and toward the close of the century by the *Canon* of Avicenna, which makes a large folio volume in the Latin edition of 1582, and which remained until our own time the standard cyclopaedia of medicine for the Mohammedan world. We have here substantially the *corpus* of mediaeval medicine, from which the university curriculum usually selected for concentrated study the *Aphorisms* of Hippocrates, the *Tegni* of Galen, the *Pantegni* of Ali-ben-Abbas, the works of Isaac the Jew, and, later, Avicenna. Fundamentally Greek, it had been enriched by much fruitful observation of diseases and their medicines among the Arabs.

Unfortunately, the scholastic habit of mind and the mediaeval reverence for the written word put these texts into a position of absolute authority, to be expounded and interpreted literally and dogmatically rather than experimentally in laboratories or clinics, so that medical science advanced very slowly in the period which immediately followed. By a statute of Frederick II three years of logic must precede the study of medicine. From the classrooms of the fourteenth century as they are depicted on the Bolognese monuments, with the textbook lying open before master and students, it is a long way to Rembrandt's "Lesson in Anatomy."

Nevertheless, dogmatic and academic as was the study of medicine in the mediaeval university, some progress seems to have been made toward a saner practice of the art. In the early Middle Ages there was no professional class of physicians as we understand the term, for the usual practice consisted in the domestic applications of incantations, charms, and old wives' remedies of every sort. Thus we read in the Old English leechdoms: [1]

For head ache, take willow and oil, reduce to ashes, work to a viscid substance, add to this hemlock and carline and the red nettle, pound them, put them then on the viscid stuff, bathe therewith. Against head ache; burn a dog's head to ashes, snip the head; lay on . . . .

For fellon, catch a fox, strike off from him while alive the tusk [or canine tooth], let the fox run away, bind it in a fawn's skin, have it upon thee. . . .

For flying venom and every venomous swelling, on a Friday churn butter, which has been milked from a neat or hind all of one color; and let it not be mingled with water, sing over it nine times a litany, and nine times the *Pater noster*, and nine times this incantation. . . . That is valid for every, even for deep wounds. Some teach us against bite of adder to speak one word, that is, Faul; it may not hurt him. Against bite of snake, if the man procures and eateth rind, which cometh out of paradise, no venom will damage him. Then said he that wrote this book, that the rind was hard gotten.

---

[1] T. O. Cockayne, *Leechdoms* (Rolls Series), ii. 19–21, 105, 113–115.

Now if the school of Salerno was not wholly scientific in the modern sense, its treatment was at least simple and sensible, while the Arabs showed much skill in the actual healing of diseases and their practice gradually spread with the growth of the medical profession. Moreover, Jewish and Arab physicians were in great favor when they could be had; Henry I of England is said to have had the services of a converted Jew, Petrus Alphonsi, as well as a Christian named Grimbald, while "in Spain the life of the Catholic princes was intrusted to the skill of the Saracens." The contrast between Oriental skill and the older Christian superstition is instructively brought out in the narrative of a Syrian physician, Thabit, preserved in the memoirs of Usama:[1]

They brought to me a knight with an abscess in his leg, and a woman troubled with fever. I applied to the knight a little cataplasm; his abscess opened and took a favorable turn. As for the woman, I forbade her to eat certain foods, and I lowered her temperature. I was there when a Frankish doctor arrived, who said, "This man can't cure them!" Then, addressing the knight, he asked, "Which do you prefer, to live with a single leg, or to die with both of your legs?" "I prefer," replied the knight, "to live with a single leg." "Then bring," said the doctor, "a strong knight with a sharp axe." The knight and axe were not slow in coming. I was present. The doctor stretched the leg of the patient on a block of wood, and then said to the knight, "Cut off his leg with the axe, detach it with a single blow." Under my eyes, the knight gave a violent blow, but it did not cut the leg off. He gave the unfortunate man a second blow, which caused the marrow to flow from the bone, and the patient died immediately.

---

[1] French version by H. Derenbourg (Paris, 1895); as translated by D. C. Munro, in *Essays on the Crusades* (Burlington, 1903), pp. 19–20. See also E. G. Browne, *Arabian Medicine*, pp. 69–73.

As for the woman, the doctor examined her and said, "She is a woman with a devil in her head, by which she is possessed. Shave her hair." They did so, and she began to eat again, like her compatriots, garlic and mustard. Her fever grew worse. The doctor then said, "The devil has gone into her head." Seizing the razor he cut into her head in the form of a cross and excoriated the skin in the middle so deeply that the bones were uncovered. Then he rubbed her head with salt. The woman, in her turn, expired immediately. After asking them if my services were still needed, and after receiving a negative answer, I returned, having learned from their medicine matters of which I had previously been ignorant.

The veterinary medicine of this age was practical rather than academic. Treatises upon the diseases of hawks and dogs meet us in the twelfth century and continue throughout the Middle Ages, while contemporary knowledge respecting horses is summed up at the instance of Frederick II by a Calabrian knight, Giordano Ruffo, whose manual of the veterinary art was translated into many languages and widely imitated. Under Manfred a version of the veterinary work of Hierocles was made from the Greek.

The learned zoölogy of the twelfth century still rested on Pliny, and its popular ideas on the bestiaries. A more scientific treatment came in the early thirteenth century with the translation, by Michael Scot, of the Aristotelian books on animals and their Arabic abbreviation by Avicenna. There was, as we shall see below, much observation of the common animals, and kings begin to have their menageries of the more rare and strange beasts. Although the early Norman sovereigns had their forests — did not William the Conqueror 'love the tall stags as if he were their father'? — the leopards of England came in with the Angevins, and Henry II had a gift of camels from the Saracen king of Valencia. Frederick II, like his Mohammedan contemporaries, had a great menagerie, which he carried with him about Italy and even into Germany. In 1231 he came to Ravenna "with many animals unknown to Italy: elephants, dromedaries, camels, panthers, gerfalcons, lions, leopards, white falcons, and bearded owls." Five years later a similar procession passed through Parma, to the delight of a boy of fifteen later known as Salimbene. The elephant, a present from the sultan, stayed in Ghibelline Cremona, where he was put through his paces for the Earl of Cornwall and died thirteen years later "full of humors," amid the popular expectation that his bones would ultimately turn into ivory. In 1245 the monks of Santo Zeno at Verona, in extending their hospitality to the Emperor, had to entertain with him an elephant, five leopards, and twenty-four camels. The camels were used for transport and were even taken over the Alps, with monkeys and leopards, to the wonder of the untravelled Germans. Another marvel of the collection was a giraffe from the sultan, the first to appear in mediaeval Europe. Throughout runs the motif of ivory, apes, and peacocks from the East, as old as Nineveh and Tyre and as new as the modern 'Zoo,' with the touch of the thirteenth century seen in the elephant which Matthew Paris thought rare enough to preserve in a special drawing in his history, and the lion which

Villard de Honnecourt saw on his travels and carefully labelled in his sketchbook, "drawn from life"! That Villard's observations were not limited to such grand occasions is seen from others of his sketches, which range all the way from the swan and the parrot to the snail and the grasshopper.

The contribution of the twelfth century to botany lay chiefly in the field of *materia medica*. Here the Greek tradition had for some reason been more persistent, as is seen in the current versions of Dioscorides; the early translations of medical works were often accompanied by Graeco-Arabic glossaries of botanical terms, while much of the Arabic knowledge of plants came in with the *Canon* of Avicenna. In this field, too, the observation of the unlearned was active. The depiction of foliage and fruit in Gothic sculpture is so exact that modern naturalists have identified a large number of the originals among the flora of modern France: plantain, arum, buttercup, fern, clover, coladine, hepatica, columbine, cress, parsley, strawberry, ivy, snapdragon, the leaf of the oak, and the flower of the broom — spring flowers and buds for the most part, so that "all the spring delights of the Middle Ages live again in the work" of these artists of an epoch often considered indifferent to natural beauty.[1]

In agriculture the twelfth century cannot show any treatises either practical or theoretical; books like Walter

[1] E. Mâle, *L'art religieux du XIII° siècle en France*, third edition (Paris, 1910), pp. 70–71.

of Henley's *Husbandry* and the *Ruralium commodorum libri XII* of Peter de Crescentiis belong to a later age. Latin antiquity contributed occasional copies of Varro, Palladius, and Columella, while Burgundio the Pisan translated a fragment on viticulture from the Greek *Geoponica*, but agriculture remained still, and for many centuries later, a severely practical art. Resting on Roman traditions, and spreading from the Roman lands northward, it was in our period extended by the monastic colonization of Eastern Germany and enriched by the new products which came west in the Mediterranean as a consequence of the Crusades; but all this had no scientific character. The agricultural experiment station was a thing of the far future.

In one form of applied science the twelfth century stands in the forefront, namely in architecture. This was not based on the perusal of ancient writings or the imitation of classical models, although Vitruvius was copied and even excerpted,[1] but upon the traditions and practices of the art of building itself. In this the twelfth century stands out as the culminating period of Romanesque and the beginning of the Gothic style, the latter not only an artistic achievement of the highest significance, but an engineering feat as well, in the measure of strain and stress and in the skilful use of materials and the balance and harmony of the whole. Unfortunately

[1] Vatican MS. Reg. Lat. 1286, ff. 43–50 v; MS. Barberini Lat. 12, ff. 98–110.

for us, this knowledge was handed down in practice rather than in any theoretical manuals for our information. Even the artist's sketchbook fails us before the time of Villard de Honnecourt, and for long thereafter.

There remains the matter of scientific observation and experiment. How far were the men of this age satisfied with the teachings of the Greeks and Arabs and how far did they seek to verify and enlarge this knowledge? There was plenty of precedent for further study in the work of the Greeks and their successors. Aristotle's descriptions of animals are highly regarded by modern zoölogists, indeed, they often reached the limits attainable without a microscope; Hippocrates observed diseases with accuracy and discernment; Galen performed a famous experiment on the spinal cord of a frog; Eratosthenes and the astronomers of Bagdad measured a degree on the earth's surface; Greek and Arab observatories marked the movements of the heavenly bodies as the basis of astronomical tables. The Christians of the Middle Ages had only to follow such illustrious examples. In the main, however, it must be said, they took the results of Greek and Arabic science rather than its methods. Medicine became the study of the writings of Galen and Hippocrates scholastically interpreted; physics the logical interpretation of Aristotle's treatises; geography the study of books, not travel or even maps. Aristotle became in course of time a hindrance rather than a help, stereotyping knowledge rather than furnishing a method for its extension, and imposing theories of the universe which science had to abandon as a preliminary to further progress. His logic tended to crush his natural science and the method by which his natural science came into being. The universities of the Middle Ages studied their medicine and natural history out of books, not out of laboratories and observatories, and scientific knowledge could not grow in this fashion.

All this, however, is apt to be exaggerated in our current impressions of mediaeval science, impressions which take insufficient account of the advance made from the early twelfth century onward. Our period can show many examples of observation and experiment, like Walcher of Malvern seeking in 1092 to fix the difference of time in England and Italy from an eclipse; Aristippus examining at some personal danger an eruption of Etna; Giraldus Cambrensis recording the height of the tide in Ireland and Wales; Michael Scot describing the volcanic phenomena of the Lipari Islands. If the physicians of Salerno did not dissect the human body, they at least studied the anatomy of the pig. For an early example let us take Adelard of Bath in the first forty years of the century. To him authority is a halter, and God an explanation to be used only when all others have been exhausted. Travelling through the Mediterranean world in search of knowledge, he acquired something of the scientific and realistic temper of the Arabs and Greeks. He reports seeing an earthquake in Syria, a pneumatic experiment in Magna Graecia, and notes that light travels faster than sound. He or another contemporary tries to determine the spot where the sun is directly overhead at midday. Adelard was clearly a pioneer of scientific inquiry.

A century later perhaps our best example appears in the Emperor Frederick II. Writing on birds, he tells us that Aristotle relies too much on hearsay and must be corrected from personal observation — *non sic se habet.* Aristotle has "rarely or never had experience in falconry, which we have loved and practised all our lives." The Emperor's own treatise on falconry is compact of personal observation of the habits of birds, especially falcons, carried on throughout a busy life of sport and study, and verified by birds and falconers brought from distant lands. Indeed, his systematic use for such inquiries of the resources of his royal administration constitutes an interesting example of the pursuit of research by governmental agencies. "Not without great expense," he tells us, "did we call to ourselves from afar those who were expert in this art, extracting from them whatever they knew best and committing to memory their sayings and practices." "When we crossed the sea we saw the Arabs using a hood in falconry, and their kings sent us those most skilled in this art, with many species of falcons."

The Emperor not only tested the artificial incubation of hens' eggs, but, on hearing that ostrich eggs were hatched by the sun in Egypt, he had eggs and experts brought to Apulia that he might test the matter for himself. The fable that barnacle geese were hatched from barnacles he exploded by sending north for such barnacles, concluding that the story arose from ignorance of the actual nesting-places of the geese. Whether vultures find their food by sight or by smell he ascertained by seeling their eyes while their nostrils remained open. Nests, eggs, and birds were repeatedly brought to him for observation and note, and the minute accuracy of his descriptions attests the fidelity with which his observations were made.

This experimental habit of mind, the Emperor's desire to see and know for himself, lies behind those *superstitiones et curiositates* at which the good Salimbene holds up his hands. There is the story of the man whom Frederick shut up in a wine-cask to prove that the soul died with the body, and the two men whom he disembowelled in order to show the respective effects of sleep and exercise on digestion. There were the children whom he caused to be brought up in silence in order to settle the question "whether they would speak Hebrew, which was the first language, or Greek or Latin or Arabic or at least the language of their parents; but he labored in vain, for the children all died." There was the diver, Nicholas, surnamed the Fish, hero of Schiller's *Der Taucher*, whom

he sent repeatedly to explore the watery fastnesses of
Scylla and Charybdis, and the memory of whose exploits
was handed on by the Friars Minor of Messina, not to
mention the "other superstitions and curiosities and mal-
edictions and incredulities and perversities and abuses"
which the friar of Parma had set down in another chronicle now lost.

All in all, quite enough to demolish the legend that
Roger Bacon was the first experimenter of the Middle
Ages! Frederick is, of course, an exceptional figure, and we
shall look far before finding many similar manifestations
of the experimental spirit in mediaeval times. Nevertheless, he points us in one direction where observation was
particularly active, namely; domestic animals and the
beasts of the chase; not only in royal menageries, but in
every farm and forest observation was going on. Most of
it was naturally unrecorded. Something found its way
into books of hunting and husbandry as well as into more
general works. Men might take their dragons and dog-
men from Pliny and their griffins from the bestiaries, but
their horses and dogs and hawks they derived from their
own knowledge. The same Bartholomew the Englishman
who is so sure of griffins and the resurrection of the pelican has an oft quoted description of the domestic cat
which, so far as it goes, can hardly be improved upon:

> He is a full lecherous beast in youth, swift, pliant, and merry, and
> leapeth and reseth on everything that is to fore him: and is led by a
> straw, and playeth therewith: and is a right heavy beast in age and

full sleepy, and lieth slyly in wait for mice: and is aware where they be more by smell than by sight, and hunteth and reseth on them in privy places: and when he taketh a mouse, he playeth therewith, and eateth him after the play. In time of love is hard fighting for wives, and one scratcheth and rendeth the other grievously with biting and with claws. And he maketh a ruthful noise and ghastful, when one proffereth to fight with another: and unneth is hurt when he is thrown down off an high place. And when he hath a fair skin, he is as it were proud thereof, and goeth fast about: and when his skin is burnt, then he bideth at home; and is oft for his fair skin taken of the skinner, and slain and flayed.[1]

What most shocks the modern mind in such a writer is the juxtaposition of cats and griffins, the extraordinary mixing of fact and fable. To a certain extent this is inherent in the limitations of mediaeval knowledge. Adam of Bremen knows his Norway and Denmark, but he colonizes the lands to the east of the Baltic with blue men and dark men, Amazons and men with heads between their shoulders, all out of Pliny and books of fable. There was always a sea of darkness beyond the known world. This, however, is not all: Frederick II, sceptical of barnacle geese and the existence of the soul, believes implicitly the predictions of the royal astrologers, like a Hapsburg of the seventeenth century. Even at its highest point the scientific spirit of Christian Europe in the Middle Ages did not emancipate itself from the respect for authority which was characteristic of the epoch. The critical sense had been only partially awakened, and it did not penetrate far or in all directions. There was no systematic testing of authorities, no subjection of all statements to

[1] Robert Steele, *Mediaeval Lore*, p. 165.

verification and proof. To demand all of this is, of course, to demand much of any age, far too much, unhistorically too much, for the age we are considering. To ask something of the sort is not, however, to violate the historical spirit, for it is suggested by the thirteenth century itself in admitting that statements of Aristotle might be erroneous.

BIBLIOGRAPHICAL NOTE

There is no authoritative history or bibliography of mediaeval science, and much of the preliminary investigation has still to be done. The best guide to the newer material as it appears is the current bibliography in *Isis* (Brussels, since 1913). Of works covering considerable portions of the field, special mention should be made of Pierre Duhem, *Le système du monde de Platon à Copernic* (Paris, 1913–17); and Lynn Thorndike, *History of Magic and Experimental Science* (New York, 1923), valuable for all things connected with magic and for many individual writers, but weak on experimental science, e. g., alchemy. Certain phases of the subject are treated in my *Studies in the History of Mediaeval Science*. The important *Introduction to the History of Science* of George Sarton extends as yet only to the end of the eleventh century (i, Washington, 1927). On popular science, see Ch. V. Langlois, *La connaissance de la nature et du monde* (Paris, 1927: *La vie en France au moyen âge*, iii).

Of the encyclopedists, Isidore is discussed, with liberal excerpts in translation, by E. Brehaut, *An Encyclopedist of the Dark Ages* (New York, 1912); Lambert's *Liber floridus*, by L. Delisle, in *Notices et extraits des MSS.*, xxxviii, 2, pp. 577–791 (1906). See also the extracts translated by Robert Steele, *Mediaeval Lore from Bartholomaeus Anglicus* (London, 1907). There are various editions of Vincent of Beauvais, the most accessible being published at Douai in 1624; the *Speculum morale* included therein is not his. On Albertus Magnus, cf. Thorndike, ch. 59. Besides the editions of his complete works (latest by A. Borgnet, Paris, 1890–99), there are critical annotated editions of the *De animalibus* by H. Stadler (Münster, 1916–20); of the *De vegetabilibus* by E. Meyer and C. Jessen (Berlin, 1867).

On mathematics, see M. Cantor, *Vorlesungen über Geschichte der Mathematik*, i (third edition, Leipzig, 1907), ii, 1 (second edition, 1899), with the numerous corrections of G. Eneström in *Bibliotheca Mathematica*; and D. E. Smith, *History of Mathematics* (Boston, 1923–24). The most convenient example of the new mathematics will be found in L. C. Karpinski's edition and English translation of *Robert of Chester's Latin Translation of the Algebra of al-Khowarizmi* (New York, 1915). See also Smith and Karpinski, *The Hindu-Arabic Numerals* (Boston, 1911). The account of twelfth-century astronomy and physics in Duhem may be supplemented by my *Mediaeval Science*, chs. 2, 3, 5, and 6; and by the monograph of

C. A. Nallino on al-Battani, in *Pubblicazioni del R. Osservatorio di Brera in Milano*, xl (1904). Thorndike is full on the astrology of this period; see also Nallino, in J. Hastings's *Encyclopaedia of Religion and Ethics*, xii. 88–101; and T. O. Wedel, *The Mediaeval Attitude toward Astrology* (New Haven, 1920).

The general background of mediaeval geography is sketched by C. R. Beazley, *The Dawn of Modern Geography*, i, ii (London, 1897–1901); an excellent account of our period, with bibliography, is J. K. Wright, *Geographical Lore of the Time of the Crusades* (New York, 1925).

There is no satisfactory general work on mediaeval alchemy. M. Berthelot, *La chimie au moyen âge* (Paris, 1893), needs to be supplemented and corrected by special investigations; the writings of E. O. von Lippmann are weak on the mediaeval side. The Greek texts are appearing in the *Catalogue des manuscrits alchimistes grecs*, ed. J. Bidez (Brussels, 1924–   ); the Latin are being listed by Mrs. Dorothea Singer; cf. also G. Carbonelli, *Sulle fonti storiche della chimica e dell' alchimia in Italia* (Rome, 1925). The best recent studies are those of E. Wiedemann; E. J. Holmyard (*Isis*, vi. 293–305, 479–497; viii. 403–426); E. Darmstaedter, *Die Alchemie des Gebet* (Berlin, 1922), cf. *Archiv für Geschichte der Medizin*, xvii. 181–197 (1925); and J. Ruska, *Arabische Alchemisten* (Heidelberg, 1924–   ). I have examined the *Alchemy* ascribed to Michael Scot in a forthcoming number of *Isis*.

For medicine, besides the general histories of M. Neuburger, J. L. Pagel, K. Sudhoff, and F. H. Garrison, see E. G. Browne, *Arabian Medicine* (Cambridge, 1921). The two volumes of Donald Campbell, *Arabian Medicine and its Influence on the Middle Ages* (London, 1926), are uncritical and disappointing. The Old English *Leechdoms* are edited and translated by Cockayne in the Rolls Series (London, 1864–66). The Salernitan physicians have recently been the object of many special studies on the part of Karl Sudhoff and his pupils, e. g., Friedrich Hartmann, *Die Literatur von Früh- und Hochsalerno* (Leipzig, 1919). The most famous product of this school, the poem entitled *Regimen sanitatis Salernitanum*, is available, in the quaint English version of Sir John Harington, in *The School of Salernum*, ed. F. R. Packard (London, 1922); Sudhoff has shown that its date is comparatively late (*Archiv für Geschichte der Medizin, passim*). On Gilles de Corbeil, see the volume of C. Vieillard (Paris, 1909); and S. d'Irsay, in *Annals of Medical History*, vii. 362–378 (1925). On early Salerno, see C. and D. Singer, in

History, x. 242–246 (1925); also G. W. Corner, *Anatomical Texts of the Earlier Middle Ages* (Washington, 1927).

The standard history of botany for the early period is that of E. H. F. Meyer (Königsberg, 1854–57); there is nothing so good for zoölogy. For agriculture, see Walter of Henley's *Husbandry*, published by the Royal Historical Society (London, 1890).

For Adelard of Bath, see my *Studies in Mediaeval Science*, ch. 2; for Frederick II, chs. 12–14.

CHAPTER XI

THE REVIVAL OF PHILOSOPHY

IN the Middle Ages, as in ancient Greece, philosophy and science were closely allied, if not inseparable; indeed in most mediaeval classifications of knowledge science was only a branch of philosophy. The methods of the two were similar, at a time when science was largely abstract and deductive; similar, too, were their problems when so much attention was given to cosmology, in which the two disciplines met. And there was the powerful example of Aristotle, who was not only the 'Prince of Philosophers' but the accepted master in many fields of natural science as well, and who mingled the two in the almost universal cyclopaedia of his writings. To the Middle Ages the universe was closed and symmetrical, not open and irregular, as it seems to many of our contemporaries, and philosophy was the supreme integrator of the whole, the sum and system of all the sciences. Such a degree of coherence and unity was not achieved before the thirteenth century and Thomas Aquinas; the earlier Middle Ages, possessing only fragments of ancient philosophy, seized upon one aspect or another of this material, with many contradictions and inconsistencies in the process. The twelfth century marked the turning-point. Together with the years immediately following, it saw the full recovery of the philosophy and science of Aristotle, as well as the chief Platonic revival of the Middle Ages; the triumph of logic over literature; and the elaboration of scholastic method by Abaelard, Gratian, and Peter Lombard, so that it furnished the necessary foundation and something of the superstructure for the great synthesis of the thirteenth century. Indeed, says De Wulf, it worked out "whole groups of doctrines relating to God, to the pluralism of beings, to the activities of the soul, ready for incorporation into more comprehensive philosophies." [1]

Of the two principal philosophers of the ancient world, the sympathy of the Middle Ages lay with Aristotle rather than with Plato. An age which strove to reconcile its authorities at any cost would have derived comfort from those recent writers who minimize the differences between these two and remind us that Aristotle is at times quite Platonic. Nevertheless the two are not the same, and the conscious preference of the Middle Ages was for Aristotle. Gibbon would have it that the Arabs adopted the philosophy of the Stagirite because it was "alike intelligible or alike obscure for the readers of every age," while "Plato wrote for the Athenians, and his allegorical genius is too closely blended with the language and religion of Greece"; but this is not the whole story. It is perhaps evading the question to say that the mediae-

[1] *Histoire de la philosophie médiévale* (1924), i. 177–178.

val mind had a natural affinity for Aristotle, since this mind had been early formed on the Aristotelian logic of Boethius; but it is true that the later centuries turned with avidity to Aristotle's dialectic and stretched themselves on the frame of his thought. The discursive manner of Plato, letting his mind play freely about a subject in the form of dialogue, never became fully domesticated in the Middle Ages, indeed the only work of Plato then widely known, the *Timaeus*, has relatively little dialogue. Aristotle, on the other hand, through his compact, clear-cut, and systematic style of presentation, appealed to an age which loved manuals and textbooks and found these under Aristotle's name in almost every field of philosophy and science. The 'father of textbooks' easily became 'the grandfather of the commentator,' so naturally did his works lend themselves to exposition, comment, and gloss. Moreover, he came with the indorsement of the Arabs, elucidated by their commentaries and exalted by their chief philosophers. In an age of few authorities, he stood for the greater part and the higher part of knowledge, easily overtopping all others. No wonder that Aristotle early became 'the Prince of Philosophers,' 'the Master of them that know.'

Nevertheless, a thin stream of Platonism runs through the Middle Ages, broadening out occasionally into short-lived schools, and it so happens that the most active period of mediaeval Platonism falls in the twelfth century. Not that this age made large additions to the body of available Platonic literature, for the versions of the *Meno* and *Phaedo* made by Aristippus of Catania *ca.* 1156 were not widely influential, in spite of perhaps a dozen surviving manuscripts, and the only other Platonic dialogue then directly accessible to the West was the *Timaeus*, or rather its first fifty-three chapters in the fourth-century translation of Chalcidius with its accompanying commentary. Acquaintance with Plato was mainly indirect, through Cicero and Boethius, Macrobius and Apuleius and St. Augustine, and in the later years of the century through Arabic versions of certain Neoplatonic material. Though he is always mentioned with great respect, Plato never had a fair chance in the Middle Ages, for he was not directly accessible. This period knew nothing of Plato the literary artist, knew very little of the human Socrates. While Anselm had a certain affinity of spirit with Plato, Platonic idealism in the twelfth century is chiefly represented by the school of Chartres. Its chief Platonists were Bernard and Thierry of Chartres, William of Conches, and Gilbert de la Porrée, with whom may be grouped such writers as Adelard of Bath, Bernard Silvester, and Hermann of Carinthia, the latter a pupil of Thierry, and the authors of certain anonymous treatises on cosmology. Thus Bernard of Chartres, whose works are lost but whom John of Salisbury calls the most perfect Platonist of his time, develops a theory of eternal ideas from which proceed the *forme native* which combined with matter to form the transitory world of things, matter being viewed as the primordial and chaotic mass described in the *Timaeus*. The cosmology of the *Timaeus* also appears explicitly in the account of Creation given in the *De sex dierum operibus* of Thierry of Chartres; but such doctrines disappear in the course of the century before the triumph of the Aristotelian physics. Indeed the high reputation of Plato in the twelfth century, when Abaelard calls him *maximus omnium philosophorum*, was due in part to the prevailing ignorance of Aristotle, then known only as a dialectician, and Plato's influence fades rapidly before the universal genius revealed by the full recovery of the works of Aristotle.

Aristotle's influence, on the other hand, depended upon the gradual reception of the several portions of the Aristotelian *corpus*. Of his works the early Middle Ages had access only to the six logical treatises of the *Organon* as translated by Boethius, and as a matter of fact all of these except the *Categories* and the *De interpretatione* dropped out of sight until the twelfth century. These two surviving treatises came to be known as the *Old Logic*, in contradistinction to the *New Logic* — the *Prior* and *Posterior Analytics*, *Topics*, and *Elenchi*—which reappeared in various forms soon after 1128. By 1159 the most advanced of these, the *Posterior Analytics*, was in course of assimilation, and the whole of the Aristotelian logic was absorbed into European thought by the close of the century. The *Physics* and lesser works on natural science, such as the *Meteorology*, the *De generati-*

one, and *De anima* were translated not long before 1200, though, as we have seen, traces of their teachings can be found somewhat earlier, coming from both Greek and Arabic sources. About 1200 came the *Metaphysics*, first in a briefer and then in the complete form. In the course of the thirteenth century the rest of the Aristotelian *corpus* was added: the various books *On Animals*, the *Ethics* and *Politics*, and, imperfectly, the *Rhetoric* and *Poetics*, accompanied and followed by a considerable mass of pseudo-Aristotelian material, so that by *ca.* 1260 the surviving works of Aristotle were known and men were busy comparing the texts of the versions from the Arabic with those derived immediately from the Greek.

The welcome extended to the Prince of Philosophers was, however, chilled by the company in which he came. Whereas the *New Logic* was derived solely from the Greek under orthodox auspices, the metaphysics and natural science came also from the Arabic accompanied by various commentaries and expositions which rendered them suspect to Christian Europe. With Aristotle there arrived Averroës. After all, Aristotle was not a Christian, nor even a Hebrew, writer, and there are doctrines in his philosophy, such as the eternity of the universe, which run counter to the view of Creation upheld by Jewish, Christian, and Mohammedan orthodoxy, and had to be explained away by the scholastics of all three religions. Indeed the parallel development is very striking: "the mysticism of all three religions is essentially Neoplatonic,

the scholasticism of all predominatingly Aristotelian." [1]
So the more conventional philosophers, like the Mohammedan Avicenna and the Hebrew Maimonides, softened
the differences between Aristotle and orthodox theology,
thus to a certain extent denaturing Aristotle; but such a
thinker as Averroës (1126–98) refused to turn aside in
his path for any such purpose, and even brought into the
foreground elements which, although contained in the
Aristotelian philosophy, had not been emphasized by the
Stagirite himself. Such were the doctrine of the eternity
of matter and the theory of the unity of the intellect
which denied individual immortality. The influence of
Averroës, strangely enough, was greater in the Christian
than in the Mohammedan world, and the first impact of
his writings on Christendom produced a shock which
extended to those of Aristotle himself. In 1210 the newly
arrived natural philosophy of Aristotle and the commentaries thereon were forbidden by a provincial council at
Paris; in 1215 the prohibition was repeated and specifically applied to the *Metaphysics*; in 1231 the Pope prohibited the study of these works at Paris until they should
have been purged of all error by a special commission.
No actual expurgation, however, seems to have taken
place; the difficulties were simply smoothed out and explained away, and the Arabic interpretations were swept
aside, until, by 1255, the whole of the new Aristotle is
prescribed at the University of Paris for the degree of

[1] G. F. Moore, *History of Religions*, ii (New York, 1919), p. ix.

Master of Arts. Moreover, while Averroës does not appear in these statutes, his commentary on Aristotle remained in regular use down to the seventeenth century and earned him a place with the great philosophers of antiquity in Dante's *Inferno*, where he is celebrated as the author of the *Great Commentary* — *che il gran commento feo*. Dante, however, also preserved the memory of a follower of Averroës, one Siger de Brabant, "who syllogized invidious truths in the Street of Straw" at Paris, and the revival of Latin Averroïsm at Paris in the later thirteenth century left a strong taint of heresy about the master's memory. The most vigorous efforts of Albertus Magnus and Thomas Aquinas were needed to check this new heterodoxy, whose tenets have been handed down in a long list of two hundred and nineteen errors condemned at Paris in 1277. Here, along with much else, we find the Averroïstic doctrines of the eternity of matter and the denial of personal immortality. When the contradiction between such doctrines and orthodox belief was pointed out, Siger and many of his followers brought forward the comfortable theory that what was necessary in philosophy might be false in theology, and vice versa. Meanwhile the teachings of Averroës were supposed to have infected that suspicious character, the Emperor Frederick II, while his later reputation can be seen from a fresco in the Campo Santo at Pisa which represents him suffering torment with Mohammed and Antichrist.

Philosophy and theology also came to blows in the

case of other heretical doctrines of the twelfth century, the pantheisms of Amauri de Bène and David of Dinant, and the dualism of the Albigenses. The Pantheists, perhaps also connected with the Averroïsts, were included in the Paris condemnation of 1210. The Dualists, Manichaeans, or Cathari, were the chief object of the Albigensian crusade and the Dominican Inquisition. As the name indicates, Manichaeism goes back to the heretics of the Roman empire and ultimately to the dualism of the Persians. Perhaps surviving from early times in Gaul, it was in any event also spread from the East through the Balkans to the North of Italy and the South of France, where it broke out violently in the twelfth century. It does not particularly affect the philosophic thinking of the age, but it had a wide popular influence, and its anti-sacerdotal character called into activity all the agencies of the church for its suppression. Unfortunately for us, the destruction of this heretical literature was carried out so thoroughly that the teachings of its authors are scarcely known outside of the citations and refutations of its enemies.

We must not, however, suppose that the philosophical activity of the twelfth century was entirely or even mainly due to Greek and Arabic influence. Indeed Anselm and Abaelard, the chief philosophical minds of the age, antedate the introduction of the new material, while that great problem of scholasticism, the question of universals, had been raised by Roscellinus before 1092.

Anselm (d. 1109), "last of the Fathers and first of the scholastics," is both a follower of St. Augustine and the spiritual ancestor of St. Bonaventura and St. Thomas. His philosophy is fundamentally concerned with theological speculation, especially the existence of God. This he seeks to establish by objectifying the human conception of the greatest possible being, a form of extreme realism which he applies to prove the independent existence of such abstract ideas as justice and truth. As the opponent of Roscellinus, he plunges us into the midst of the question of universals when he says, "he who does not understand how several men are in species but a single man cannot understand how several persons can be one God, yet each a perfect God." He does not, however, support those who have no place whatever for dialectic. His famous principle, "I believe in order that I may understand," leaves much room for understanding: "the proper order requires that we should believe with profound faith before we presume to discuss by our reason, but after we are strengthened in the faith we should not neglect to study to understand what we believe." His faith is ever seeking to understand, *fides quaerens intellectum*.

The importance of liberal learning is also emphasized by the great mystical philosopher of this period, Hugh of St. Victor (1096–1141), but chiefly as a means to the understanding of the hidden meaning of the Scriptures. His great treatise *On the Sacraments* has something of the organic and logical system of the later *summae*, but it takes us rather into the world of symbolism and allegory. With him the material universe is a symbol, Scripture is an allegory, the sacraments are "perfected and potent symbols which have been shadowed forth in the unperfected sacramental character of all God's works from the beginning." [1] He can even find in the ark of Noah a symbol of the church in which every detail has its allegorical meaning. If, like Anselm, he starts with Augustine, the mystic soon triumphs over the philosopher, and the allegorical interpretation resolves the contradictions which perplex his more dialectically minded contemporaries.

In Abaelard (1079–1142) we have one of the most striking figures of the mediaeval renaissance. Vain and self-conscious, as we have found him in his autobiography, his defects of temperament must not blind us to his great mental gifts. He was daring, original, brilliant, one of the first philosophical minds of the whole Middle Ages. First and foremost a logician, with an unwavering faith in the reasoning process, he fell in with the dialectic preoccupations of his age, and did more than any one else to define the problems and methods of scholasticism, at least in the matter of universals and in his *Sic et non*. The question of universals, the central though not the unique theme of scholastic philosophy, is concerned with the nature of general terms or conceptions, such as man,

[1] Taylor, *The Mediaeval Mind* (1925), ii. 90.

house, horse. Are these, as the Nominalists asserted, mere names and nothing more, an intellectual convenience at the most? Or are they realities, as the Realists maintained, having an existence quite independent of and apart from the particular individuals in which they may be for the moment objectified? A mere matter of logical terminology, you may say, of no importance in the actual world. Yet much depends upon the application. Apply the nominalistic doctrine to God, and the indivisible Trinity dissolves into three persons. Apply it to the Church, and the Church ceases to be a divine institution with a life of its own and becomes merely a convenient designation for the whole body of individual Christians. Apply to it the State, and where does political authority reside, in a sovereign whole or in the individual citizens? In this form, at least, the problem is still with us. Practical thinking cannot entirely shake itself free from logic, and, conversely, logic has sometimes practical consequences not at first realized.

The debate respecting universals has its roots in Boethius and Porphyry, but it comes into the foreground with Roscellinus, an extreme Nominalist, condemned in 1092 for tritheism at the instance of Anselm. Against the extreme realism represented in various forms by William of Champeaux, Abaelard maintained a more moderate view, a doctrine which he worked out with his usual brilliancy and which we have just begun to understand with the publication, now proceeding, of his *Glosses on Porphyry*. As here explained, this resembles closely the doctrine of later orthodoxy. In an age, however, when theology was a prime object of attention, the logicians were always under the temptation of applying their dialectic to fundamental problems concerning the nature of God, and it is not surprising to find that Abaelard, like Roscellinus before him, ran into difficulties on the subject of the Trinity, being condemned for heresy at Soissons in 1121 and at Sens in 1141. Such conflicts were inevitable with one of Abaelard's radical temper, who courted opposition and combat; but the dangers of mixing dialectic and theology were even more apparent in the instance of Gilbert de la Porrée, bishop of Poitiers, a man of great weight and authority, whose *Liber sex principiorum* was studied along with the *Organon* of Aristotle in the mediaeval universities, but whose exposition of Boethius *On the Trinity* brought him before a church council in 1148. Fortunately for him, he knew more than his opponents, who, he declared, did not understand Boethius; and he retained the respect of the more discriminating of his contemporaries, such as Otto of Freising and John of Salisbury.

In another way Abaelard contributed to the formation of scholasticism, namely, in his *Sic et non*, or *Yes and No*. True, the method of collecting and arranging passages from the Fathers on specific topics had been used before, as in the *Sentences* of Anselm of Laon, but Abaelard gave it a pungency and a wide popularity which associate it permanently with his name. Like everything he did, it was well advertised. His method was to take significant topics of theology and ethics and to collect from the Fathers their opinions pro and con, sharpening perhaps the contrast and being careful not to solve the real or seeming contradiction. Inerrancy he grants only to the Scriptures, apparent contradictions in which must be explained as due to scribal mistakes or defective understanding; subsequent authorities may err for other reasons, and when they disagree he claims the right of going into the reasonableness of the doctrine itself, of proving all things in order to hold fast that which is good. He has accordingly collected divergent sayings of the Fathers as they have come to mind, for the purpose of stimulating tender readers to the utmost effort in seeking out truth and of making them more acute as the result of such inquiry. "By doubting we come to inquiry, and by inquiry we perceive truth." The propositions cover a wide range of topics and of reading; some are dismissed briefly, while others bring forth long citations. Thus:

1. That faith is to be supported by human reason, *et contra*.
5. That God is not single, *et contra*.
32. That to God all things are possible, *et non*.
55. That only Eve, not Adam, was beguiled, *et contra*.
58. That Adam was saved, *et contra*.
106. That no one can be saved without baptism of water, *et contra*.
115. That nothing is yet established concerning the origin of the soul, *et contra*.
122. That marriage is lawful for all, *et contra*.
141. That works of mercy do not profit those without faith, *et contra*.

145. That we sin at times unwillingly, *et contra*.
154. That a lie is permissible, *et contra*.
157. That it is lawful to kill a man, *et non*.

Some of these questions, like the last two, one can almost imagine briefed on either side in modern manuals for the training of debaters. Some such purpose, the stimulating of discussion among his pupils, seems to have been Abaelard's primary object, but the emphasis upon contradiction rather than upon agreement and the failure to furnish any solutions, real or superficial, tended powerfully to expose the weaknesses in the orthodox position and to undermine authority generally. Gratian, the next to employ this method, was careful to bring the authorities into agreement, however formal or hollow it might be, in his *Concord of Discordant Canons*. Thus used, it became the regular form of scholastic exposition — proposition, opposition, and solution — as we find it most elaborately worked out by St. Thomas Aquinas.

The stimulus given to dialectic by the masters of the early part of the century, reënforced later by the recovery and absorption of the *New Logic* of Aristotle, made the twelfth century preëminently an age of logic. The earlier *trivium* had preserved a balance between logic on the one hand and grammar and rhetoric on the other, but this was now destroyed by the addition of a large body of new material to be mastered in dialectic, so that less time and still less inclination were left for the leisurely study of grammar and literature, as they had been pursued in the school of Chartres. By 1159, John of Salisbury, whose humane philosophy, *moderatrix omnium*, is the ripe product of the older type of balanced culture, is protesting in vain against the neglect of classical learning in favor of the newer studies and against the 'Cornifician' masters who offer practical short cuts in education. He can also satirize the futility of excessive logical debate in the person of those who discuss whether the pig is led to market by the rope or by the driver. Dialectic is to him a means, not an end: while it furthers other studies, "if it remain by itself it lies bloodless and barren, nor does it quicken the soul to yield fruit of philosophy, except the same conceive from elsewhere." Yet logic is already driving letters from the schools, and the thirteenth century will have no place for the Latin classics in the curriculum of the universities.

While dialectic thus dominates the thinking of the new age, the logical works of Aristotle are forced to share the field with his other writings, and a curriculum like the Paris course of 1255 which includes the *Physics* and lesser works on natural science, the *Ethics* and *Metaphysics*, is far more than a training in logic. It has found some place for science, in a way that will react upon the philosophic thinking of the thirteenth century, and it has prepared, as we shall see, potential conflicts with theology.

The revival of philosophy in the twelfth century was accompanied by renewed activity in the allied field of theology, indeed the two were not easily separable in the thinking of that age, and the philosophers, as we have seen, were pretty certain to have their fling at purely theological questions. The logical method of the age quickly affected the formulation and organization of theological thought. The translation of John of Damascus by Burgundio added something to the stock of Latin theology, and the writings of the Pseudo-Dionysius contributed to Western mysticism and angelology, but after Anselm the twelfth century devoted itself chiefly to the systematization of earlier material. Thus the influence of Abaelard's *Sic et non* and of Gratian showed itself in the *Sentences* of Peter Lombard, who died bishop of Paris in 1160, a systematic theology in four books covering respectively God and the Trinity, Creation and the Fall, the Incarnation and morals, and the sacraments and last things. Whereas Abaelard emphasized the contradictions between his authorities, the Lombard's temperament was conservative and harmonizing, eschewing the "garrulities of the dialecticians," and softening and reconciling the differences and disagreements to a degree that made the 'Magister Sententiarum' the standard authority for many centuries to come. By 1205 the *Sentences* have been glossed by Peter of Poitiers, in 1215 they are stamped with the approval of the Lateran Council. They were the textbook for two years of the course in theology, indeed the usual library of a student in theology, when he could afford a library, became the Bible and these *Sentences*, fifty copies of which with one hundred and eighteen volumes of commentaries were in the library of the Sorbonne in the year 1338. Albertus Magnus even assumes a 'summary' knowledge of the Bible and the *Sentences*, as well as of the liberal arts, on the part of the Virgin Mary.

This example of successful systematization was followed in a host of *summae* or systematic outlines of theology and related subjects, somewhat as the years after the Great War saw the appearance of outlines of history, literature, science, gastronomy, and almost everything else. Such was the manual of sacred history, the *Historia scholastica* of Peter Comestor, chancellor of Paris until 1178, a veritable devourer of books only to be devoured himself by worms, as his epitaph reminds us (*dictus comestor nunc comedor*), whose work was in every library and passed through eight printed editions by 1487. Such, too, were the summary of ethics in the *Verbum abbreviatum* of the Paris professor Petrus Cantor (d. 1197), written "against the superfluity and prolixity of glosses and futile questions"; the canonistic *summae* of Robert de Courçon and others; and a large body of theological *summae* and sentences which carry us into the thirteenth century and prefigure the great *Summa* of Thomas Aquinas in which they are completed and synthesized. Contemporary with the great Gothic cathedrals, these architectonic *summae* have well been called cathedrals of human thought.

On the side of political theory the twelfth century has less to show. Throughout the Middle Ages the theory of politics lagged far behind its practice, and the twelfth century was no exception. Indeed, save in the realm of church and state, there is little relation between theory and practice, no attempt to derive a theory from the facts of current observation; men practiced feudalism, but studied Aristotle and the Fathers. There is, accordingly, no literary reflection of the revival of the state in the twelfth century in England, Sicily, Aragon, and somewhat later in France. At the same time the newer philosophical critics leave the state alone; we do not meet a nominalist doctrine of the state before Marsiglio of Padua and William of Ockham. Indeed the twelfth century is rather a slack period in the history of political theory, for the pamphlet literature dealing with church and state had just spent its force during the controversy over investiture, and the more systematic discussion awaited the translation of Aristotle's *Politics ca.* 1260 and the *Summa* of Thomas Aquinas. Of this intervening period the chief product is the *Policraticus*, or *Rulers' Book*, of John of Salisbury, written in 1159. "The first attempt to look apart from surrounding conditions and to produce a coherent system which should aspire to the character of a philosophy of politics," it "bears no reference to contemporary forms of government." Its author had a wide experience of the papal curia and the court of Henry II, yet he scarcely mentions either; "his examples are those of the Old Testament or of the ancient Roman empire," [1] and so is his political terminology throughout. If his theory of kingship seems affected by the feudal idea that the king is below the law, the authorities cited are from the Roman law and the ancient historians, and they give the color to his views of tyranny and tyrannicide. John writes throughout as a humanist, not as an observer, concerned less with the difficulties of contemporary statesmen than with the difficulty of remaining a philosopher in their company; his work is of the twelfth century by virtue of its literary and civilian background rather than its political atmosphere. It could not have been written earlier, neither could it have been written much later, for its scholasticism is literary rather than Aristotelian.

Any account of mediaeval philosophy must take into consideration the matter of intellectual liberty, the freedom of the thinker to follow his conclusions to the end. In general, this freedom was far greater than is commonly believed. Within the limits of the doctrines of the church, men were free to speculate as they would, and these limits were not felt as a restriction to the degree we might imagine. Teachers of law and medicine, of grammar and logic, of mathematics and astronomy, did not find themselves held down by prescribed rules. As Thorndike has shown, experiment and research were much freer

[1] R. L. Poole, *Illustrations of the History of Medieval Thought and Learning* (1920), p. 204.

than has been supposed. Nor, in the absence of the social sciences, were there any of those conflicts with civil authority which have disturbed writers on these subjects in recent times. When Bury [1] speaks of the Middle Ages as "a millennium in which reason was enchained, thought was enslaved, and knowledge made no progress," he goes far beyond the facts of the case.

What the authors of such statements appear to mean is that conformity to any fixed and authoritative body of doctrine constitutes an intolerable limitation on free thought, and, since mediaeval Europe had such a system, the human reason was in prison. Historically, or pragmatically, formulated, however, the question is not how such restrictions on inquiry would be felt today, but how far they were actually felt in the Middle Ages. Freedom is a relative matter. If men did not consider themselves fettered, they were for practical purposes free, and the fact seems to be that the amount of actual conflict of reason with authority was comparatively small. It was almost wholly confined to philosophy, and was apparently far less than a modern philosopher would expect. For good or ill, mediaeval philosophy was less interested in the foundations of knowledge than in its processes, so that it found no hardship in accepting certain propositions as axiomatic and applying its energy to drawing conclusions therefrom. Even when Abaelard shows the inconsisten-

[1] J. B. Bury, *History of Freedom of Thought* (London and New York, 1913), p. 52.

cies of authority in his *Sic et non*, he is not molested for this. Both the reverent John of Salisbury and the irreverent Frederick II seem to have led untrammelled lives. John ranged at will through ancient literature, pagan and Christian, and wrote freely on the philosophy of the state and of life; Frederick discussed the immortality of the soul with Jews and Mohammedans, and while men shook their heads, no one punished him or his companions. For the most part intellectual life went its way unhindered.

Freedom of course engenders variety, and here again current impressions are likely to mislead us by giving a false idea of the uniformity of mediaeval thought. Scholasticism was a method rather than a single system of doctrine, and in different hands this method might and did lead to different conclusions. To our distant eyes the differences within scholastic philosophy may often seem minute, but they bulked large in the view of contemporaries, and they were so considerable as to excite and maintain active controversy in every period throughout the age. If these controversies are more acute in the thirteenth and fourteenth centuries, they have their roots in the preceding age, the age which formulated the problem of universals and developed the dialectic method of Abaelard and his successors. Nothing would have astonished mediaeval philosophers more than to be told that they all thought alike.

Philosophy, then, was free, save where it trespassed upon theology, but philosophy at all times has a way of trespassing upon theology, and the result must not be overlooked in any view of our period. The difficulty is inherent in any authoritative system of religious doctrine, and the conflict showed itself in the case of Judaism and Mohammedanism as clearly as in that of Christianity. Even the Athenians condemned Socrates to death for denying the official gods of the city. In our period the chief instances of restriction upon philosophical freedom concern, as we have seen, the application of logic to the Trinity by Roscellinus, Abaelard, and Gilbert de la Porrée, and the interdiction of the new Aristotle until it should be 'purged of error' — as it never was. The instrument in these *causes célèbres* was a church council; the penalty was recantation or imprisonment, in the case of the Amalrician heretics of 1209 it was death. Later on, the Latin Averroïsts likewise tried to mix philosophy and theology, or rather to maintain that the two were independent disciplines which might well lead to contradictory conclusions without prejudice to faith; but this way out was condemned by ecclesiastical authority, and professors of arts at Paris were forbidden to meddle with theology, a supreme as well as a separate discipline. On this occasion academic authority and the Inquisition were brought to bear.

The plight of the Latin Averroïsts illustrates the fundamental difficulty of the position in which philosophers found themselves after the reception of the Aristotelian science and metaphysics. "Whereas an Abaelard had nothing more to say when he had finished teaching his dialectic and was forced to become a theologian if he wished to attack other problems, in the thirteenth century the humblest master of arts found himself in possession of a vast domain which included, besides the older dialectic, psychology, physics, ethics, and metaphysics." In expounding the texts of the new curriculum in arts, the professor "found himself compelled to examine as a philosopher and from the point of view of natural reason alone problems which up to that time had been considered as reserved to theology and theologians," [1] problems, too, of which Aristotle's solutions did not always accord with those of Christian theology. At the same time, not being a professor of theology, the master of arts lacked the competence for resolving the contradiction authoritatively in the orthodox sense. Here theology took decisively the upper hand, as 'Madame la haute science' to which philosophy was only the handmaiden, the captive taken from the enemy. The theological intellect should dominate all other faculties of a university, said Gregory IX in 1228, and guide them in the path of righteousness as the spirit rules the flesh; and the Faculty of Arts at Paris in 1272 forbade discussion of any purely theological question like the Trinity, and pronounced sentence of exclusion from their body as a heretic against any master or bachelor who should transgress the due bounds of the faculty by disputing concerning any ques-

[1] E. Gilson, *Études de philosophie médiévale* (Strasbourg, 1921), pp. 56–57.

tion touching both faith and philosophy and should determine it contrary to faith. Henceforth any debatable common territory was to be occupied by theology alone.

With the Cathari and, to a less degree, the Waldenses, the problem takes a different form. It is not a question of individual speculation, but of the popular acceptance of doctrines which struck at the base of the sacramental system and the power of the keys, and the endemic character of the movement in Southern France required new organs of suppression. To supplement and finally to take the place of the local council and the local bishop, the centralized machinery of the papal or Dominican Inquisition was created by Gregory IX between 1227 and 1241, and the regular penalty for obdurate heretics now became death by burning. In this the church had the support of popular opinion as well as of the civil authority, for the heretic was regarded as a sort of anarchist, an anti-social person who struck at the foundations of society, and his punishment by fire was held to symbolize and prefigure his eternal fate in hell. The first civil legislation on heresy since Roman days is a section of Henry II's Assize of Clarendon in 1166; death by burning makes its appearance in the code of the freethinking Frederick II, to whom the heretic was a traitor, guilty of lese-majesty against the Divine Emperor, God himself. The limitations of mediaeval tolerance are nowhere more evident.

BIBLIOGRAPHICAL NOTE

As a guide to the philosophy of our period one may use the fifth edition of M. De Wulf, *Histoire de la philosophie médiévale*, i (Louvain, 1924; translated, London, 1925), with excellent bibliographical apparatus by A. Pelzer; a more detailed bibliography is in Ueberweg-Baumgartner, *Grundriss der Geschichte der Philosophie*, ii (tenth edition, Berlin, 1915). B. Hauréau, *Histoire de la philosophie scolastique* (Paris, 1872–80), is still fundamental. Brief accounts by masters are E. Gilson, *La philosophie au moyen âge de Scot Érigène à G. d'Occam* (Paris, 1925); C. Baeumker, in *Die Kultur der Gegenwart*, i, 5 (Berlin, 1913), pp. 288–381; and M. Grabmann, *Die Philosophie des Mittelalters* (Berlin, 1921). For a still briefer summary, see *Cambridge Medieval History*, v, ch. 23. Many texts and studies relating to the twelfth century are published in Baeumker's *Beiträge zur Geschichte der Philosophie des Mittelalters* (Münster, 1891 ff.), e.g., the *De eodem* of Adelard of Bath and the *Glosses* of Abaelard on Porphyry.

Important studies of particular aspects of the period are M. Grabmann, *Geschichte der scholastischen Methode* (Freiburg, 1911–13); E. Gilson, *Études de philosophie médiévale* (Strasbourg, 1921); R. L. Poole, *Illustrations of the History of Medieval Thought and Learning* (second edition, London, 1920); C. C. J. Webb, *Studies in the History of Natural Theology* (Oxford, 1915); J. de Ghellinck, *Le mouvement théologique du XIIᵉ siècle* (Paris, 1914). For Platonism, see C. Baeumker, *Der Platonismus im Mittelalter* (Munich, 1916); for the reception of Aristotle, my *Mediaeval Science*, especially ch. 11, and the works there cited. On Siger de Brabant the fundamental monograph of P. Mandonnet (Louvain, 1911) should be supplemented by the recent discoveries of M. Grabmann, *Sitzungsberichte* of the Munich Academy, p.-p. und hist. Klasse, 1924, no. 2, and *Miscellanea Ehrle*, i. 103–147; and F. M. Powicke (*Mélanges Ferdinand Lot*, Paris, 1925, p. 656). For the Cathari, consult P. Alphandéry, *Les idées morales chez les hétérodoxes latins au début du XIIIᵉ siècle* (Paris, 1903); and E. Broeckx, *Le catharisme* (Hoogstraten, 1916). On David of Dinant, see the volume of G. Théry in the *Bibliothèque Thomiste*, vi (1925), who distinguishes David's doctrines sharply from those of Amauri.

The standard history of mediaeval political theory is that of R. W. and A. J. Carlyle, *A History of Mediaeval Political Theory in the West*, i–iv (London, 1903–   ). The important portions of John of Salisbury's *Policraticus* (ed. C. C. J. Webb, Oxford, 1909) are translated with an excellent introduction by John Dickinson (New York, 1927). For the political theories of civilians and canonists, see O. Gierke, *Das deutsche Genossenschaftsrecht*, iii (Berlin, 1881).

The best history of the Inquisition in the Middle Ages is that of H. C. Lea (New York, 1887, also French and German editions). The procedure is analyzed by Ch. V. Langlois, *L'inquisition d'après des travaux récents* (Paris, 1902). A scholarly and fair-minded Roman Catholic account is that of the Abbé E. Vacandard, *The Inquisition* (New York, 1908). I have discussed the beginnings of the new procedure in Northern France in the *American Historical Review*, vii. 437–457, 631–652.

CHAPTER XII

THE BEGINNINGS OF UNIVERSITIES

THE twelfth century was not only an age of revival in the field of learning, it was an age of new creation in the field of institutions, most of all in the institutions of higher education. It begins with the monastic and cathedral schools, it ends with the earliest universities. We may say that it institutionalized higher learning or at least determined that process. In 1100 'the school followed the teacher,' by 1200 the teacher followed the school. At the same time these intervening years created a more advanced type of school by the very fact of the revival of learning. At the close of the eleventh century learning was almost entirely confined to the seven liberal arts of the traditional curriculum; the twelfth century filled out the *trivium* and *quadrivium* with the new logic, the new mathematics, and the new astronomy, while it brought into existence the professional faculties of law, medicine, and theology. Universities had not existed hitherto because there was not enough learning in Western Europe to justify their existence; they came into being naturally with the expansion of knowledge in this period. The intellectual revolution and the institutional revolution went hand in hand.

Besides producing the earliest universities, the twelfth century also fixed their form of organization for succeeding ages. This was not a revival of some ancient model, for the Graeco-Roman world had no universities in the modern sense of the term. It had higher education, it is true, really superior instruction in law, rhetoric, and philosophy, but this was not organized into faculties and colleges with the mechanism of fixed curricula and academic degrees. Even when the state took on the responsibility of advanced instruction in the state-paid teachers and public law schools of the later Roman empire, it did not establish universities. These arise first in the twelfth century, and the modern university is derived in its fundamental features from them, from Salerno, Bologna, Paris, Montpellier, and Oxford. From these the continuity is direct to our own day, and there was no other source. The university is a mediaeval contribution to civilization, and more specifically a contribution of the twelfth century.

The word university originally meant a corporation or gild in general, and the Middle Ages had many such forms of corporate life. Only gradually did the term become narrowed so as to denote exclusively a learned corporation or society of masters and scholars, *universitas societas magistrorum discipulorumque*, as it is expressed in the earliest and still the best definition of a university. In this general sense there might be several universities in the same town, just as there were several craft gilds, and these separate universities of law or of medicine were each jealous of their corporate life and were slow to coalesce into a single university with its special faculties. Speaking broadly, the nucleus of the new development was in Northern Europe a gild of masters and in the South a gild of students, but in both cases the point of chief importance centres about admission to the gild of masters or professors. Without such admission there could be no license to teach; until then one could be only a student, thereafter one was a master, in rank if not by occupation, and had passed out of the journeyman stage. In order to guard against favoritism and monopoly, such admission was determined by an examination, and ability to pass this examination was the natural test of academic attainment in the several subjects of study. This license to teach (*licentia docendi*) was thus the earliest form of academic degree. Historically, all degrees are in their origin teachers' certificates, as the names doctor and master still show us; a Master of Arts was a qualified teacher of arts, a Doctor of Laws or Medicine was a certified teacher of these subjects. Moreover the candidate regularly gave a specimen lecture, or, as it was said, incepted, and this inception is the origin of the modern commencement, which means commencing to teach. An examination presupposes a body of material upon which the candidate is examined, usually a set of standard textbooks, and this in turn implies systematic teaching and a minimum period of study. Curriculum, examinations, commencement, degrees, are all part of the same system; they are all inherited from the Middle Ages, and in some form they go back to the twelfth century.

The background of the early universities is the monastery and cathedral schools, as these had been reorganized and extended by the Carolingian legislation. As the primary purpose of this reform was an educated clergy, it occupied itself directly only with schools for monks and cathedral clerks. There was also apparently the possibility of an 'external' school for others, but in the nature of the case this was supplementary or incidental and could not be generally counted on as a regular institution of learning. Even with the internal schools there was great variation from place to place. The seven liberal arts were an ideal often very imperfectly realized; schools like Monte Cassino and Bec were brilliant exceptions, not representative examples. Moreover, as we have seen, the monasteries as centres of culture decline as we pass into the twelfth century, and most of the monastic schools decline likewise, so that the revival of learning and the new institutional development found little aid in this quarter. Indeed the monasteries were by their nature ill prepared to house any considerable body of non-monastic students, and the presence of these in any number might prove prejudicial to the maintenance of discipline for those living under the rule. The cathedral, urban by its nature, did not suffer from these disadvantages, and the growing importance of the cathedrals in this age is reflected in the greater activity of their schools. Even here we must not exaggerate the amount of provision for regular instruction: a Lateran decree of 1179 which prescribes the reservation of a benefice for a schoolmaster in every cathedral has to be renewed in 1215 because of its neglect in many churches.

The most important cathedral schools of the twelfth century are those of Northern France. Some of these, like Rheims and Chartres, represent an earlier development which reached its climax in this period; others, like Laon and Tours, were of but temporary importance; still others, like Paris and probably Orleans, went on to form universities. All were influenced in greater or less degree by the revival of learning, some especially by its classical phase, others chiefly by its dialectic and theology. In all of them the teacher at first counted for more than the school, indeed Paris is the only such centre which now acquired a momentum independent of the individual master and drew students by its own attractive power. And Paris is the only one which in this period fully became a university. The freer conditions of the pre-university epoch, when men moved in leisurely fashion from place to place in search of eminent masters, careless of curriculum or fixed periods of study or degrees, are portrayed in a famous passage of John of Salisbury which covers the years 1136–47: [1]

---

[1] *Metalogicus*, ii. 10, as translated by R. L. Poole, *Illustrations of the History of Medieval Thought and Learning* (1920), pp. 177–186.

When as a lad I first went into Gaul for the cause of study (it was the next year after that the glorious king of the English, Henry the Lion of Righteousness, departed from human things) I addressed myself to the Peripatetic of Palais [Abaelard], who then presided upon Mount Saint Genovefa, an illustrious teacher and admired of all men. There at his feet I acquired the first rudiments of the dialectical art, and snatched according to the scant measure of my wits whatever passed his lips with entire greediness of mind. Then, when he had departed, all too hastily, as it seemed to me, I joined myself to master Alberic, who stood forth among the rest as a greatly esteemed dialectician, and verily was the bitterest opponent of the nominal sect.

Being thus for near two whole years occupied on the Mount I had to my instructors in the dialectical art Alberic and master Robert of Melun (that I may designate him by the surname which he hath deserved in the governing of schools; howbeit by nation he is of England): whereof the one was in questions subtil and large, the other in responses lucid, short, and agreeable. [They were in some sort counterparts of one another; if the analytical faculty of Alberic had been combined in one person with Robert's clear decision] our age could not have shown an equal in debate. For they were both men of sharp intellect, and in study unconquerable. . . . Thus much for the time that I was conversant with them: for afterwards the one went to Bologna and unlearned that which he had taught; yea, and returned and untaught the same; whether for the better or no, let them judge who heard him before and since. Moreover the other went on to the study of divine letters, and aspired to the glory of a nobler philosophy and a more illustrious name.

With these I applied myself for the full space of two years, to practice in the commonplaces and rules and other rudimentary elements, which are instilled into the minds of boys and wherein the aforesaid doctors were most able and ready; so that methought I knew all these things as well as my nails and fingers. This at least I had learned, in the lightness of youth to account my knowledge of more worth than it was. I seemed to myself a young scholar, because I was quick in that which I heard. Then returning unto myself and measuring my powers, I advisedly resorted, by the good favour of my preceptors, to the Grammarian of Conches [William], and heard his teaching by the space of three years; the while teaching much: nor shall I ever regret that time. [While at Chartres John also studied with Richard l'Évêque] a man whose training was deficient almost in nothing, who had more heart even than speech, more knowledge than skill, more truth than vanity, more virtue than show: and the things I had learned from others I collected all again from him, and certain things too I learned which I had not before heard and which appertain to the Quadrivium, wherein formerly I had for some time followed the German Hardwin. I read also again rhetoric, which aforetime I had scarce understood when it was treated of meagrely by master Theodoric. The same I afterwards received more plenteously at the hand of Peter Helias.

Since I received the children of noble persons to instruct, who furnished me with living — for I lacked the help of friends and kinsfolk, but God assuaged my neediness, — the force of duty and the instance of my pupils moved me the oftener to recall what I had learned. Wherefore I made closer acquaintance with master Adam [du Petit-Pont], a man of exceeding sharp wits and, whatever others may think, of much learning, who applied himself above the rest to Aristotle: in such wise that, albeit I had him not to my teacher, he gave me kindly of his, and delivered himself openly enough; the which he was wont to do to none or to few others than his own scholars, for he was deemed to suffer from jealousy. . . .

From hence I was withdrawn by the straitness of my private estate, the instance of my companions, and the counsel of my friends, that I should undertake the office of a teacher. I obeyed: and thus returning at the expiration of three years, I found master Gilbert [de la Porrée] and heard him in logic and divinity; but too quickly was he removed. His successor was Robert Pullus, whom his life and knowledge alike recommended. Then I had Simon of Poissy, a trusty lecturer, but dull in disputation. But these two I had in theologics alone. Thus, engaged in diverse studies near twelve years passed by me.

And so it seemed pleasant to me to revisit my old companions on the Mount [at Paris], whom I had left and whom dialectic still detained, to confer with them touching old matters of debate; that we might by mutual comparison measure together our several progress. I found them as before, and where they were before; nor did they appear to have reached the goal in unravelling the old questions, nor had they added one jot of a proposition. The aims that once inspired them, inspired them still: they only had progressed in one point, they had unlearned moderation, they knew not modesty; in such wise that one might despair of their recovery. And thus experience taught me a manifest conclusion, that, whereas dialectic furthers other studies, so if it remain by itself it lies bloodless and barren, nor does it quicken the soul to yield fruit of philosophy, except the same conceive from elsewhere.

John is here speaking of Paris and Chartres, to which we shall return in a moment, though he may also have visited Rheims and Provins. Of the less conspicuous schools Rheims was most remarkable under Albericus, head of the school from 1121 to 1136, a theologian of some eminence, praised by the Primate for his devotion to Scripture rather than to Priscian or the poets:

> Non leguntur hic poete,
> Sed Iohannes et prophete.

While Rheims seems to have had some further importance under Archbishop William (1176–1202), a distinguished patron of letters, at no time did it have any such standing or influence as it had enjoyed under Gerbert in the tenth century. Laon we hear of in the days of Albericus's master Anselm (d. 1117), 'the old man of Laon,' of whom Abaelard speaks in terms of much disrespect, but who has a considerable place in the development of the theological method of 'sentences,' and of Anselm's brother Ralph, who is noted as a mathematician; but after their time it lapses into obscurity. Still earlier another mathematician, Adelard of Bath, had studied and taught at Laon and seems to have had some connection with Tours, whose most famous master was the Platonist philosopher Bernard Silvester. Of Orleans we know little that is specific in this period beyond the fact that it was a celebrated centre of literary studies and rhetoric,[1] an eminence which it retained into the thirteenth century

[1] See Chapters IV–VI.

when it became known rather as a university of law. The constitutional side of Orleans is very obscure, so that we cannot speak with assurance of the connection between the older schools of rhetoric and the newer university.

Chartres clearly did not become a university, indeed its flourishing period is over by the middle of the twelfth century, when the ascendancy of Paris is well established. It is a centre of canon law as well as of theology under the distinguished canonist St. Ivo, bishop from 1089 to 1115, in whose time we have an engaging picture of school life in the letters of two nephews of Dean Arnold — working at a Psalter, copying a book on dialectic, and making glosses; sending home for parchment and chalk, 'for their own chalk is worth nothing,' as well as for their father's boots and the material for a lambskin cloak; and not omitting requests for money from their mother, Leticia, on whose name they played in Latin verse:

> Nomen tuum,
> Nomen letum,
> Prebet nobis gaudia.

Over the schools of Chartres stood a series of eminent chancellors: Bernard the grammarian, "the most abounding spring of letters in Gaul"; Gilbert de la Porrée, logician and theologian, remembered at Chartres also for his special care for the books of the library; Thierry, to whom Bernard Silvester dedicates his treatises on cosmology, and Hermann the Dalmatian his translation of Ptolemy's *Planisphere*. A wide knowledge of the seven liberal arts appears in Thierry's *Eptatheuchon*, or *Book of the Seven Arts*, *ca.* 1150, in which Thierry sought to marry the *trivium* and *quadrivium* "for the multiplication of the noble tribe of scholars"; and the general reputation of Chartres lay, as we have seen,[1] in literary studies, where the thorough methods of Bernard have been already described by John of Salisbury as they were carried on in his time by William of Conches and Richard l'Évêque. Chartres, we have also seen,[2] was the chief centre of twelfth-century Platonism. The death of Thierry, *ca.* 1155, marks the end of the great period of Chartres: by the time its cathedral church, with its "dedicated shapes of saints and kings," has taken on something of the form we know, the school has passed its zenith. From Our Lady of Chartres,

> Silent and gray as forest-leaguered cliff
> Left inland by the ocean's slow retreat,

men turn to Our Lady of Paris, amid the bustling activity of what is fast becoming the capital of the French monarchy.

At Paris the situation was complicated by the presence of three schools: that of the cathedral of Nôtre Dame, that of the canons regular of Saint-Victor, of which William of Champeaux at the beginning of this century was the first known master, and that of the collegiate church of Sainte-Geneviève, which passed into the hands

---

[1] See Chapters IV, V, and the extract from John of Salisbury on pp. 373-374.   [2] Chapter XI.

of canons regular in 1147. Thus Abaelard began his
studies and teaching at Nôtre Dame, where he seems to
have become canon, later listened in the external schools
of William of Champeaux at Saint-Victor, but in his
maturer years taught on the Mount of Sainte-Geneviève
where John of Salisbury heard him in the passage quoted
above. The fame of Abaelard as an original and inspiring
teacher, with a ready command of the ancient authorities and a quick perception of their inconsistencies, and
withal "able to move the minds of serious men to laugh-
ter," had much to do with the resort of students to Paris,
although Abaelard was for one reason or another absent
from Paris for long stretches of time and was followed by
large bodies of students to Melun and Corbeil and even
into the desert. Still it was in his day that Paris became
the great centre of dialectic study, and if his later teaching was associated only with Sainte-Geneviève and its
direct influence suffered from the decline of this school, in
a larger sense he contributed powerfully to the habitual
resort of students to Paris for advanced study. It is true
that our fullest description of his success as a teacher is
given by himself, but this receives general confirmation
from unimpeachable witnesses like John of Salisbury and
Otto of Freising, as well as by more casual evidence. It
will be noted in John of Salisbury's account that Abaelard
is only one of many masters with whom he studied at
Paris, so that already we see signs of the change which
Rashdall observes in the next generation, when "Paris

became a city of teachers — the first city of teachers the medieval world had known." [1] The masters, like the students, came from many lands. John of Salisbury had been preceded shortly by Otto, future bishop of Freising and uncle of Frederick Barbarossa, and by Adalbert the future archbishop of Mainz; a list of masters *ca.* 1142 mentions not only Bretons like Abaelard and Thierry of Chartres and a Norman like William of Conches, but Englishmen such as Robert of Melun, Adam of the Little Bridge, and the future bishop of Exeter, and an Italian in the person of Peter Lombard. A little later we hear of students from still more remote countries, the nephews of the archbishop of Lund in Sweden and an Hungarian friend of Walter Map who becomes archbishop of Gran.

In the second half of the century Paris grows and consolidates its position. When John of Salisbury comes there again in 1164 on behalf of Becket, he is obliged to hire his rooms for a whole year, nor can he sufficiently admire the glories of the city, the splendor of its new cathedral, and 'the various occupations of its philosophers' who remind him of the angels ascending and descending Jacob's ladder. "Verily," he concludes, "the Lord is in this place, and I knew it not"; but his correspondent and superior, the abbot of Celle, sees fit to remind him of the dangers and temptations of Paris for the devout soul, advice which reappears somewhat later

[1] *Universities*, i. 289.

when the bishop of Paris prohibits his country priests from spending their weekdays in Paris and only Sundays in their parishes. About 1175 Guy de Bazoches writes an enthusiastic account of the city "raised above others by the royal diadem," with its island in the Seine an ancient centre of philosophy, law, and the seven arts, connected with the right bank by the Grand-Pont with its boats and merchandise, and with the left bank by the Petit-Pont, "set apart for the disputes of logicians as well as for strollers and passers-by." The intellectual preponderance of Paris is further attested by John of Salisbury's pupil, Peter of Blois, who studied civil law and theology there, lamenting the tendency to neglect the classics for professional studies, but asserting that the most intricate knots of difficult questions are here untangled. That vain and amusing Welshman, Giraldus Cambrensis, also studies law in Paris and has left us a boastful account of his Sunday lectures as a canonist, when almost all the doctors and scholars came "to hear his pleasing voice" discuss whether a judge should decide according to the evidence or according to his own opinion. The civilians of Paris disgusted Daniel of Morley, who turned to Toledo in order to listen to the 'wiser philosophers of this world,' but any possible danger that the new university might become a centre of the Roman law was ended in 1219 when the Pope forbade its study at Paris. The triumph of theology had long since been assured, for the masters mentioned in the poem of 1142 are mostly theologians,

and before his death in 1160 Peter Lombard had fixed
the form of theological discussion in his *Sentences* which
became the standard textbook for many generations.
Denifle remarks that the roots of the great theological
systems of the thirteenth century must be sought in the
twelfth century, and that all the great *summae* of theology point directly or indirectly to Paris. Indeed, by the
turn of the century Stephen of Tournai complains that
theological discussion has there become too active, dis-
secting the indivisible Trinity on the street corners and
pouring forth scandal and blasphemy in every lecture
hall and public square; and the Popes were quick to
check the vagaries of the philosophers and subordinate
them to the supreme faculty of theology. It was as a
school of theology that Paris became the first school
of the church. Already Paris was identified with that
Canaanitish city Kirjath-Sepher which mediaeval exegesis interpreted as a 'city of letters'; and in 1231 Pope
Gregory IX adds to this the name *Parens scientiarum*,
'parent of the sciences.'

Among all these indications of considerable bodies of
masters and students and of vigorous intellectual life, we
find very little evidence of formal university organization. Even the name university eludes our search before
the thirteenth century, when it appears incidentally in
1208–09 in the letters of a former student, Pope Innocent III. Here, as so often in the history of institutions,
the name follows after the thing itself. But while we

cannot find in the earlier period such full-fledged institutions as the four organized faculties, the nations, or the
rectorship, we can discern some traces of common university life. The subjects of study are grouped by faculties, whether or not the faculties themselves existed, and
the students seem to live in local groups, even if these
are not yet technically the nations of later times. The
first college also appears about 1180. There is some
suggestion of fixed terms of study, while for all schools a
canon of the Lateran Council of 1179 requires free admission of competent candidates to the rank of master.
Herein at Paris lay the germ of university organization,
in the control of teaching by the chancellor of the cathedral, who alone conferred the right to teach, *licentia
docendi*, and in the gild of the licensed masters or professors which became the university. Already in Abaelard's time there are traces of such supervision of teaching
on the part of the cathedral, as illustrated by his difficulties with the authorities at Paris and at Laon, and the
control of the body of teachers over formal admission to
their ranks grew as the century advanced. Inasmuch as
such a development was necessarily gradual, we cannot
say just when Paris ceased to be a cathedral school and
became a university, or give any special date for the
university's foundation. Like all the oldest universities,
it was not founded but grew. The growth, too, was partly
physical, from the precincts of the cathedral which housed
the earliest school to the Little Bridge on which masters

and scholars lived — the 'philosophers of the Little Bridge' even form a group by themselves — and thence to the Left Bank which has ever since been the Latin Quarter of Paris.

While the University of Paris thus originated of itself, it came to depend upon royal and still more upon papal support, and with papal support came papal control. The first specific document of the university's history belongs to the year 1200, the famous charter of Philip Augustus from which the existence of a university is sometimes dated, though such an institution really existed years earlier. There is here no suggestion of a new creation, but merely the recognition of a body of students and teachers which already exists: the *prévôt* and his men had attacked a hospice of German students and killed some of their number, including the bishop-elect of Liége; the king disciplines the *prévôt* severely and provides that students and their chattels shall have justice and be exempt from the jurisdiction of lay courts. The name university is not mentioned, but the assembly of scholars is recognized as the body before which the royal officers shall take oath. In 1208 or 1209 the earliest statutes deal with academic dress and funerals and with "the accustomed order in lectures and disputations," and the Pope recognizes the corporate character of this academic society, or university. Its right to self-government is further extended by the papal legate in 1215 in a document which gives the earliest outline of the course of study in arts. With the great papal privilege of 1231, the result of another town and gown row and a prolonged cessation of lectures, the fundamental documents of the university are complete. Indeed, the chancellor has begun to complain that there is too much organization and too much time consumed with university business: "in the old days when each master taught for himself and the name of the university was unknown, lectures and disputations were more frequent and there was more zeal for study." Paris has already fallen from the traditions of the good old times!

By the thirteenth century Paris has become the mother of universities as well as the mother of the sciences, counting the first of that numerous progeny which was to comprise all the mediaeval universities of Northern Europe, in Great Britain and in Germany as well as in Northern France and the Low Countries. An even wider field is suggested in a letter of 1205, in which the new Latin emperor of Constantinople asks for aid from Paris to reform the study of letters in Greece. The eldest daughter of this large family was Oxford, mother in turn of English universities.

Just why the first English university or indeed any university should have arisen at Oxford, nobody knows. Oxford in the Middle Ages was not a cathedral city, nor was it one of the greatest towns of the realm. Saxon in origin, it had a Norman stronghold, a monastery at St. Frideswide's and three monasteries in the neighborhood at Abingdon, Oseney, and Eynsham, and a royal castle not far distant; but if one were seeking a likely site for a future university, one would be more apt to choose a better established centre such as London, York, Winchester, or Canterbury. London, particularly, whose university dates only from 1836, might seem intrinsically to have had as good a chance as Paris. As Dean Rashdall concludes, "Oxford must be content to accept its academic position as an accident of its commercial importance," and, we may add, of the ease of access which goes with trade.

Nor can any one say just when a university first arose at Oxford. Time was indeed when Oxford seemed so necessary and ancient a part of the established order that its origin was ascribed to King Alfred or the Greek philosophers brought by the first British king, Brutus, grandson of Aeneas; the memory of man ran not to the contrary. Oxford could not have 'just grown,' like Paris, for we cannot discern anything out of which it grew. Theobald of Étampes, who taught there before 1117, was an isolated master, not the head of a school, and we do not know that he had a definite successor, or that the schools of Oxford in the twelfth century differed from those of many other places, as, for example, the London schools of whose disputes FitzStephen has left so vivid a description toward the close of the century. The fact seems to be that in some unexplained way Oxford profited by the recall of English students from Paris about 1167 so as to become their chief place of resort, and that it rose quickly into the position of a university, or *studium generale*, attended by students from foreign countries as well. By 1197 King Richard is supporting a clerk of Hungary in its schools. We must not, however, think of these foreign students as the nucleus of the *studium*; while it seems to have drawn the model of its organization from Paris, the material was English, the masters and students in whom the England of Henry II abounded and of whom we have seen many at Paris, but who henceforth remain in large numbers at home. *Ca.* 1180 the presence of a considerable community of scholars is shown by the appearance of a bookbinder, a scribe, two parchmenters, and three illuminators as witnesses of a conveyance of land near St. Mary's church. *Ca.* 1188 the irrepressible Giraldus Cambrensis, "in the most flattering of all autobiographies," [1] tells how he publicly read his latest book at Oxford, "where the clergy in England chiefly flourished and excelled in clerkship," the reading consuming three successive days in the course of which he entertained in his hostel all the doctors and scholars, "a costly and noble act which renewed the authentic and ancient times of the poets, nor does the present or any past age recall anything like it in England." Alexander Neckam, who died in 1217, mentions Oxford along with Paris, Bologna, Montpellier, and Salerno, but says nothing of its characteristic studies, which did not differ notably from those of Paris.

[1] Rashdall, *Universities*, ii. 341.

Nevertheless, as compared with Paris and Bologna, Oxford in 1200 was only an inchoate university. It had as yet no famous masters, it lacked charter and statutes. Its first privilege, the legatine ordinance of 1214, in which the chancellor is first mentioned, came as the result of a town and gown riot which, five years previously, had scattered its masters and scholars — to Cambridge, among other places — and produced a real crisis in the history of Oxford. Not until the second half of the thirteenth century do we meet with the earliest colleges, Balliol, Merton, and University, an institution which had sprung up first on the Continent but was destined in time to prove the most distinctive in English university life. Cambridge, the other modern home of the collegiate system, was quite unknown before the migration from Oxford in 1209, nor can we explain on any inherent grounds why it should have become the site of the other historic English university. In any case its origin and history lie beyond our period.

In the genesis of the Mediterranean universities, along with the cathedral and monastery schools we must take into account the survival of the traditions of lay education, particularly in the professions of law and medicine. At least at the outset these institutions are less concerned with the logic and mathematics which expanded the older curriculum in arts than they are with instruction in these professional subjects, and their eminence throughout the

Middle Ages lay in the professional faculties. They are still a part of the revival of learning, but of a revival which is perhaps somewhat earlier and is certainly more obscure. The obscurity is greatest at Salerno, the oldest medical school in Europe, which goes back into the tenth century as a centre of medicine, but is very dimly known as an institution until it is put to one side by the reorganizing hand of Frederick II. Montpellier, with its university of law and university of medicine, was clearly younger, but it is likewise obscure, on the medical side connected possibly with Salerno and possibly with the science of Spain, but as a law school clearly derived from Bologna through the coming of Placentinus *ca.* 1160. Bologna is the best known of all and by far the most important.

While the University of Bologna was a direct consequence of that revival of Roman law which we have studied in a preceding chapter,[1] it does not appear to have been the earliest Italian law school. Others preceded it at Rome, Pavia, and neighboring Ravenna, but none of these grew into a university. The history of these eleventh-century schools is dim and indistinct, nor is it clear why Rome, at least, did not go on to become a university. Though not the first, Bologna possessed a natural advantage in its situation at the crossroads of Northern Italy, where the highway northward from Florence intersects the Aemilian Way which ran along the northern

[1] Chapter VII.

side of the Apennines, just as today it is a junction of the railroad lines which follow the same routes. A rich and commodious place for study it seemed to the members of the university, who as early as 1155 are represented as answering to this effect the Emperor's query as to the reason for their preference:

> Nos, ait, hanc terram colimus, rex magne, refertam
> Rebus ad utendum multumque legentibus aptam.

While Bologna had at least one eminent lawyer in the eleventh century, Pepo, it was long distinguished for the related study of rhetoric. As late as the second decade of the twelfth century a certain Albert the Samaritan is contracting with students to conduct a school of *dictamen* there rather than at Cremona, and is teaching his pupils to write letters which tell of the study of rhetoric and grammar and the new French theology rather than of law; similar letters from the middle of the century still emphasize rhetoric, and it is from Bologna that the *ars dictandi* passes to France. Still, from the time of Irnerius the great fame of Bologna lay in the field of law, and it was this reputation as a law school, with great teachers and a sound method, which brought it students from a distance.

This body of foreign and especially of Transmontane students constituted the nucleus of the university. Away from home and unprotected, they organized for defence and mutual advantage. In seeking concessions from the townspeople they used the threat of leaving the city, a

threat easy of execution when the university had no
buildings or local habitation to anchor it to any one place,
and the students early gained for their gild that right to
fix the price of lodgings and books which marks one of
the definite steps in university organization. Against
the professors their weapon was the boycott, no idle
penalty when the income of the professor depended upon
the fees paid by the students, and the professors were in
time compelled to submit to minute supervision and regu-
lation of their teaching at the behest of the students, who
demanded their money's worth of instruction. The professors also had a gild, and by controlling admission to
their number they fixed the conditions of the license to
teach which was the equivalent of a degree. Out of these
two sorts of gilds the educational institutions developed.
It is, however, significant that at Bologna the professors'
gilds were called colleges and the name universities was
reserved for the students' gilds, perhaps four but ultimately reduced to two, the Transmontane and the Cis-
montane, which really constituted the university. This
organization seems to have taken shape gradually in the
last quarter of the twelfth century, following the model
of the other gilds of the city, for Bologna, too, never had
a charter of foundation. The general privileges of the
student class granting exemption from the ordinary lay
jurisdiction rested upon a decree of Frederick I, the so-
called authentic *Habita* of 1158; but while Bolognese
jurists were doubtless active in securing this concession,

and Bolognese students had greeted the Emperor in procession three years before, it mentions no particular *studium*, and was considered the fundamental statute of the student class throughout Northern Italy. Plainly Bologna had no year of foundation, as it had no founder, and there was no valid reason for celebrating its eight-hundreth anniversary in 1888 rather than in some other year — save that the oldest of universities ought to have their anniversaries and celebrations quite as much as their upstart descendants of recent origin! *Bononia docta*, 'Bologna the learned,' it was called as early as 1119, and it has been a centre of learning ever since.

Bologna, too, was a mother of universities, parent of the institutions of higher learning in Southern Europe as Paris was in the North, although, with the exception of whatever influence Bologna had upon Montpellier, it is not clear that any of these daughters came into being in the twelfth century. The first quarter of the thirteenth century, however, sees the foundation of Bologna's neighboring rival Padua in 1222 by a secession from Bologna, not to mention the less important though somewhat earlier examples of Modena, Reggio, and Vicenza; of Frederick II's university at Naples in 1224, created with Bolognese masters for the purpose of keeping at home the students of his Sicilian kingdom; and of the earliest Spanish universities at Palencia and, probably by this time, at Salamanca. In Northern Italy this propagation was usually by fission, as in the case of

Oxford from Paris, and in any event the Bolognese type of organization was followed. To a large extent also these later universities were universities of law.

Of the curriculum and methods of study in the universities of the twelfth century we can speak only in general terms, for there are no statutes in this period, nor has any one described their instruction with the minuteness of John of Salisbury's account of the school of Chartres. As regards teaching we must be satisfied with the general statement that university exercises consisted of lectures which were largely comments on texts,[1] of elaborate note-taking, and of discussion and debate. Such exercises were held in the master's dwelling or in a hall which he hired for the purpose, since there were no university buildings or classrooms. Concerning the course of study we can be somewhat more specific, for the principal texts are otherwise known and toward 1200 we have, probably from Alexander Neckam, a systematic account of the works used in the several academic subjects. In the seven arts, Priscian and Donatus were still the authorities in grammar, supplemented by some study of the ancient poets and rhetoricians, while logic had been greatly expanded by the *New Logic* of Aristotle and was just receiving the further addition of his science and *Metaphysics*. Arithmetic and music were still dependent on Boethius; but Euclid's geometry and the Arabic com-

[1] For the lectures of Odofredus, see pp. 203–204.

pends of Ptolemy's astronomy had come into general use. In civil law the *Corpus Juris Civilis* was the basis of all teaching, and in canon law the *Decretum* of Gratian and the decretals of subsequent Popes. Medicine was still based on Galen and Hippocrates with the early translations from the Arabic, but not yet upon Avicenna. The textbook of theology was the Bible, a costly text at that, supplemented by the *Sentences* of Peter Lombard.

The human side of these early universities has also left some record of itself. If Irnerius is a rather shadowy figure, his successors in the latter part of the century are more clearly defined. Abaelard is reasonably well known, thanks to his autobiography, as is also the Primate from his poems. Of the lesser figures, Giraldus Cambrensis is only too familiar to us. Respecting the students, if we have little that is individual, we have much that is generic. The student has become an object of satire in the person of Nigel Wireker's ass who brays as before after seven years of study in Paris, an object of sympathy in the Archweeper's picture of the gray and pinched life of the Paris scholar of slender means. If some of them are clearly "the bent scholarly men" whom H. G. Wells deplores, some are full-blooded enough to satisfy any tests. Already they tell of themselves in letters and in poems. The Goliardic verse shows them on the gayer and less responsible side, wandering from school to school, "light of purse and light of heart," joyous and carefree,

greeting each other at wayside taverns or begging their
way from town to town and door to door:

> We in our wandering,
> Blithesome and squandering,
> > Tara, tantara, teino!
>
> Eat to satiety,
> Drink with propriety;
> > Tara, tantara, teino!
>
> Laugh till our sides we split,
> Rags on our hides we fit;
> > Tara, tantara, teino!
>
> Jesting eternally,
> Quaffing infernally:
> > Tara, tantara, teino!
> > > etc.
>
> I, a wandering scholar lad,
> > Born for toil and sadness,
> Oftentimes am driven by
> > Poverty to madness.
>
> Literature and knowledge I
> > Fain would still be earning,
> Were it not that want of pelf
> > Makes me cease from learning.
>
> These torn clothes that cover me
> > Are too thin and rotten;
> Oft I have to suffer cold,
> > By the warmth forgotten.
>
> Scarce I can attend at church,
> > Sing God's praises duly;
> Mass and vespers both I miss,
> > Though I love them truly.
>
> Oh, thou pride of N——,
> > By thy worth I pray thee
> Give the suppliant help in need,
> > Heaven will sure repay thee.

The letters of the students depict them in all aspects, from the naïve chalk and lambskins of the Chartres letter-book to the polished love-letters of the Orleanese *dictatores*. They show the scholars set upon by the townsmen of Paris and Oxford, praising the medicine and the climate of Montpellier, begging their way through the mud of Bologna, penning ingenious and ingenuous missives home for money and necessaries, turning the left cheek to paternal reproof, appealing artfully to a mother's affection, borrowing a Priscian from a comrade, exalting their special master and their special subject of study. One example from Oxford *ca.* 1220 must suffice: [1]

B. to his venerable master A., greeting. This is to inform you that I am studying at Oxford with the greatest diligence, but the matter of money stands greatly in the way of my promotion, as it is now two months since I spent the last of what you sent me. The city is expensive and makes many demands; I have to rent lodgings, buy necessaries, and provide for many other things which I cannot now specify. Wherefore I respectfully beg your paternity that by the promptings of divine pity you may assist me, so that I may be able to complete what I have well begun. For you must know that without Ceres and Bacchus Apollo grows cold. . . . . . .

The student of all subsequent time is here, sure proof of the existence of the new university life.

This student class is singularly mobile and singularly international, if we may use this term in an age when nations were only in process of formation. Bologna has its English archdeacons and German civilians, Paris its clerks from Sweden and Hungary, as well as from Eng-

[1] See also the Chartres letter on p. 144.

land, Germany, and Italy. Even the cathedral schools drew from beyond the Alps and across the narrow seas. Moreover the same student might attend more than one university. Adalbert of Mainz early in the century and Guy de Bazoches toward its close visit both Northern Paris and Southern Montpellier; one of John of Salisbury's masters went from Paris to Bologna where he unlearned what he had taught and then came back and untaught it. Brunellus the Ass was doubtless not the only English student who moved from Salerno to Paris. The international student of the *studium generale* is the natural accompaniment of the international language and the international culture of the twelfth century.

BIBLIOGRAPHICAL NOTE

The standard work on mediaeval universities is that of the late Hastings Rashdall, *The Universities of Europe in the Middle Ages* (Oxford, 1895); a new edition is in preparation by H. H. E. Craster and F. M. Powicke. I have given a rapid sketch entitled *The Rise of Universities* (New York, 1923). The epoch-making work of H. Denifle, *Die Universitäten des Mittelalters bis 1400*, i (Berlin, 1885), is still important. The new *History of the University of Oxford* by C. E. Mallet (London, 1924) adds nothing to Rashdall on the subject of origins.

The great collections of documents are weak on the twelfth century; the best of them all, the *Chartularium Universitatis Parisiensis* edited by Denifle and Chatelain (Paris, 1889–97), begins *ca.* 1160 and omits the earlier literary material. The principal texts concerning the early Oxford schools are conveniently collected in the Oxford *Collectanea*, ii. 137–192 (1890).

Most of the cathedral schools of the twelfth century still await monographic investigation. The best work has been done by A. Clerval, *Les écoles de Chartres* (Paris, 1895); and R. L. Poole, *Illustrations of the History of Medieval Thought and Learning* (second edition, London, 1920), and "The Masters of the Schools at Paris and Chartres in John of Salisbury's Time," in *English Historical Review*, xxxv. 321–342 (1920). See also G. Robert, *Les écoles et l'enseignement de la théologie pendant la première moitié du XIIᵉ siècle* (Paris, 1909); and A. Hofmeister, "Studien über Otto von Freising," in *Neues Archiv*, xxxvii. 99–161, 633–768. For Italian schools, see the useful work of G. Manacorda, *Storia della scuola in Italia*, i (Milan, 1915). For English schools the writings of A. F. Leach (e. g., *The Schools of Medieval England*, London, [1915]) are full of information, but must be used with caution.

For the content of learning, see the bibliographical notes to the preceding chapters. Neckam's list will be found in my *Mediaeval Science*, ch. 18. For student poetry, see Chapter VI; for letters, Chapter V. Student letters in general I have discussed in the *American Historical Review*, iii. 203–229 (1898); Albert of Samaria at Bologna, in the *Mélanges H. Pirenne* (Brussels, 1926), pp. 201–210.

INDEX

INDEX

The abbreviations 'f.' and 'ff.' indicate that the reference is to the page designated and, respectively, to that next following or to the two next following.

Mediaeval names of persons are arranged alphabetically under the English form of the Christian name.

lish, 188, 211, 385 ff.; German, 383; Transmontane, 298 f.; in plays, 174 f.

Style, 105, 148 f., 152.

Suetonius, 111, 114, 226, 244.

Suger, abbot of Saint-Denis, 120, 226; *De rebus in administratione sua gestis*, 254 ff.

Sulmona, 107, 120.

Summae, 77, 202, 210, 211, 216, 351, 358, 381.

Superstitions, 147.

Swan, the, 306, 308.

Sweden, 316, 379, 395.

Syllogism, the, 241.

Symonds, J. A., 178, note, 181, 182.

Synagogue, the, 176.

Syntax, 130.

Syria, 22, 238, 270, 271, 278, 291; cities, 64; earthquake in, 333; Greek literature in, 281 f.; Normans in, 265; translators in, 282 f.

Syriac language, 281, 282.

Tabelliones, the, 24.

Tacitus, 37, 105, 224 f., 230, 243, 263.

Taillefer, 57.

Tales, 147 f.

Tarazona, 52, 285.

Tarquins, the, 118.

Tavern, the, 181, 182, 394.

Taylor, H. O., 5, 30; quoted, 16, 25, 157, 165 f., 351.

Technical spirit, the, 99.

Tegernsee, 28, 41, 73, 87, 176.

Temple at Jerusalem, the, 176.

Temple of Jupiter, the, 123.

Terence, 37, 95, 110, 113, 130, 171, 278.

Teutonic Knights, the, 265.

Textbooks, 37, 45, 77, 81, 127, 130, 139, 184, 343; law, 215.

Thabit, 326 f.

Thais, 103.

Theatres, Roman, 121, 171.

Thebes, 56, 110, 115.

Themistius, 287.

Theobald, archbishop of Canterbury, 49 f., 211.

Theobald of Étampes, 385.

Theodore of Antioch, 61, 284, 319.

Theodoric, Master, 374.

Theodorus, 37.

Theodosian Code, 195.

Theodosius Tripolita, 287.

Theodulus, 116, 131, 132, 151.

Theology, 24, 29, 45, 50, 54, 58, 103, 134, 206, 295, 299, 300, 364 f., 368, 372, 389; in Germany, 41; at Paris, 380 f.; orthodox, 346, 347, 348; in poetry, 28; revival of, 356 ff.; scholastic, 80; theological treatises, 35, 37 f., 40, 44, 45, 64, 77, 80, 81; Greek theologians, 281; Carolingian theologians, 82.

Theudo, 231.

Thibaud, count of Blois, 248 f.

Thibaut IV, count of Champagne, 57.

Thierry of Chartres, 101 f., 114, 344, 345, 374, 376, 379; *Eptatheuchon*, 130, 377.

Thisbe, 103, 108, 115.

Thomas Aquinas, 10, 341, 348, 350, 355; *Summa*, 358, 359.

Thomas Becket, 50, 51, 212, 222, 233, 379.

Thomas Brown, 61.